LANGUAGE AND CULTURE IN ABORIGINAL AUSTRALIA

Edited by
Michael Walsh and Colin Yallop

ABORIGINAL
STUDIES
PRESS

FIRST PUBLISHED IN 1993 BY
Aboriginal Studies Press
for the Australian Institute of Aboriginal and Torres Strait Islander Studies
GPO Box 553, Canberra ACT 2601.

Reprinted 2005, 2007, 2010, 2012, 2021, 2026

The views expressed in this publication are those of the authors and not necessarily those of the Australian Institute of Aboriginal and Torres Strait Islander Studies.

NATIONAL LIBRARY OF AUSTRALIA CATALOGUING-IN-PUBLICATION DATA:
Walsh, Michael and Colin Yallop (eds)
Language and Culture in Aboriginal Australia

Includes Bibliographies.
ISBN 0 85575 241 6.

[1]. Aboriginies, Australian — Languages. [2]. Aborigines, Australia — Languages — Social aspects. [3]. Intercultural communication — Australia. I. Walsh, Michael, 1948– II. Yallop, Colin.

499.15

CONTENTS

NOTES ON LINGUISTIC CONVENTIONS

SYMBOLS USED IN AUSTRALIAN ABORIGINAL LANGUAGES

This list gives a rough guide to the pronunciation of letters and combinations of letters in Aboriginal languages. The English equivalents do not indicate the pronunciation accurately but give approximations which should be acceptable for most purposes. The list does not include letters whose values can be safely predicted from English conventions, such as *l* and *m*.

The references are to the notes following the list.

a	as in English 'spa', not as in 'tame' — see 1.1
a:	a long version of 'a' as in English 'spa' — see 1.2
ä	used in Yolngu (NE Arnhem Land) for long a: — see 1.2
aa	an alternative way of writing a: — see 1.2
ah	an alternative way of writing a: — see 1.2
[β]	the international phonetic symbol for a voiced bilabial fricative (Spanish 'v'); rare in Australian languages — see 2.7
ch	as in English 'chip' — see 2.2.2, 2.2.5
dh	as in English 'this' — see 2.2.4, 2.2.5
dj	as in English 'jam' — see 2.2.2, 2.2.5
e	used in Yolngu (NE Arnhem Land) for long i: — see 1.2; elsewhere more or less as 'e' in 'bet'
[γ]	the international phonetic symbol for a voiced velar fricative (Spanish *g* in *digo* or *luego*); rare in Australian languages — see 2.7
i	as in English 'pit' — see 1.1
i:	a long version of 'i' as in 'machine', not as in 'dine' — see 1.2
ih	an alternative way of writing i: — see 1.2
ii	an alternative way of writing i: — see 1.2
j	as in English 'jam' — see 2.2.2, 2.2.5
l	a dental 'l' with the blade of the tongue against the teeth — see 2.4
ly	a palatal 'l', as in Italian *gl* or Spanish *ll* — see 2.4; for a rough approximation pronounce as 'lli' in 'million'
[ŋ]	the international phonetic symbol for 'ng' as in 'sing'
ng	as in 'sing' or 'singer', not as in 'finger' — see 2.3.1
nh	a dental 'n' with the blade of the tongue against the teeth — see 2.3.2

ny a palatal 'n', as in Italian *gn* or Spanish *ñ* — see 2.3.2; for a rough approximation pronounce as 'ni' in 'opinion'

o used in Yolngu (NE Arnhem Land) for a long u: — see 1.2; elsewhere more or less 'o' as in 'note'

r as in Australian English, but pronounced also when final, as in American pronunciation of 'car' or 'door' — see 2.6 and see also the letter combinations rd rl rn rr rt

rd in some languages a retroflex 'd' with the tip of the tongue against the roof of the mouth — see 2.2.3, 2.2.5; in Warlpiri a retroflex flap — see 2.6

rl a retroflex 'l', with the tip of the tongue against the roof of the mouth — see 2.4

rn a retroflex 'n', with the tip of the tongue against the roof of the mouth — see 2.3.2

rr a trilled or flapped 'r', as in Scottish English or Italian — see 2.6

rt a retroflex 't', with the tip of the tongue against the roof of the mouth — see 2.2.3, 2.2.5

th as in English 'thin' — see 2.2.4, 2.2.5

tj as in English 'chip' — see 2.2.2, 2.2.5

u as in 'put' — see 1.1

u: a long version of 'u' as in 'Sue', not as in 'cue' — see 1.2

uh an alternative way of writing u: — see 1.2

uu an alternative way of writing u: — see 1.2

NOTES ON THE PRONUNCIATION AND SPELLING OF AUSTRALIAN LANGUAGES

1 Vowels

1.1 Simple Vowel Sounds

The vowels of Australian Aboriginal languages are more like those of Italian or Spanish than English. In the spelling of languages, vowel letters usually have 'continental European' values rather than English values: *i* is more like the *i* of 'machine' or 'kiwi' and not at all like the *i* of 'time' or 'dine'; *a* is more like the *a* of 'spa', not the *a* of 'tame'; and *u* is more like the vowel of 'Sue' and 'two', not as in 'cue' or 'pure'. Thus, for example, the Guugu Yimidhirr words *bayan* 'house', *dumbi* 'smashed' and *yiyi* 'this' (quoted in chapter 2) sound more or less as if pronounced in Spanish or Italian: the first syllable of *bayan* sounds more like

English 'bah' than 'bay', and the second syllable would rhyme with English 'bun' rather than 'ban'; the first syllable of *dumbi* is more like English 'doom' than 'dumb', the second more 'be' than 'by'; and *yiyi* sounds more like 'kiwi' than 'hi-fi'.

In some cases, however, the spelling of Aboriginal words does reflect English spelling. In chapter 5, Sharpe points out that the spelling of the New South Wales language Bundjalung follows English spelling conventions. And of course many Australian placenames were not only written down according to English spelling conventions but were also adapted in pronunciation. As Troy mentions in chapter 3, the Sydney place name Woolloomooloo was originally written down as Walla-mool which, if written in a modern Aboriginal orthography, would probably be Walamul. Both the spelling and the pronunciation have shifted away from this original form.

1.2 Long and Short Vowels

In many Aboriginal languages there is a difference between long and short vowels. The long vowels are sometimes written as double letters (*ii, aa, uu*) or occasionally with a following *h* (*ih, ah, uh*). In the Yolngu language (NE Arnhem Land), long *ii* is written *e*, long *aa* as *ä*, and long *uu* as *o*. It is important to note here that different spellings do not necessarily mean different pronunciations: the vowel sound that is written *ii* in one language, *ih* in another and *e* in another is more or less the same sound.

To avoid the problems of constantly trying to explain sounds in terms of various spelling systems, linguists sometimes use standardised phonetic symbols, enclosed in square brackets. In the International Phonetic Alphabet [i], [a] and [u] represent the three basic vowels of most Australian languages and their lengthened counterparts are represented as [i:], [a:] and [u:]. In this book you will only occasionally find such phonetic symbols. But note that in chapter 9 Simpson gives some Latin words in which vowel length is indicated by the colon (for example, *glo:ssa*).

1.3 Stress Patterns

The stress pattern of Australian language is in most cases rather more even than in English. In particular, it is not common to reduce unstressed syllables in the way that English does (as in, say, 'believe' or 'police', where the first syllable may almost disappear, leaving a monosyllabic 'blieve' or 'plice'). Once again, most Australian languages are more like Spanish or Italian, in which unstressed syllables still have their full vowel sounds. But there are exceptions, Bundjalung (chapter 5) being one.

2 Consonants

2.1 Types of Consonant

The kinds of consonant sound found in Australian languages are not radically different from English: there are plosive consonants (like English *p, t, k, b, d, g*), nasal consonants (like *m* and *n*), lateral consonants (like *l*) and semivowels (*w*, and *y*). English also has fricative consonants (such as *f* and *s*) and affricates (*ch* as in 'church' and *j* as in 'jam'), but these sounds are rare in Australia and totally absent from many of the languages. On the other hand, Australian languages have *r*-sounds of a kind not found in English.

Within these categories of consonant, there are important differences between English and Australian languages, and we shall look at each category in turn.

2.2 Plosive Consonants

2.2.1 p b t d k g

The six plosive consonants of English are made in three positions or gestures of the speech organs. *p* and *b* are bilabial, involving a brief closure of the lips; *t* and *d* are alveolar, involving a brief closure of the tongue tip against the gum-ridge behind the upper teeth; and *k* and *g* are velar, involving a brief closure of the back of the tongue against the soft palate. The plosives *p t k* are voiceless, *b d g* are voiced, the difference being that during a voiced plosive, the vocal folds in the larynx are vibrating as air passes up through them from the lungs; in a voiceless plosive the vocal folds are further apart allowing air to pass more freely. If you have never studied speech sounds before, test what we have just said by listening to and feeling your articulation of the following six words, each of which contains a plosive between vowels: happy, abbey, fatty, paddy, tacky, baggy.

2.2.2 Palatal Plosives (ch tj j dj)

Most Australian languages have more than the three positions of English plosives. All of them have an additional position in which the blade of the tongue makes contact with the hard palate. A plosive made in this way sounds similar to English *ch* or *j*, and is often written as *ch, j* or *tj*, but the Aboriginal sound is made with the blade of the tongue in a single gesture, whereas the typical articulation of English *ch* or *j* is not one single gesture but begins with the tip of the tongue against the gum ridge and then moves through a fricative release. The Aboriginal sound is normally described as a palatal plosive.

2.2.3 Retroflex Plosives (rt rd)

Some Aboriginal languages also have a plosive in which the tip of the tongue is raised towards the hard palate and sometimes even curled back so that the underside of the tongue tip touches the roof of the mouth. Most English speakers perceive this plosive as having an r-sound before it. This is not an accurate perception, but the plosive is commonly written as *rt* or *rd*, occasionally as a *t* or *d* with some additional marking such as a dot or a line beneath the letter. The sound is normally described as a retroflex plosive.

2.2.4 Lamino-dental Plosives (th dh)

A minority of Aboriginal languages have yet another place of articulation, one in which the tongue is pushed well forward in the mouth so that the blade of the tongue makes contact with the back of the teeth. The nearest sound in English is a dental fricative (voiceless as in 'thin' or voiced as in 'then') but the Aboriginal sound is a plosive (like *t*) not a fricative. The Aboriginal sound is commonly written as *th* or *dh* and described as a dental plosive, or more precisely as a lamino-dental plosive to indicate that the blade of the tongue is involved. Thus all Australian languages have four different positions for the articulation of plosive consonants and some have as many as six.

2.2.5 Voiced and Voiceless Plosives

Some Australian languages have — like English — the distinction between voiced and voiceless plosives. For these languages it is important to distinguish between *p* and *b*, *th* and *dh*, and so on. But most Australian languages do not have this distinction: there is only one bilabial plosive sound, which may in fact be pronounced like *p* in some circumstances (say at the beginning of words) and like *b* in others (say in the middle of words). For speakers of these languages the variation between *p* and *b* is not significant. This is the same phenomenon that occurs in English with sounds *l* and *r*. Most English speakers pronounce these sounds differently in different positions: compare the *l* in 'leap' and 'table' or the *r* in 'reap', 'tree', 'dream' and 'three'. Just as English speakers will count variant *l*s or *r*s as versions of one sound, so Aboriginal speakers may count *p* and *b* (and *t* and *d* and so on) as variants of a single sound.

2.3 Nasal Consonants

2.3.1 The Velar Nasal (ng)

Nasal consonants such as *m* and *n* are common in Australian languages. There are two particular problems for English speakers. The first is that the velar nasal, usually written *ng*, is limited in its occurrence in English: it occurs in words like 'sing', 'long', 'hanger', but never at the beginning of a word or syllable. In fact, English speakers mostly have difficulty in pronouncing an initial *ng*, and they often simplify foreign names such as Ngaio or Nguyen by pronouncing them with an initial *n*. In Australian languages, words commonly do begin with *ng*, for example the widespread word *ngali* meaning 'you and I'. If you want to pronounce this word correctly, try detaching the *ng* from the end of a word: for example try saying 'sing ah lee', then run the syllables together and repeat the sequence several times before trying to make it sound like 'sing-ngah-lee'.

Avoid inserting a *g* plosive sound. There is a clear difference in English pronunciation between the single *ng* sound of 'singer', 'ringer' and the *ng* of 'finger', 'linger'. But, given that we write *ng* in both cases, it is understandable that people are sometimes confused, for example, about how to pronounce the *ng* in 'Singapore'. The difference is important in Australian languages and is usually shown in the spelling: in reading Aboriginal material, assume that *ng* is the velar nasal (as in 'singer') and that the nasal plus stop (as in 'finger') will be written as *ngg*.

English spelling is not very helpful here. We've just seen that the spelling *ng* is ambiguous, and we should also note that the velar nasal is written as *n* in words like 'sink' and 'bank'. From the spelling of an English word like 'incorporate' we can't tell whether the *n* is pronounced as *n* or *ng* (and it probably doesn't matter to most people). In Australian languages, however, it may be necessary to distinguish carefully between words like *rinka* (pronounced with *n-k*) and *ringka*. In the spelling of some languages, an apostrophe may be used to make it clear that *n* not *ng* is intended (as in *rin'ka*). And for even greater clarity, some transcriptions use the phonetic symbol [ŋ], called 'eng'.

2.3.2 Nasal Consonants Not Found in English (ny rn nh)

A second difficulty for English speakers is that Australian languages generally have nasal consonants at the same places of articulation as plosives. Thus, a language may have not only *m n ng* but also a palatal *ny*, a retroflex *rn* and a lamino-dental *nh*. Despite its common spelling as *ny*, the palatal nasal is not a sequence of *n* plus *y*, although this is a reasonable approximation if you are speaking an Aboriginal language with an English accent. It is in fact the sound written as *gn* in French and Italian and as *ñ* in Spanish. (Alternative spellings in Australian languages include *ñ* and *nj*.) The retroflex *rn* should be pronounced in the same way as *rt*, with the tongue tip curled up into the roof of the mouth, the lamino-dental *nh* in the same way as *th*, with the blade of the tongue pressed against the back of the upper teeth. Most English speakers find it very hard to hear the difference between *nh* and *n*.

2.4 Lateral Consonants (l ly rl lh)

As with nasal consonants, many Australian languages have more lateral sounds than the one *l* of English. *ly* represents a palatal lateral, which is not identical to a sequence of *l* plus *y* of the kind heard in English 'full-year' but is a single consonant as represented by *gl* in Italian or *ll* in standard Spanish. *rl* is a retroflex lateral, with the tongue tip curled up into the roof of the mouth, and *lh* a lamino-dental lateral, with the blade of the tongue touching the back of the upper teeth.

2.5 *Semivowels (w y)*

Both *w* and *y* are common in Australian languages and are pronounced as in English. Notice that both sounds can occur between vowels: the word *mayi* sounds like 'mah-yee', somewhat like 'my' or 'my-ee', the word *kawu* like 'kah-woo', somewhat like 'cow' or 'cow-oo'.

2.6 *R-sounds (r rr rd)*

All Australian languages distinguish two sorts of r-sound, one very similar to the Australian English *r* of 'run' or 'around', the other a trilled or flapped *rr* of the kind heard in Scottish English or Italian or Spanish. The two sounds are quite distinct, as different to Aboriginal speakers as *l* and *r* or *n* and *ng*. The spelling usually differentiates them as single *r* versus double *rr*. Australian English speakers should be aware here of their habit of not pronouncing final r-sounds. It is normal in Australian English (and in New Zealand and much of Britain) to drop *r* in final position. Thus, there is no r-sound on the end of 'car' or 'ear', although the sound is restored when a vowel follows, as in 'car-alarm' or 'ear-ache'. This habit should not be imported into Aboriginal languages: the Yir-Yoront word *larr* 'ground', for instance, should be pronounced with a trilled or flapped r-sound on the end, as in a Scottish pronunciation of 'car' or 'bar'.

A few Australian languages have yet another r-sound, one in which the tongue starts from a retroflex position, with the tongue tip up in the roof of the mouth, and then flaps forward striking the gum ridge as it passes. This sound occurs in Warlpiri (in addition to *r* and *rr*) and is written *rd*.

2.7 *Fricatives*

As mentioned earlier, most Australian languages have no fricative consonants such as English *f* and *s*. A few do, and in chapter 7 you will find the word *ef* 'tongue' quoted from a Cape York language. You will also find that in a few languages, plosive sounds are sometimes pronounced as fricatives. This is the case in Bundjalung (chapter 5), where, very much as in Spanish, plosives between vowels are pronounced as fricatives — for example, *b* as a bilabial fricative [β] (like [v] but made with both lips, not with teeth and lip), and *g* as a velar fricative [ɣ] (like the *ch* of Scottish 'loch' but with voicing).

CONVENTIONS FOR THE GRAMMATICALITY/ACCEPTABILITY OF SENTENCES

Linguists need to signal the different reactions that speakers have about expressions in a language. Some expressions are simply ungrammatical because they conflict with the rules of grammar which may be implicit but reflect our understanding of how the language works:

*Me like bananas.
*Harry like bananas.

In one sentence the form of the pronoun 'me' is inappropriate in that position in the sentence while in the other it is a rule of English grammar that the verb form must be 'likes' in such a sentence.

But there are other expressions where speakers might not reject the sentence out of hand although they feel dubious about its acceptability:

Max gave the fence a new coat of paint.
?Max gave a new coat of paint to the fence.

Nigel was kicked by his father.

?Nigel was wanted by his father.
??Nigel was resembled by his father.

And there may be sentences where speakers feel uncertain as to whether the expression breaks the structural rules and is ungrammatical or merely seems strange and is therefore unacceptable:

?*Harry and me like bananas.

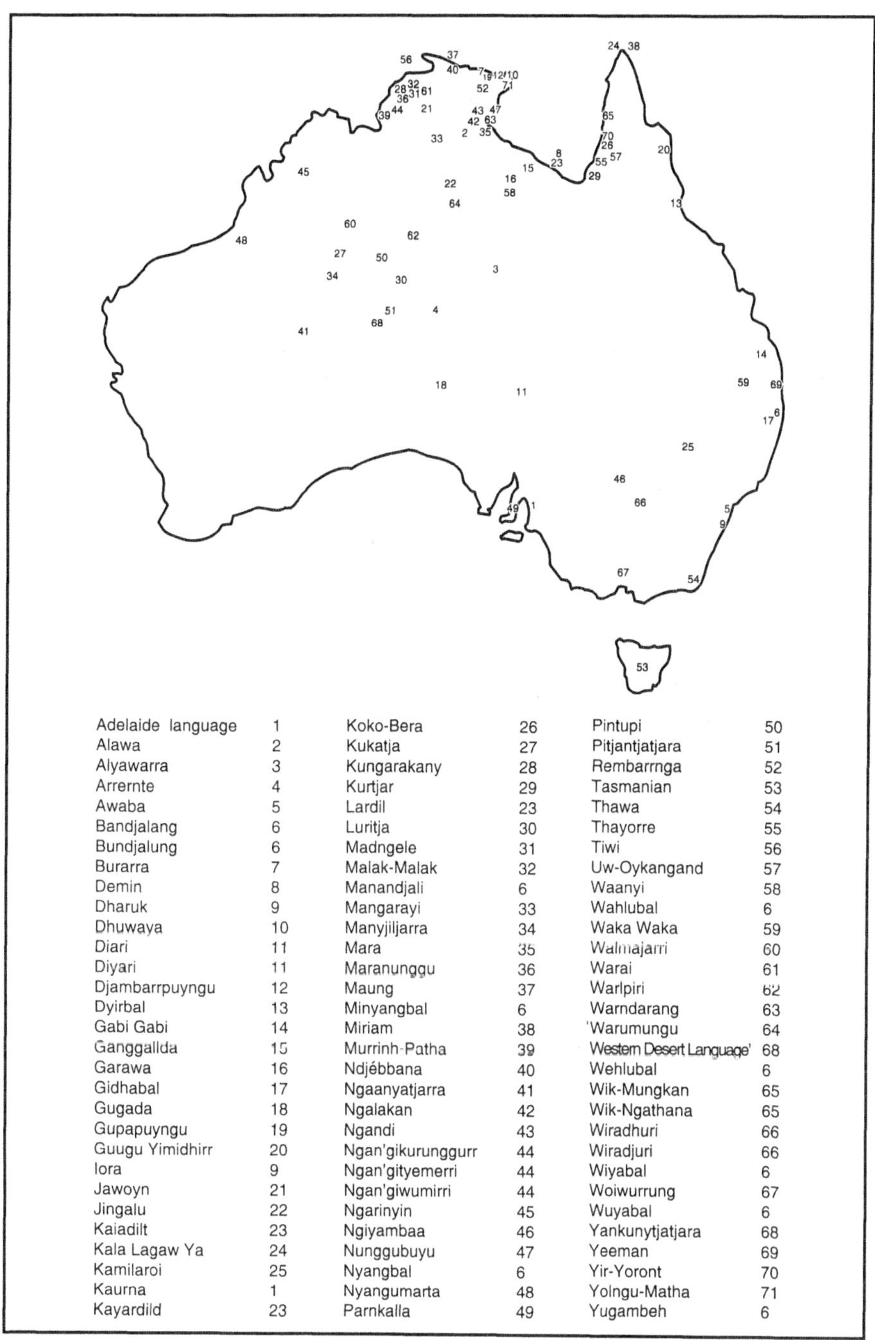

Map 1: Approximate locations of languages referred to in this volume (based on Dixon 1980, xviii–xix).

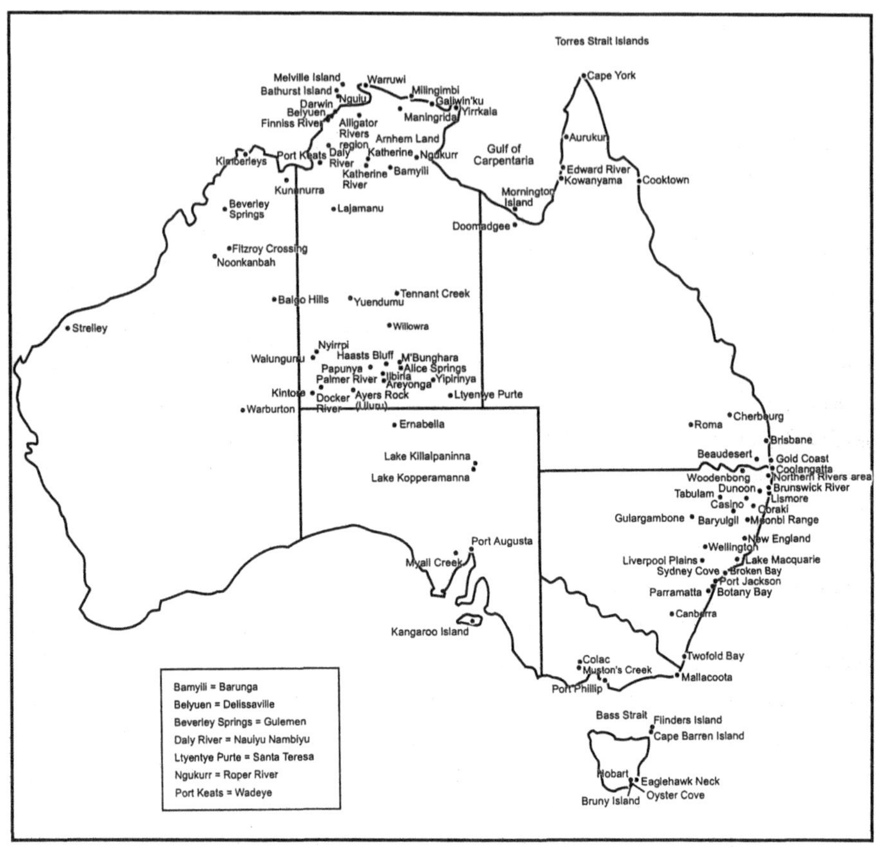

Map 2: Location of placenames referred to in this volume.

PREFACE

The initial impetus for this volume arose from a belief that there were many important issues concerned with language in Aboriginal Australia which were not known to a wide enough audience. Over the last twenty years a tremendous amount of work has been carried out on the languages of Aboriginal Australia. But much of this is not readily accessible to non-specialists even though a number of general, overview accounts have appeared. Among these are Barry J. Blake's basic introduction (*Australian Aboriginal Languages*, Angus and Robertson, Sydney 1981, with a second edition from University of Queensland Press, St Lucia, in 1991), R.M.W. Dixon's *The Languages of Australia* (Cambridge University Press, Cambridge, 1980) and Colin Yallop's *Australian Aboriginal Languages* (André Deutsch, London 1982). These are representative of the potential range of such coverages. Blake (1981, 1991) is very accessible but is quite brief and therefore cannot address issues in any detail. Dixon (1980) is not only an important reference but presents original research on the classification of Australian languages. While parts of the book are accessible to the public, a substantial portion is challenging even to the specialist and so this volume, for all its strengths, cannot reach a very wide audience. Yallop (1982) falls somewhere between Blake and Dixon and succeeds in giving a brief but less than elementary account of language in Aboriginal Australia. For those of us involved in teaching basic, overview courses on Australian languages to students in linguistics or in Aboriginal Studies, none of these works was entirely satisfactory.

One problem was the potential audience at which general works have been pitched. Some are clearly too basic for use in an academic context, others require a background in linguistics even if rather basic. What was needed was an account that had sufficient depth to excite the continuing interest of students but was not so technical as to exclude a large number of them.

Another problem is the coverage of issues. There are a number of recurring questions put to so-called specialists on Australian Aboriginal languages (sometimes to the point of posing an occupational hazard!): how many Aboriginal languages are there? are they written down? where did they come from? why did they die out? where are they now spoken? what are they like? how many words do they have? how do they manage in the modern world (in terms of language)? Each of these questions inevitably leads to numerous others, so that giving a satisfactory answer can be a daunting task. Because an apparently simple question often stems from a number of mistaken assumptions, one has to alter the assumptions before one can begin to answer the question effectively. Often the literature is not much help, not so much because the answers are lacking as that the chain of connection from the original question to underlying assumptions to an eventual answer is scattered in such a way that one must recommend snippets of reading from a number of disparate sources.

A major purpose of this volume is to satisfy these two concerns: accessibility and coverage. As editors we approached potential contributors with a fairly specific request based on our knowledge of their interests and expertise. We wanted to provide answers to some of these recurring questions and at the same time refer to the varying language situations across Aboriginal Australia. Inevitably there was a certain amount of negotiation involved so that some contributors ended up offering us something that we might not have otherwise included. It was also predictable that some contributors fell by the wayside so that some issues that are worthy of mention have not appeared. But in each case we emphasised that the topic agreed upon should be accessible to people without a specialist knowledge of linguistics or of Aboriginal Studies.

The editors had other requirements as well. Each contributor was asked to make their chapter free-standing. Although there are occasional references from one chapter to another, any of the chapters in this volume should provide a brief, accessible, self-contained introduction to the topic under consideration. Contributors were also invited to provide a section of points for discussion. Envisaging that this volume might well be used in a teaching context, this section provides questions and raises issues which are closely linked to the content of the chapter. Obviously these should only be treated as a guide. We hope that many other points for discussion will be triggered by reading these chapters. Some readers may choose to skip over this section altogether.

The result is a somewhat heterogeneous collection in which each chapter tries to address some of the recurring issues of interest in the broad area of language and culture in Aboriginal Australia. With the growth of interest in Aboriginal Studies, we see an important pedagogic function in this volume. But people who are already specialists in Aboriginal Studies should find plenty to interest them. Much of the material has not appeared before and certainly some of it challenges previously held views on the role of language and culture in Aboriginal Australia.

Michael Walsh and Colin Yallop
August 1992

CHAPTER

1 LANGUAGES AND THEIR STATUS IN ABORIGINAL AUSTRALIA

Michael Walsh

NUMBER OF LANGUAGES

It is thought that around 250 distinct languages were spoken at first (significant) European contact in the late eighteenth century. Most of these languages would have had several dialects, so that the total number of named varieties would have run to many hundreds. This contradicts the still popular view that there is just one Aboriginal language, perhaps with a number of dialects.

It is difficult to be precise about the numbers of dialects and languages because the information available is often poor and terms like 'dialect' and 'language' can shade into each other. For the English language we can recognise dialects like Australian English, Canadian English, New Zealand English, and so on. The differences between these dialects may not be so great as to interfere with communication. But what of Scots English and Jamaican English? Here the differences may be sufficient to create difficulties in communication — at least in the short term — even though we refer to them as kinds of English. On the other hand, we also recognise forms of speech which are clearly separate languages, such as German and Spanish, Irish and Armenian or Hindi and Greek. Despite their current differences these languages all go back to a single ancestral language spoken thousands of years ago. In Aboriginal Australia there are languages which are clearly distinct, like Tiwi (from Bathurst and Melville Islands, off the north coast of Australia) and Pitjantjatjara (from the desert areas of South Australia and Western Australia). There are also forms of speech which share much the same grammar but differ in pronunciation and vocabulary just as various dialects of English do. Examples of such forms of speech are Gugada, Ngaanyatjarra, Luritja, Pintupi and Pitjantjatjara, which linguists have classified as belonging to the 'Western Desert Language'. This was not a term used by the native speakers themselves any more than a cover term like the 'Scandinavian Language' is used by speakers of closely related forms of speech like Danish and Norwegian. Danes and Norwegians feel that they have a separate language with a separate territory and that their language is a reflection of their group identity. The dialects of the Western Desert Language were spoken over a vast area of well over a million square kilometres in the Northern Territory, South Australia and Western Australia. Not surprisingly there would be difficulties in communication between speakers of dialects which were widely separated. Rumsey takes up questions of language, territory and group identity in Aboriginal Australia (in chapter 14).

THE DECLINE OF AUSTRALIAN LANGUAGES

Soon after the arrival of the Europeans, Australian languages began to decline. A recent study of the language situation in Australia indicates that 160 languages are extinct, seventy are under threat and only twenty are likely to survive (at least in the short term).

The question must be asked: why did they die out? The contributions by Crowley (in chapter 4) on Tasmanian and Troy (in chapter 3) on the Sydney area go some way toward answering this question. From the earliest days of European contact there was often an assumption that Aboriginal languages were of less value than English and this view soon hardened into government policy, which was reinforced through education and employment practices. Aboriginal people were positively discouraged from speaking their ancestral languages and made to feel ashamed of using them in public. Eventually the link between generations of speakers was broken, so that young children had little or no knowledge of ancestral languages, their parents were partial speakers of these languages and their grandparents were the only remaining speakers of languages that may have been passed on from generation to generation over hundreds of years.

Once this intergenerational link is broken an unwritten language may disappear very quickly. Evans (forthcoming), for example, reports that varieties of English have taken over within forty years of significant white contact on Mornington Island in the Gulf of Carpentaria. One of the traditional languages, Kaiadilt, now has no fluent speakers under forty-five years of age. Younger speakers retain active command of a small vocabulary, but speak Kaiadilt with varying degrees of fluency.

THE NATURE OF AUSTRALIAN LANGUAGES

People often ask: what are Aboriginal languages like? In a sense this is like asking what European languages are like. In Europe there are languages as diverse as Spanish, German and Russian. So too in Australia there are languages which are very different in nature even though they can be traced back to a common source. Warlpiri, a language spoken to the northwest of Alice Springs, can be likened to Latin in that it has an elaborate array of case suffixes (endings indicating different functions of nouns). Murrinh-Patha, spoken on the coast south of Darwin, can be likened to Turkish in that a single word contains many clearly separable chunks of meaning. For example, the single Murrinh-Patha word *manhipurlnu* translates into English as 'I'm going to wash you/I will wash you' (as might be said by a parent to a child). English spreads the intended meaning across four (or more) separate words; Murrinh-Patha links the separate pieces of meaning in one word, somewhat like beads on a string:

> ma-nhi-purl-nu
> I-you-wash-will
> 'I will wash you'

In English we can change meaning by substituting one word for another and adding others, but in Murrinh-Patha the change may be handled within a single word:

> ma-nhi-ma-purl-nu-ngani
> I-you-hand-wash-will-I do habitually
> 'I will keep on washing your hand'
>
> ma-nanku-ma-purl-nu-ngani
> I-you two siblings-hand-wash-will-I do habitually
> 'I will keep on washing the hands of you two sisters'
>
> ma-nanku-ma-purl-nu-ngintha-ngani
> I-you two-hand-wash-will-two not being sisters, at least one being female-I do habitually
> 'I will keep on washing the hands of you two who are not sisters and one or both are female'

Murrinh-Patha grammar is not simple. In fact, no language has a particularly simple grammar, although some aspects of some languages seem less complex than others. The grammar of any language is always shifting. In some respects, for example, the current grammar of English is simpler than it was 800 years ago, but this does not mean that there are no longer any complexities in modern English. Secondly, the grammar is significantly different from that of English – it is neither better nor worse, just different. Thirdly, differences in grammar between languages create difficulties in translation. In the examples above it can be seen that Murrinh-Patha has three ways of expressing 'you-ness': *nhi* 'you singular'; *nanku* 'you two brothers/sisters (siblings)'; *nanku ngintha* 'you two who are not brothers or sisters and one or both are female'. (And there are four other ways of expressing 'you-ness' in this language). By contrast English normally has just one form 'you' whether one is referring to one person or more and regardless of how they might be related to each other or what sex they are. The translation thus becomes awkward. On the other hand, Murrinh-Patha does not usually indicate for nouns whether there is exactly one or more than one, as the grammar of English usually requires. So a stricter translation of the Murrinh-Patha expressions would indicate 'hand/hands'. It is always possible in Murrinh-Patha to specify that just one hand is meant rather than a number of hands but the grammar does not require this specification as English grammar does. In the same way, English can resort to wording such as 'you two' or 'the two of you' but the grammar does not require these details.

Further details of language structure are outlined by Yallop (in chapter 2), and some of the richness of vocabulary in Australian languages is covered in the contribution by Simpson (in chapter 9).

THE HISTORY OF AUSTRALIAN LANGUAGES

We know that people have been in Australia for at least 40,000 years (and much longer periods have been suggested). Many Aboriginal people believe that their ancestors have always been here. Archaeologists, however, think that there has been more than one influx of people. Until around 7,000 or 8,000 years ago Papua New Guinea was joined by a land bridge to Australia. We can safely assume that there would have been contact between the people of Australia and land to the north.

The Torres Straits Islands still form an island link between Queensland and Papua New Guinea, the northernmost islands being in sight of the New Guinea coastline. This raises the question of whether the languages of Australia are related to those of New Guinea. In terms of physical type and culture the people of the Torres Straits Islands are Papuan, but linguistically the islands divide up into two quite distinct types. Miriam, a Papuan language, is spoken in the east and Kala Lagaw Ya, clearly an Australian language, is spoken in the west. Kala Lagaw Ya shows some unusual features for an Australian language but it is clearly of the Australian type in terms of its grammar.

Archaeologists have claimed that the most recent influx of people was about 4,000 years ago, probably occurring at the same time as the dingo came into Australia. This raises the question of how the Australian languages developed. Have the languages come from one relatively recent source, have they developed out of earlier migrations, or are there layers reflecting successive migrations of people speaking quite different languages? Questions of this kind are intriguing but for the most part unanswerable. For languages in Europe we sometimes have written records going back thousands of years. For Australian languages the record is much sparser: for many languages our earliest records are measured in decades while the first known recording of an Australian language is 1770. Even if the ancestry of present day Aboriginal languages goes back only 4,000 years, it is unlikely that careful study could establish links with languages outside.

Most of the possible connections between Australian languages and other languages of the world have been considered and rejected. Even the connection with Papua New Guinea, which seems likely given its proximity to the

Australian mainland, is yet to be established: it is not so much ruled out, as unproven. A comparison between Papuan and Australian languages *suggests* that there might have been some connection but there is not sufficient evidence to be sure (Foley 1986, 296–375).

For reasons of this kind the position of Tasmanian is unknown and will probably remain unknown. The Tasmanian people were subjected to horrific treatment from government authorities and their languages suffered an early decline (although the Tasmanian people have survived as Crowley describes in chapter 5). We might expect that Tasmanian languages would have something in common with languages across the Bass Strait. Until about 10,000 years ago Bass Strait was dry land but then the sea level rose, cutting off Tasmania from the mainland (see Map 3).

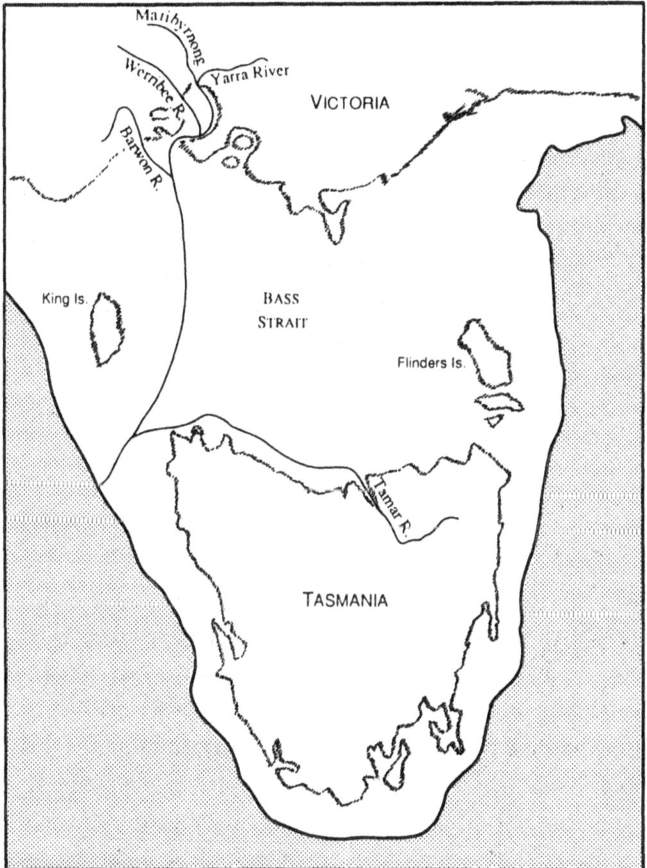

Map 3: The coastline of southeastern Australia during the height of the iceage. 18,000 years ago Bass Strait was dry land and the mainland took in Tasmania and the area shown in white (from Blake 1991, 32).

Even if the records for languages of Tasmania and southern Victoria were extensive, the connection would be very hard to establish after a separation of 10,000 years. The written records are quite meagre, especially for Tasmanian.

There is evidence of contact between Indonesia and northern Australia in relatively recent times. Towards the end of the seventeenth century traders from around what is today known as southern Sulawesi began to visit the shores of northern Australia to collect and process a much-prized commodity variously known as trepang, bêche-de-mer or sea-cucumber. These Macassan traders set up seasonal camps on the northern Australian coast for months at a time, mingling with the local Aboriginal population. Some Aborigines seem to have travelled back to Indonesia with the boat crews, returning to Australia on later trading expeditions. This contact is demonstrated linguistically by a sizeable stock of words in some Aboriginal languages of northeast Arnhem land, such as *rrupiya* 'money' — distantly derived from 'rupee' (Walker and Zorc 1981). In addition, it may be that a Macassan-based pidgin developed for use not only between Aborigines and the boat crews but also for casual contact among Aborigines along the coast who did not have a language in common (Urry and Walsh 1981).

Although our understanding of outside connections is limited, most linguists now believe that the 250 Australian languages are genetically related and can be traced back to a common source called proto-Australian. For further comments, see the opening section of Yallop's chapter 2.

THE EFFECTS OF CONTACT ON AUSTRALIAN LANGUAGES

European contact has had a profound impact on Australian languages. We have already seen (in the second section of this chapter) that the languages have declined. In this section we consider the rise of pidgins, creoles and lingua francas, as well as the influence of English.

From earliest European contact pidgins developed when the settlers and the local people tried to communicate with each other. A pidgin is born out of the needs of this contact where neither people has learnt the language of the other fully and might not need to. If its purposes are limited, the pidgin itself will remain limited. It will be a simplified form of speech employing some of the features of both languages with a predominance from the dominant language, in this case English. If there are greater needs for the pidgin, it will become more complex. With extended contact, a creole may arise which is still English-based but has a much wider application, being used to meet all the communicative requirements of its speakers.

Troy (chapter 3) describes early contact in the Sydney area while Harris and Rhydwen (chapters 10 and 11) outline the rise of the widespread English-based creole called Kriol in northern Australia. Kriol varies over the vast area in which it is used by having an input from the local Aboriginal language in a particular area. Nevertheless, Kriol is largely intelligible over this whole area. Some of the English-based pidgins contributed to the development and spread of creoles and some have now died out, but there were also pidgins which arose from contact between Aboriginal people and non-Europeans. The following map (Map 4) gives an idea of the spread of contact varieties:

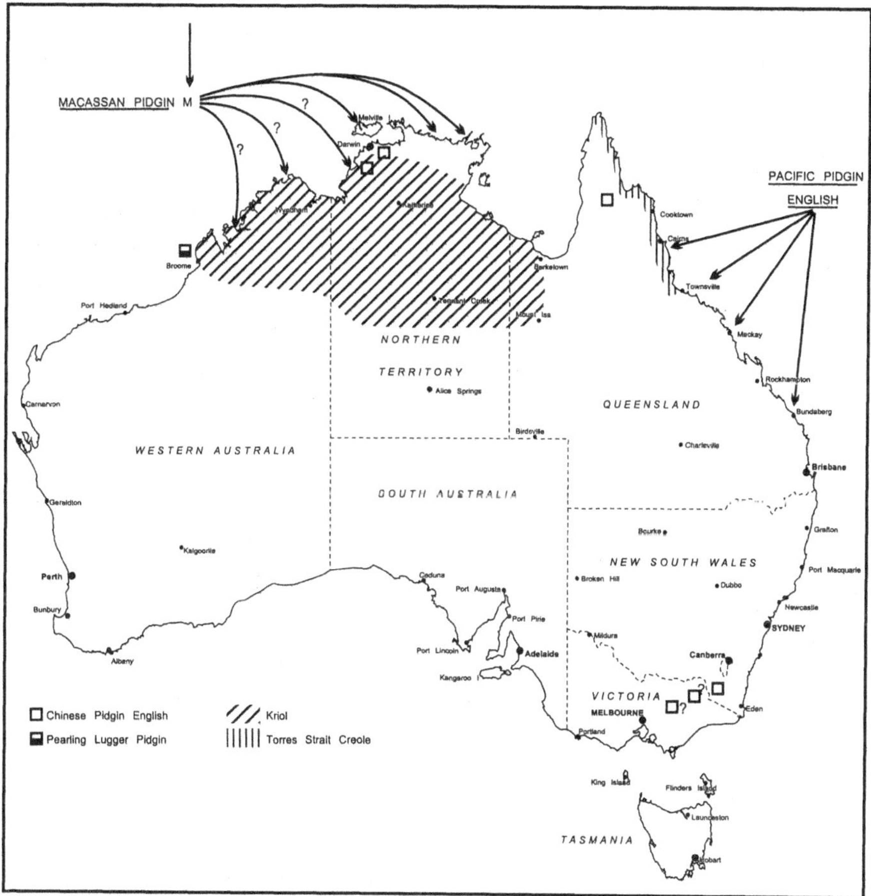

Map 4: Pidgins and creoles in Australia (adapted with permission from Wurm and Hattori 1981, Map 24).

Another effect of European contact is the emergence of indigenous lingua francas. These are traditional Aboriginal languages which have emerged as a common means of communication for a community or region. For example, at Wadeye (on the west coast of the Northern Territory) from 1935 missionaries brought together speakers of a number of mutually unintelligible languages. Over the past fifty years one of these, Murrinh-Patha, emerged as the lingua franca for the area and is now used as the medium for the local bilingual education program.

English has had a linguistic effect through its contribution to pidgins and creoles, but it has also had important consequences in its own right. English has been adopted by many Aboriginal Australians but may differ in subtle ways from English as used by other Australians (see Eades in chapter 13). And, of course, English words have been taken into Aboriginal languages to meet new needs (see the contributions by Black and Simpson in chapters 15 and 9).

One important feature of the English used by Aboriginal Australians is the use of terms to describe groups of people, especially Aborigines and non-Aborigines. Elsewhere in this volume you will find terms such as Koori and Murri, which are used by some Aborigines to refer to themselves. This reflects a dissatisfaction with the identifier labels which have been imposed upon them from outside their culture:

> The word 'Aborigine' comes from the Latin word *ab origine* meaning 'from the beginning'. It should be a proud word, because our peoples have occupied this land since the Dreamtime began, not merely for 150 years. But for many people it has become debased, part of the negative perception of us and our heritage. (Mattingley and Hampton 1988, xv)

Most of the terms are based on Aboriginal words for 'person' or 'man'. The fact that there are several is a reminder that Aboriginal languages differ across the continent. The most common words are:

Koori	New South Wales and Victoria
Murri	Queensland
Nyoongah	southwestern Western Australia
Yammagee	Western Australia, around the Murchison River

A LINGUISTIC CONTRIBUTION TO AUSTRALIAN ENGLISH

Australian languages have also contributed to English. Perhaps the best known loan word from an Australian language into English is 'kangaroo', used to refer to a creature that was quite unfamiliar to Europeans. The word is derived from Guugu Yimidhirr, a language spoken around Cooktown in northern Queensland. Many well-known loan words come from the Aboriginal people of the Sydney area: billabong, dingo, koala, kookaburra, nulla nulla (a kind of wooden club) and woomera (spear-thrower). Others, understandably, come from a region where the things the words refer to occur: so words like 'jarra' and 'quokka' come from languages of Western Australia. For many non-Aboriginal Australians their most frequent encounter with Australian languages is with placenames like Canberra, Coolangatta, Kununurra, Mallacoota, Parramatta and Uluru. In some instances the sources for these place names are not clear: Canberra, for example, is said to have meanings as different as 'breasts' and 'meeting place'. Sometimes connections between words sharing a common source are not obvious. The first part of the place name Gulargambone is the same as the word for the distinctively Australian bird, the galah. These related terms, Gulargambone and galah, are found in Ngiyambaa, a language traditionally spoken in western New South Wales.

In recent years there have been moves to reinstate Aboriginal placenames. In the Northern Territory, Ayer's Rock is also referred to as Uluru, Roper River has become Ngukurr, Delissaville has become Belyuen and Port Keats is now Wadeye. This process is not without problems. Ngukurr is difficult for many non-Aboriginal Australians, starting with a sound which can only occur at the *end* of a syllable in English and finishing with a trilled 'r' sound. Wadeye is problematic because there is a tendency to interpret the word from the perspective of English spelling: wad-eye. In fact, it is a three syllable word with the last two vowels pronounced like the 'e' in 'egg'. This can result in two pronunciations: one as the local Aboriginal people say it; the other transformed by the spelling of the word and by the lack of fit between the sound system of English and the local Aboriginal language.

RECORDING AUSTRALIAN LANGUAGES

The recording of Australian languages began with white contact but the results have been very uneven. In 1770 Captain Cook and Joseph Banks took down word lists from people living in Cape York in the area that has come to be called Cooktown. It was from this source that 'kangaroo' passed into English. In the early days of settlement some of the more detailed recordings of Australian languages were carried out by missionaries who eventually hoped to produce translations of the Bible. Unfortunately some languages were not recorded in any detail. Thawa, the language of Twofold Bay in the southeastern corner of New South Wales, is known only from a few word lists while Yeeman, formerly spoken near Brisbane, is known only by its name. Valuable work was carried out by people from varied backgrounds: policemen, surveyors, farmers and clergymen. One of the most significant contributions was made by a Victorian sheep farmer, Edward Micklethwaite Curr. In the latter part of the nineteenth century Curr widely distributed a questionnaire seeking information on local languages. His four-volume work, *The Australian Race* (1886–87), was the most comprehensive compilation of knowledge on Australian languages in its day. In some instances most of what we now know about a particular language is to be found in Curr's collection.

It is only quite recently that the systematic study of Australian languages has become more widespread. Separate departments of linguistics only came into being in Australian universities in the mid-1960s. The establishment of the Summer Institute of Linguistics in Australia in the late 1950s was an important development for a fuller knowledge of Australian languages. This organisation is devoted to the translation of the Bible into local languages but also has contributed strongly to indigenous (secular) literacy and to the description of Aboriginal languages. Perhaps the most exciting initiative in recent times has been the setting up of the School of Australian Linguistics in 1974. This institution provided training for Aboriginal and Torres Strait Islander people in techniques of linguistic analysis as well as skills for literacy work and translating and interpreting. Apart from the assistance such skills could provide in applied linguistic work in Aboriginal communities, there is tremendous potential for a more detailed understanding of Australian languages. No matter how talented, a linguistic researcher cannot compete with native-speaker knowledge.

The scope of investigation for any given Australian language varies considerably. For the bulk of Australia's ancestral languages one must rely on early written records, there being no surviving fluent speakers. This can amount to detective work of a linguistic kind. The records will always be incomplete, often difficult to interpret because of the recording techniques of non-specialists in linguistics, and frequently conflicting. Some of the difficulties involved in coming to understand these early records are brought out in the chapters by Crowley on Tasmanian (chapter 4) and by Sharpe on Bundjalung (chapter 5).

For languages still in everyday use the challenges for adequate documentation are rather daunting. In chapter 2 Yallop briefly indicates some of the details of language structure that can be investigated. In chapter 9 Simpson explores some of the possibilities for modern dictionaries, while in chapter 15 Black looks at some of the needs encountered by Australian languages as they accommodate to the introduced culture of the Europeans. Increasingly there are collections of text material appearing in Australian languages. These range from transcriptions of traditional stories and life histories to announcements about forthcoming events such as elections, and instructions on how to repair a gearbox. In the development of this new literature there is increasing Aboriginal involvement, some of it focused in regionally based language resource centres. Such centres provide a venue for language policy including the control by Aborigines of linguistic research in their area.

RESPONDING TO NEW CHALLENGES

In chapter 15 Black concentrates on some of the new uses for Australian languages. Writing and literacy are not yet universal in the English-speaking community in Australia and were much less widespread even a few generations ago. For many Aboriginal Australians these skills have only appeared in the last fifty years or less. But there is the dual challenge of taking on these new skills in their own languages as well as English. Some of the problems involved are discussed by Rhydwen (in chapter 11). Aboriginal people have also had to accommodate to new forms of communication of technology: cameras, radio, television and telephones. They have also had to respond to new communication situations, including Western-style education, the law, land rights and negotiations. These latter areas are considered by Christie, Eades and Rumsey (in chapters 12,13,14) while a more general account is given by Walsh (1991).

LANGUAGE AND ABORIGINALITY

What effect has the decline of Australian languages had on Aborigines today? One European commentator has claimed (Dixon 1980, 79):

> If a minority group is to maintain its ethnic identity and social cohesion it must retain its language (the Basques and the Jews provide two quite diverse examples). Once a group has lost its language, it will generally lose its separate identity and will, within a few generations, be indistinguishably assimilated into another, more dominant political group.

At first glance this statement may seem reasonable but it requires some interpretation. It is true that Hebrew has played an important role in Jewish ethnic identity, but there are many Jews who do not speak Hebrew with any fluency and this does not detract from their Jewishness. Of course they may regret their lack of knowledge of the language and strongly favour its maintenance but the loss of language does not automatically signal a loss of identity.

Language in Aboriginal Australia continues to play an important role in Aboriginal identity despite the decline of many ancestral languages. Asked how important language was in preserving culture one Aborigine has said:

> Oh, it's our lifeblood. This is what we tell the young people. You have to know your language because you'll never be able to learn your Dreaming and if you don't know your Dreaming you can't identify where you belong. If you don't identify where you belong you may as well say you're dead. As an Aboriginal person you have to know your language to be able to learn your Dreamings. (Bowden and Bunbury 1990, 32–33).

Black (chapter 15) points out that Aboriginal culture is not static and varies across the continent. Aboriginal people who have grown up and lived their whole lives in the towns and cities of 'settled' Australia can still retain an Aboriginal identity. Eades (in chapter 13) shows that such people may have a quite distinctive form of English which at once sets them apart from other Australians and at the same time marks them as members of one group. Crowley (in chapter 4) points out that Aboriginality can survive the loss of traditional languages. Rumsey (in chapter 14) demonstrates that language can play a crucial role in group and territorial identity whether one knows that language or not. In chapter 5, Sharpe describes the efforts made by Aboriginal people to maintain their linguistic heritage. In these and other chapters it should become clear that Aboriginality is not reliant merely on knowledge of an ancestral language but may involve the use of a creole or of a distinctive form of English.

FOR DISCUSSION

1. Why are there now so few Aboriginal languages? Is this recent decline in linguistic diversity unusual in other areas in the region around Australia? Or the world?
2. Many ethnic groups are recognised in multicultural Australia. To what extent is knowledge of language associated with ethnicity? Consider various groups such as Dutch, Greek, Italian, Scots and Vietnamese. How do some of these groups differ from each other?
3. Which of the following words have been borrowed from Aboriginal languages? — boomerang, cockatoo, dinkum, humpy, jacaranda, wattle, woomera. (If you don't know, consult a good dictionary such as the *Macquarie*.) Try to identify more borrowings from Australian Aboriginal languages into English.
4. Imagine that you are one of a few hundred speakers of English living on a small island. English is spoken nowhere else in the world. Suppose now that speakers of a totally different language come and visit and settle your island. How might you try to communicate? How could you go about learning the newcomers' language? How might you try to teach or explain English to the newcomers?

REFERENCES

Blake, B.

1991 Woiwurrung, the Melbourne Language. In R.M.W. Dixon and B.J. Blake (eds), *The Handbook of Australian Languages*, vol 4, Oxford University Press, Melbourne.

Bowden, R. and B. Bunbury

1990 *Being Aboriginal. Comments, Observations and Stories from Aboriginal Australians*, ABC Books, Sydney.

Curr, E.M.

1886–87 *The Australian Race: Its Origin, Languages, Customs, Place of Landing in Australia, and the Routes by Which It Spread Itself over That Continent*, 4 vols, J. Ferres, Government Printer, Melbourne.

Dixon, R.M.W.

1980 *The Languages of Australia*, Cambridge University Press, Cambridge.

1983 *Searching for Aboriginal Languages: Memoirs of a Field Worker*, University of Queensland Press, St Lucia.

Evans, N.

forthcoming Age, Sex and Language Shift among the Kayardild. In P. McConvell and R. Amery (eds), *Can Aboriginal and Islander Languages Survive?*, University of Queensland Press, St Lucia, Qld.

Foley, W.

1986 *The Papuan Languages of New Guinea*, Cambridge University Press, Cambridge.

Mattingley, C. and K. Hampton

1988 *Survival in Our Own Land. 'Aboriginal' Experiences in 'South Australia' since 1836*, ALDAA in association with Hodder and Stoughton, Adelaide.

Urry, J. and M. Walsh

1981 The Lost 'Macassan' Language of Northern Australia, *Aboriginal History* 5, 91–108.

Walker, A. and D. Zorc

1981 Austronesian Loanwords in Yolngu-Matha of Northeast Arnhem Land, *Aboriginal History* 5, 109–134.

Walsh, M.

1991 Conversational Styles and Intercultural Communication: An Example from Northern Australia, *Australian Journal of Communication* 18(1), 1–12.

Wurm, S.A. and S. Hattori

1981 *Language Atlas of the Pacific Area: Part 1*, Australian Academy of the Humanities and the Japan Academy, Canberra.

CHAPTER

THE STRUCTURE OF AUSTRALIAN ABORIGINAL LANGUAGES

Colin Yallop

CLASSIFICATION

Many of the world's languages show similarities to each other. Similarities may be just coincidences, and linguists are not persuaded that languages have a historical connection until they find reasonably systematic evidence. For example, the fact that the English word 'three' sounds and looks somewhat like the Dutch *drie* and German *drei* is of itself no proof that English, Dutch and German are historically related. It is only when we find a pattern of correspondences that we can take languages to be related. One of the relevant patterns here is that many English words beginning with *th* have counterparts in Dutch and German with *d*:

English	Dutch	German
thank	danken	danken
thin	dun	dünn
think	denken	denken
three	drie	drei
through	door	durch
thunder	donder	Donner

To establish that English, Dutch and German are part of a wider Indo-European family of languages, we need to pursue such regular patterns further, noting for example that Latin has a corresponding *t* in words such as *tenuis* (thin), *tres* (three), and so on. A painstaking search for correspondences such as these lies behind the assumption that the Indo-European languages of Europe and South Asia constitute a related family.

Closer to Australia, research of a similar kind has established that a large number of Pacific and Southeast Asian languages form a family usually known as Austronesian. This family includes languages as far apart as Hawaiian, Fijian, Maori, Indonesian, Javanese and Malagasy. Note, for example, the correspondences in:

English	Indonesian & Malay	Javanese	Fijian
moon	bulan	wulan	vula
fruit	buah	woh	vua
iron	besi	wesi	vesi

Linguists have not found evidence to demonstrate a historical relationship between Australian Aboriginal languages and languages outside Australia. Aboriginal languages show no special similarity to Austronesian languages, for instance. On the other hand, Aboriginal languages probably are all related to each other. Of course the languages do differ from each other quite substantially, just as English, Dutch and German do, or Indonesian, Javanese and Fijian, despite their historical connections.

Often the words of Australian languages — the vocabulary or lexicon, as linguists would say — are strikingly varied. There are a few examples of words that can be found in similar form over a large number of languages. The word for 'hand', for instance, is often *mara, mala* or *maa*, and the word for 'you and I' is *ngali* in many languages. But often vocabulary is surprisingly diverse. Even neighbouring languages that seem closely related in pronunciation and grammar may reveal differences in quite common words. For example, in Arrernte, spoken around Alice Springs, the word for 'dog' is *kngulya*. In the Western Desert languages to the west of Arrernte, the word is *tjitutja* or *papa*; in Warlpiri to the northwest of Arrernte, the word is *maliki*; and even in closely related languages to the east and northeast of Arrernte, the word is *aringka* or *alika*. Despite this lexical diversity, there is enough evidence, from pronunciation and grammar as well as from a small number of related words, to persuade most linguists to treat Australian Aboriginal languages as one large family.

There have been attempts to classify Australian — to establish groupings within the family, just as Indo-European languages are grouped into Indo-Iranian, Celtic, Germanic, Romance, Slavonic, and so on. But these attempts have not provided a useful and lasting classification, other than to divide languages spoken in the far north from the rest of the country. To be more precise, Australian languages other than those from the north of Western Australia and the north and northwest of the Northern Territory show considerable similarities in pronunciation and grammar. They are known as Pama-Nyungan, a term based on words for 'man' in the far north of Queensland (*pama*) and the southwest of Western Australia (*nyunga*) (see Map 5). The northern languages, usually referred to simply as non-Pama-Nyungan, not only differ from Pama-Nyungan but are also more diverse among themselves.

GRAMMAR

We have already referred to grammar several times and need to explain the term. In recent years, grammar has not figured prominently in many schools. Those who have had little or no instruction in grammar may assume that it is something technical and obscure, and even those who have been taught something called

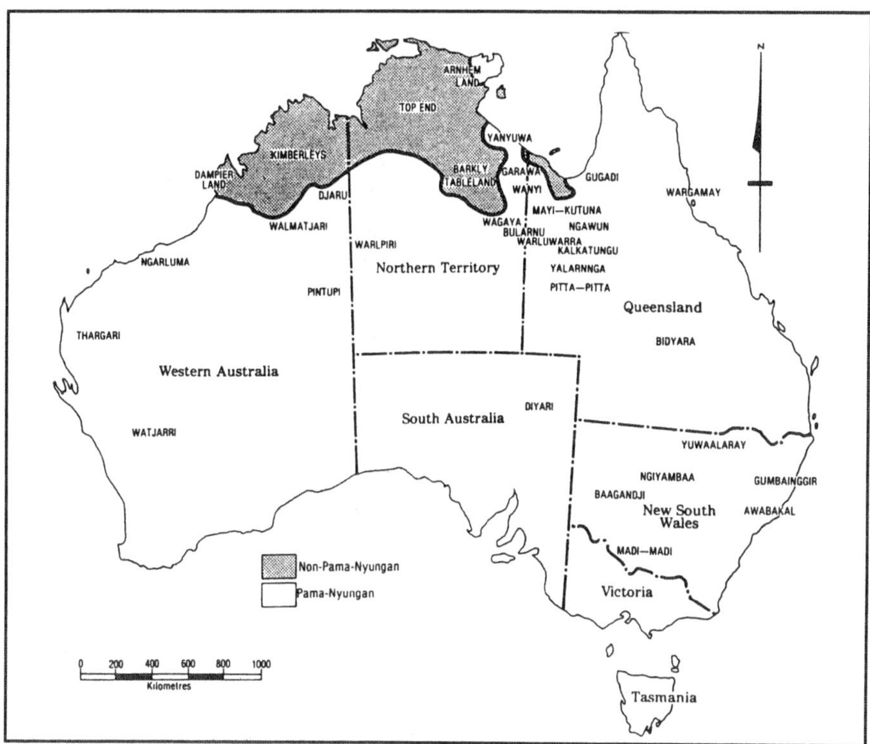

Map 5: Distribution of Pama-Nyungan and non-Pama-Nyungan languages (from Blake 1988, 87).

'grammar' may have gained the impression that it is a matter of learning a set of terms (such as 'noun' and 'transitive verb') and mastering difficult rules governing whether to say 'it is I' or 'it is me', or 'for you and I' or 'for you and me'.

It is true that 'grammar' can mean something like a grammar book or a set of grammatical rules, particularly rules that people will keep breaking unless they are firmly taught them. But there is another sense of the word that means something like 'the way in which a language is organised'. In this second sense all of us have a command of grammar, even if we speak only one language and have never consciously learned any grammatical rules or terms.

This point is not always readily accepted in English-speaking countries, partly because of an educational tradition of concentrating on only some parts of the language. In speaking English, we all follow many 'rules of grammar' which rarely if ever attract much attention. For example, we all obey certain 'rules' of word order. Anyone who speaks English says:

Did you hear that huge explosion last night?

No one who grew up speaking English needs formal instruction in putting these words in the right order, nor is tempted to break the pattern by saying, for instance, 'did hear you' instead of 'did you hear' or 'that explosion huge' instead of 'that huge explosion'. There are many other such patterns underlying our normal usage. Even this one example is sufficient to illustrate a pattern for asking a question ('did you hear' compared with 'you did hear' or 'you heard') and a pattern for certain kinds of processes and things (in English you can ask people whether they heard something, as you can ask whether they saw something, but you would be asking different questions if you asked whether they heard or read 'about' something).

These rules or patterns can be described as part of English grammar. They are part of how we express ourselves in English. Other languages may or may not have similar patterns. In some languages, such as Dutch and German, a word like 'huge' would precede 'explosion', as in English; in others, such as Spanish and Indonesian, the order would be the reverse. Few languages happen to have anything like the English question pattern represented by 'did you hear?'; in many languages the pattern would simply be a reversal of the corresponding statement: 'heard you?'. In fact this was once the pattern in English but it has been replaced. Only in old texts, such as the 1611 translation of the Bible, do we find patterns like:

> Know ye what I have done to you?
> Sayest thou this thing of thyself?
> Why baptizest thou then?

where more modern equivalents would be:

> Do you know what I have done to you?
> Do you say this thing of yourself?
> Why do you baptise then?

Grammar as taught in schools in the past often had little or nothing to say about patterns such as these. And in a way this was understandable since most of us learned the patterns quite unconsciously before going to school. What was taught as grammar was often directed towards understanding and learning the patterns of other languages, such as Latin and French. That was also understandable, given the importance of these languages in the educational system of the time. It was unfortunate, however, that English grammar tended to be judged in the light of Latin grammar: in some instances grammarians and teachers actually tried to make English conform to Latin patterns, in others they imposed rules for which there seems to have been very little justification at all, and in general they fostered the idea that you needed to learn special rules to be able to speak English properly — or more particularly to be able to produce elegant written English. Many people still have an uneasy feeling that the way they normally use English cannot be quite right and that they need to remember and apply artificial rules to their written English.

THE GRAMMAR OF AUSTRALIAN LANGUAGES

Australian Aborigines had no tradition of writing grammars or rule books. On the other hand, their languages certainly had grammar in the sense of organised and patterned expression. Some of the patterning seems similar enough to English, but there are surprises for those who might assume that every language should be like English.

For a first look at the grammar of one language, some simple sentences are given below in Guugu Yimidhirr, a Pama-Nyungan language spoken by the people with whom Captain Cook made contact in 1770 in the area we now call Cooktown in northern Queensland. The examples are based on Haviland's account of the language (Haviland 1979).

ngayu buli	I fell down
nyundu buli	you fell down
yugu buli	the tree fell down
gudaa buli	the dog fell down
ngayu nhina nhaadhi	I saw you
nyundu nganhi nhaadhi	you saw me
ngayu yugu nhaadhi	I saw the tree

Some features of these sentences are similar to English (*ngayu* precedes *buli*, just as 'I' precedes 'fell down', for example) but there are also many differences. There is nothing corresponding to 'the', and the word order in the last three sentences differs from English ('I you saw', 'you me saw', 'I tree saw'). Moreover, Guugu Yimidhirr has different forms of 'you' depending on whether you are doing something ('you saw me') or whether you are on the receiving end of the action ('I saw you'). Note that English makes such a difference between 'I' and 'me' but not between forms of 'you', whereas Guugu Yimidhirr makes a difference in both cases. The word for 'tree', however, remains the same in both Guugu Yimidhirr and English, whether it is doing something ('the tree fell down') or not ('I saw the tree').

Some more examples of Guugu Yimidhirr begin to reveal how different the patterning really is:

gudaangun nhina nhaadhi	the dog saw you
gudaangun nganhi nhaadhi	the dog saw me
nyundu bayan nhaadhi	you saw the house
yugungun bayan dumbi	the tree smashed the house

Here we find something that is quite unusual compared with the English patterning. To account for it, we need to introduce some grammatical concepts. Firstly we need to distinguish things such as dogs and houses and trees from words referring directly to persons such as 'I', 'me' and 'you'. Using common grammatical terms we call the first 'nouns' and the second 'personal pronouns'. Secondly, we need to distinguish actions or processes like falling, from those like seeing and smashing. One way of describing this difference is to say that the first type are simple actions in which someone or something does something, while the second type involves a further participant, someone or something on the receiving end of the action. Again, there are grammatical terms often used for these two types of action word: 'intransitive verb' for the first, where there is no recipient or goal; 'transitive verb' for the second, where the action does, so to speak, affect or pass on to a second participant. Here are some examples of intransitive and transitive processes in English:

intransitive	**transitive**
I fell down	I saw you
the dog barked	the dog bit me
the girl laughed	the girl hit the dog
a strong wind was blowing	a strong wind blew the tree down

With these terms at our disposal, we can say that in Guugu Yimidhirr, personal pronouns have the same form when they refer to the performer of an action, whether transitive or intransitive, but they have a different form as recipient or goal of a transitive action. On the other hand, nouns take the suffix *-ngun* only when they represent the performer of a transitive process, otherwise nouns have the same unsuffixed form, whether serving as doer of an intransitive process or goal of a transitive process.

If we look again at Guugu Yimidhirr sentences like:

ngayu buli	I fell down
gudaa buli	the dog fell down
gudaangun nganhi nhaadhi	the dog saw me
ngayu gudaa nhaadhi	I saw the dog

we can summarise the patterning of the personal pronoun and the noun in the following chart.

<table>
<tr><th></th><th>pronoun</th><th>noun</th></tr>
<tr><td>performing a transitive process</td><td rowspan="2">ngayu</td><td>gudaangun</td></tr>
<tr><td>performing an intransitive process</td><td rowspan="2">gudaa</td></tr>
<tr><td>undergoing a transitive process</td><td>nganhi</td></tr>
</table>

Most Pama-Nyungan languages have the same general kind of patterning as Guugu Yimidhirr. Many have a suffix that marks a noun as the agent of a transitive process, like *-ngun* in Guugu Yimidhirr, usually referred to as the 'ergative' suffix. Some have a suffix that marks pronouns (and sometimes some nouns as well) as the goal of a transitive process, usually referred to as the 'accusative' suffix. Most languages have a variety of other suffixes, which mark nouns for other roles besides agent and goal. In Guugu Yimidhirr, the noun *bayan* ('house') can take suffixes like *-bi* and *-nganh*:

bayanbi — in the house
bayannganh — from the house

The different forms of a noun or pronoun, suffixed to signal roles such as agent or goal or location, are referred to as 'cases'.

BEING AND HAVING IN AUSTRALIAN LANGUAGES

Here are a few more sentences from Guugu Yimidhirr:

yiyi bayan — this is a house
yiyi yugu — this is a tree
yugu munhi — the tree is black

What may be surprising to English speakers here is that there is nothing at all in Guugu Yimidhirr corresponding to English 'is' (or 'are' or 'was', et cetera). In Guugu Yimidhirr — and, in general, in most Australian languages — we do not say 'X is Y' but simply 'X Y'. Thus, a language like Guugu Yimidhirr makes a fairly radical difference among three types of process: (1) intransitive processes in which someone or something acts; (2) transitive processes in which an agent acts on a goal or recipient; and (3) processes of being in which there is actually no expression of a process at all, nothing like English 'is' or 'are'. English does not distinguish these types nearly as sharply. In English, for instance, there is no difference in form between the actor of an intransitive process and the agent of a transitive process. Moreover, by the very fact of having 'is' and 'are' English also tends to make 'being' seem more like other processes of 'doing'.

To illustrate some points about 'having', or possession, we turn to another Australian language for variety. Alyawarra is spoken in Central Australia, northeast of Alice Springs, and is closely related to other languages in the area, the most famous of which is Arrernte. The first few examples below show some structural similarities with what we have seen in Guugu Yimidhirr, notably the absence of any word matching 'am' or 'is', different forms of the pronoun 'I' and 'me', and an ergative suffix to mark a noun serving as agent of a transitive process (in Guugu Yimidhirr the suffix was *-ngun*, in Alyawarra it is *-ila*; details of Alyawarra can be found in Yallop 1977).

ayinga ngayakwa	I am hungry
aringka ngayakwa	the dog is hungry
aringka apmpima	the dog is hot
awiya apmpima	the boy is hot
aringkila ayinha utnhika	the dog bit me
awiyila aringka atuka	the boy hit the dog

The part of the grammar that we are now going to look at concerns the expression of possession. If we want to say 'my dog', a word corresponding to 'my' is added after the noun; if we want to say 'the boy's dog', the word for 'boy' takes a possessive suffix (like the English -'s) and again follows the noun 'dog':

aringka atjinha	my dog
aringka awiyikinha	the boy's dog

Phrases like these can serve as actors and goals, in the same way as simple nouns. If the phrase is agent of a transitive process, the whole phrase takes the suffix *-ila*, just as a simple noun would:

aringka atjinha ngayakwa	my dog is hungry
awiyila aringka atjinha atuka	the boy hit my dog
aringka atjinhila awiya utnhika	my dog bit the boy

What is strikingly different from English, however, is what happens with phrases like 'the boy's hand' and 'my hand'. Since 'hand' is *iltja*, we might expect the Alyawarra to be *iltja awiyikinha* and *iltja atjinha*. In fact, we find the language works as follows:

awiya iltja apmpima	the boy's hand is hot
ayinga iltja apmpima	my hand is hot
aringkila awiya iltja utnhika	the dog bit the boy's hand
aringkila ayinha iltja utnhika	the dog bit my hand

Literally, viewed through English, the Alyawarra wording is:

the boy the hand hot
I the hand hot
the dog bit the boy the hand
the dog bit me the hand

Here possession is not marked at all, but the two words are simply placed alongside each other. In other words, in Alyawarra you would not hold the boy's hand, you would hold the boy the hand, as if you were holding both the boy and the hand. If we are willing to think this through from the Alyawarra perspective, it does not seem unreasonable. After all, my hand is not something that I possess in the same way that I possess my dog or my car. My hand is part of me. When a dog bites my hand it does not bite some separate object that happens to belong to me, it bites me. The Alyawarra wording expresses this as the dog biting both me and the hand. In general, Alyawarra uses these two different patterns to distinguish between possession and a part–whole relationship. Anything that is a part of something will not be treated as a possession but will be expressed by putting the two words alongside each other, exactly in the manner of *awiya iltja*.

To look at it in another way, we might ask what it would mean to the Alyawarra to use English-style constructions. In fact, you could say 'my leg' in Alyawarra, using the possessive construction, but it would imply either that my leg is somehow detached from me or that the leg is not part of me (as if you were, for instance, sharing the meat of a bird and claiming a leg — 'that's my leg').

Many of the world's languages are in fact more like Alyawarra than English in this respect. We might say that they project a narrow view of possession. Indeed, it may be fairer to say that English and some other European languages are unusual in the extent to which they allow the possessive construction to cover all sorts of relationships that are not really possessive at all. Having looked at how a language like Alyawarra works, we may wonder why English so readily accepts phrases like 'my arm', 'my name' and 'my father'. (This question is taken up in the second point for discussion at the end of this chapter.)

QUESTIONS

Another area of grammar in which there are significant differences between Australian languages and English is that of questioning. As we mentioned earlier in this chapter, English has its own ways of distinguishing between statements and questions, for example:

statement	**question**
you heard me	did you hear me?
Jenny likes coffee	does Jenny like coffee?
Harry doesn't like tea	doesn't Harry like tea?

In fact, English grammar allows for various kinds of question. In addition to what you might call a direct question, open to a 'yes' or 'no', we also have questions that seem to expect 'yes' rather than 'no' or 'no' rather than 'yes', as well as the possibility of merely repeating something with questioning intonation to check whether we have heard correctly:

does Jenny like coffee?	(open to 'yes' or 'no')
Jenny likes coffee, doesn't she?	(expecting 'yes')
Jenny doesn't like coffee, does she?	(expecting 'no')
Jenny likes coffee?	('is that what you said?')

The grammar of questions in Australian languages is, of course, different from English. Here are some examples of statements and questions from Walmajarri, a language spoken around Fitzroy Crossing in the north of Western Australia. (Basic information about the language also written 'Walmatjari', is in Hudson and Richards 1978; but point 4 for discussion at the end of this chapter gives more examples and you may find it useful to tackle that now, to work out what each element means, including for instance the *-lu* in *palu* and *ngalu*.)

yanku palu	they will go
yanku ngalu	will they go?
yani palu	they went
yani pa	he or she went
yani nga	did he or she go?
yani pa manga	the girl went
yani palu mangawarnti	the girls went
yani ngalu mangawarnti	did the girls go?

There is yet another type of question in many languages — the information-seeking question that contains a question word such as 'who?' or 'where?' or 'when?' In Walmajarri, the words corresponding to 'where' and 'when' are *wanyjurla* and *nyangurla*:

wanyjurla palu yani	where did they go?
nyangurla palu yanku	when will they go?

The word for 'who' is *ngana*. Like other nouns and pronouns in most Pama-Nyungan languages, *ngana* takes an ergative suffix when it is agent of a transitive process. In Walmajarri the relevant suffix is *-ngu*:

ngana pa pinya mangangu	who did the girl hit?
nganangu pa pinya parri	who hit the boy?

It seems that in most Australian languages words like 'who?' and 'what?' actually have an indefinite meaning, so that 'who?' could be reinterpreted as 'someone or other, I don't know who', and 'what?' could be reinterpreted as 'something or other, I don't know what'. Thus, a speaker of an Australian language might appear to be asking:

> who took this photo and sent it to my brother?

when a better translation into English might be:

> someone took this photo and sent it to my brother.

Now, there are two ways of approaching this grammatical phenomenon. We could say, more or less as we have just said above, that an Australian word for 'who?' actually means both 'who?' (questioning) and 'someone' (indefinite, unspecified). But we should stop to ask whether this twofold meaning of the word is really a consequence of approaching the language via English. Suppose we try to forget the English distinction between 'who?' and 'someone' and ask what it means to speak a language that has no such distinction. It would mean — and we cannot entirely forget English grammar when we use English to talk about another language — that you don't really ask questions that seek specific information but you reveal gaps in your own knowledge to allow other people to fill them in. In this connection, we could compare two styles of interacting. The first would include direct questioning, expecting straight answers, and a conversation in this style might go something like this:

Who took the photo?	–My sister
Does she do a lot of photography?	–No, not a lot
Where does she live?	–Oh, in Queensland

The second style of interaction would not ask any direct questions but would, so to speak, allow the other person to supply information:

Someone took this photo	–Yes, my sister took it
Perhaps she takes lots of photos	–Not so many really
She maybe lives in South Australia	–She lives in Queensland

There is a sense in which this second style makes no distinction between information-seeking questions and statements. It's a style in which you leave it open to someone else to add information. Persons who are used to the first style are likely to find the second style far too casual and indirect, while those who are accustomed to the second style might find the first too demanding, even aggressive.

Suppose, at the very least, that Aboriginal languages make far less use of direct questioning than English does. Then consider how important questions and answers are in English-speaking Australia. They figure prominently in all kinds of education — children are expected at an early age to recognise and answer questions, especially questions asked by adults, even when it is quite obvious that the adult already knows the answer (teachers' questions like 'what do we call a shop where you buy meat?' or 'what is thirteen plus twelve?', or parents' questions like 'did you draw this beautiful picture?' or, in a sterner context, 'who's left their room in a mess again?', and so on). Later in the educational process, students are expected to ask questions themselves and we place great value on learning to inquire. We even make games and television programs out of questioning — quizzes, and so on. But this is not a universal pattern of life. Once we have taken the basic step of recognising that languages may be fundamentally different in their grammar, it is not so difficult to see how a society might build quite differently, regarding information as something to be shared rather than pursued, developing conventions for inviting information without demanding it, and so on. Eades has written about this difference in styles of interaction (Eades 1991, see also Walsh 1991) and she brings out the practical relevance of it in chapter 13.

SOME OTHER POINTS OF GRAMMAR

Some readers may be familiar with terms that are used in talking about the grammar of English or other European languages, and should not expect all of these terms to apply, or to apply in the same way, to Australian languages. For example, the term 'preposition' is used to describe English words like 'in', 'at' and 'for'. But it should be clear from earlier mention of cases, that the Australian Aboriginal equivalent of a preposition plus a noun (for example, 'in Darwin' or 'for mother') is often a suffixed noun (that is, something like 'Darwin-in' or 'mother-for'). Thus, especially in Pama-Nyungan languages with elaborate case systems, the term 'preposition' may not be needed at all.

We have already seen that terms like 'noun', 'pronoun' and 'verb' are relevant, even if the concepts are not quite as in English. Similarly the terms 'adjective' (for words like 'big', 'heavy' and 'good') and 'demonstrative' (for pointing words like 'this' and 'that') do prove useful in describing Australian languages. Again, there are significant differences as well. For example, the demonstratives of Australian languages are usually much more complex than those of English: there are often different words for 'this (very near)' and 'this (not very near)' or for 'that (distant but still visible)' and 'that (not visible)'. The English distinction between demonstrative pronouns ('that') and demonstrative adverbs ('there') may also not apply. For instance, 'there' may be translated as 'that' with a locative case suffix: looking at it through English wording, you say 'that-at' rather than 'there'.

In many Australian languages, there is no distinction between singular and plural nouns. In other words, all nouns behave like English 'sheep' or 'deer'. But some languages, including many non-Pama-Nyungan, have complex systems of gender or noun class which may include number marking. One of the simpler examples is Tiwi, spoken on Bathurst and Melville Islands off the north coast of the Northern Territory. All nouns belong to one of two genders, masculine or feminine. For example, *thangkinangki* 'white-breasted sea eagle' is masculine and *ngaringa* 'black cockatoo' is feminine. But human nouns may have a masculine, feminine and plural form (where the plural is not marked as masculine or feminine):

tini	'man'	mantani	'male friend'
tinga	'woman'	mantanga	'female friend'
tiwi	'people'	mantawi	'friends'

Walsh gives details of a more elaborate noun class system in a non-Pama-Nyungan language (chapter 8).

Even in languages without noun class systems, number may be evident in other areas of the grammar. As we saw earlier in the Walmajarri examples, number may be marked within or next to the verb. In the following example both the *-lu* attached to the interrogative element *nga* and the *-warnti* suffix on the noun are signals of the plural:

yani ngalu mangawarnti	did the girls go?

The personal pronouns of Australian languages are also marked for number, dual as well as singular and plural. Some languages also distinguish inclusive and exclusive first person, where an inclusive 'we' includes the addressee, and an exclusive 'we' doesn't. Some examples from Warlpiri are given to clarify the meanings and conventional grammatical terminology:

ngaju	I	first person singular
nyuntu	you	second person singular
ngali	you & I	first person dual inclusive
ngajarra	we two (excl. you)	first person dual exclusive
nyumpala	you two	second person dual
ngalipa	you & I & other(s)	first person plural inclusive
nganimpa	we (3+, excl. you)	first person plural exclusive
nyurrula	you (3+)	second person plural

Third person forms (omitted from the Warlpiri examples above) correspond to English 'she', 'he' and 'they'. In fact, third person pronouns are not as common in Australian languages as in English, and absence of any pronoun may be enough to signal third person. In other words, 'told me' may be equivalent to 'he or she told me'. When a third person pronoun does appear, there is commonly a single form for both male and female. In other words, there is a single word corresponding to both 'he' and 'she'. (Bundjalung, described by Sharpe in chapter 5 is an exception to this generalisation, as are some of the northern languages with noun class systems including masculine and feminine.)

Finally, verbs may be extremely complex in Australian languages. The verb itself may carry a variety of suffixes to signal such distinctions as present and past (not unlike English 'walk' and 'walked'). The verb may also be accompanied by various auxiliary elements (again not unlike English, where elements such as 'have' and 'will' contribute to the total meaning of verb groups like 'have walked', 'will walk' and 'will have walked'). We have already seen in Walmajarri that the element *pa* or *nga* following the verb distinguishes a statement from a question. For a quite different auxiliary system, see the following Warlpiri examples. (Note that both *ngaju* and *-rna* mean 'I': the suffix represents a kind of agreement with the independent pronoun and is attached to the verb auxiliary, or if there is no auxiliary, to the pronoun itself.)

ngajurna purlaja	I shouted, I have shouted
ngaju lparna purlaja	I was shouting
ngajurna purlami	I'll shout, let me shout
ngaju karna purlami	I'll shout, I'll be shouting

CONCLUSION

In this chapter we have looked at just a few aspects of the grammar of Australian languages. In some ways grammar may seem to be merely a matter of how this language or that puts words together. But we have also seen that the grammar of a language contains fundamental patterns that may have a lot to do with how we view the world and how we think about reality. In particular, the assumptions of English-speaking Australians about such things as possession and questioning are not independent of the way we habitually express ourselves in language. We do not want to overstate or exaggerate this point, but neither do we want to overlook the role that language plays. The exercises below include some further opportunities to explore the questions raised in this chapter.

Not all of the points we have mentioned here are unique to Australia. The use of a single pronoun for both 'she' and 'he', for example, is found in many languages around the world, including languages as diverse as Hindi, Indonesian and Japanese. And a final reminder: there are numerous Australian languages, each with its own grammar, and although many of them show significant similarities, we should be very cautious about generalising across all of Australia. Subsequent chapters of this book will continue to demonstrate the rich variety.

FOR DISCUSSION

1. The second section of this chapter (on 'Grammar') mentions grammatical rules which are sometimes considered important in elegant written English but which many people don't understand or don't obey. The particular example given was that of the use of 'I' and 'me', where the traditional rules are strongly influenced by Latin grammar. It is interesting in this regard that there are some similarities between Latin and Australian languages. We saw above that many Australian languages have different pronoun forms for actors and goals. For example in Guugu Yimidhirr:

ngayu nhina nhaadhi	I saw you
nyundu nganhi nhaadhi	you saw me

Latin had a similar pattern of different pronoun forms:

ego te amo	I love you
tu me amas	you love me

In both Latin and Guugu Yimidhirr you would use the 'I' form of the pronoun after a process of being (but remember that in Guugu Yimidhirr there is actually no process expressed). In Latin you would say (for example, pointing at a photograph) 'this is I', in Guugu Yimidhirr 'this I'. English obviously has a different pattern here, since we say 'this is me', but there were attempts to make English follow the Latin pattern and many people still have an uneasy feeling that 'this is I' is really what they ought to say. Such has been the confusion on this point that some people now over-correct, using 'I' instead of 'me' in many instances where the traditional rules happily accepted 'me'. For example, it was once usual to say 'please inform my colleague or me': Latin would have used the accusative form of 'me' here and traditional grammar therefore accepted the use of 'me'. But some people now seem to feel it is 'more correct' to say 'please inform my colleague or I'.

For discussion, here are some examples of modern colloquial use of 'I' and 'me':

I'll be seeing you
I can't tell you
Me? I won't do it!
John and me will call round
You'll tell me tomorrow?
You'll tell John and me tomorrow?

As a first exercise, check what you know about Guugu Yimidhirr and see which of these occurrences of 'I' and 'me' would translate as *ngayu* and which as *nganhi*.

As a second exercise, try to work out what the pattern of modern colloquial English actually is — how can you explain the use of 'I' in 'I won't do it' but 'me' in 'John and me won't do it'? (You may find you have to explain it by the position of the word rather than by the role which the word plays in the sentence; and if you have access to a French grammar you may find an interesting parallel in the French use of *moi* and *je.*)

A third point for discussion relates to the suggestion that a language like Guugu Yimidhirr makes a sharp distinction between a relationship of being something and an action of doing something. What is the relevance here of the modern English pattern of saying 'this is me' rather than 'this is I'? Does the pattern help to make being more like doing (since 'me' seems to be the goal of an action)? You might like also to look at the following English examples, where it might be argued that 'being' is treated as 'doing' something:

What did you do yesterday?– I was at my brother's place.
I know I'm being a nuisance, but I want to ask you a favour.
Will you be the spokesperson?
I'll volunteer if you'll be my supporter.

2. Review the discussion in the section about the grammatical treatment of possession ('Being and Having in Australian Languages'). In the light of the grammar of Australian languages, is it fair to say that English projects a wide-ranging view of possession? Consider examples of the way in which we refer to owning our bodies, for instance in talking about donating one's body to medical research. Or consider the way in which people to whom we are related may be treated as possessions in our language: 'my friend', 'my father', 'my daughter', and so on. Is this unconnected with our social behaviour and attitudes? Add other examples that might occur to you in this connection and discuss the implications for our view of the world. The point is not simply to praise or condemn the English language for being different from Australian languages, but rather to explore what social and cultural differences might be related to grammatical differences.

3. Pursuing the discussion in this chapter about questions and statements, think about the consequences of not distinguishing between 'who took my radio?' and 'someone took my radio', or between 'what did you find?' and 'you found something'. Add other examples of your own, again with a view to exploring just what the differences might be between Aboriginal and English-speaking Australia. Here, too, the point is not to reach sweeping and oversimplified generalisations about black Australia or white Australia, but to consider how societies and languages can differ and how they might misunderstand each other.

4. See how much you can work out about Walmajarri grammar from the following:

yanku palu	they will go
yanku ngalu	will they go?
yani palu	they went
yani ngalu	did they go?
yani pa	he or she went
yani nga	did he or she go?
yani pa manga	the girl went
yani nga manga	did the girl go?
yani palu mangawarnti	the girls went
yani ngalu mangawarnti	did the girls go?
yani palu parriwarnti	the boys went
yani ngalu parriwarnti	did the boys go?
yani palu, payi	they went, didn't they?
yani pa manga, payi	the girl went, didn't she?
yani palu parriwarnti, payi	the boys went, didn't they?
yani palu	they went
yani ngalu	did they go?
yani pa	he went
yanta	go!
yantalu	go (plural)
yanana pa	he is going
yanku pa	he'll go
yanany pa	he regularly goes

REFERENCES

Blake, B.

1988 Redefining Pama-Nyungan. In N. Evans and S. Johnson (eds), *Aboriginal Linguistics* 1, University of New England Press, Armidale, 1–90.

Eades, D.

1991 Communicative Strategies in Aboriginal English. In S. Romaine (ed), *Language in Australia*, Cambridge University Press, Cambridge, 84–93.

Haviland, J.

1979 How to Talk to Your Brother-in-law in Guugu Yimidhirr. In T. Shopen (ed), *Languages and Their Speakers*, Winthrop, Cambridge MA, 160–239.

Hudson, J. and E. Richards

1978 *The Walmatjari: An Introduction to the Language and Culture*, Summer Institute of Linguistics, Darwin.

Walsh, M.

1991 Conversational Styles and Intercultural Communication: An Example from Northern Australia, *Australian Journal of Communication* 18(1),1–12.

Yallop, C.

1977 *Alyawarra: An Aboriginal Language of Central Australia*, Australian Institute of Aboriginal Studies, Canberra.

CHAPTER

LANGUAGE CONTACT IN EARLY COLONIAL NEW SOUTH WALES 1788 TO 1791

Jakelin Troy

THE BEGINNING OF CONTACT

It is well-known that on 26 January 1788 England established its first settlement in Australia at Sydney Cove in Port Jackson. Less well-known are the linguistic consequences of that settlement. The aim of this chapter is to describe some of the earliest linguistic interactions between the indigenous people of the Sydney region and the members of the First Fleet who, led by Governor Arthur Phillip, established the colony of New South Wales.

Contact between Aboriginal people and colonists first occurred at Botany Bay where, by 20 January 1788, the First Fleet was anchored. Simple verbal exchanges and much use of gesture seemed to achieve the desired results, at least from the colonists' point of view:

> This appearance [of a large number of Aboriginal people] whetted curiosity to its utmost, but as prudence forbade a few people to venture wantonly among so great a number, and a party of only six men was observed on the north shore, the Governor immediately proceeded to land on that side, in order to take possession of his new territory, and bring about an intercourse between its old and new masters... At last an officer in the boat made signs of a want of water, which it was judged would indicate his wish of landing. The natives directly comprehended what he wanted, and pointed to a spot where water could be procured... As on the event of this meeting might depend so much of our future tranquillity, every delicacy on our side was requisite. The Indians, though timorous, shewed no signs of resentment at the Governor's going on shore; an interview commenced, in which the conduct of both parties pleased each other so much, that the strangers returned to their ships with a much better opinion of the natives than they had landed with; and the latter seemed highly entertained with their new acquaintance, from whom they condescended to accept of a looking glass, some beads, and other toys. (Tench 1979, 35)

The author of this account, a senior officer named Watkin Tench, also described an encounter during the exploration of Botany Bay:

> We were met by a dozen Indians... Eager to come to a conference, and yet afraid of giving offence, we advanced with caution towards them, nor would they, at first, approach nearer to us than the distance of some paces. Both parties were armed; yet an attack seemed as unlikely on their part, as we knew it to be on our own... After nearly an hour's conversation by signs and gestures, they repeated several times the word whurra, which signifies, begone, and walked away from us to the head of the bay. (Tench 1979, 36)

The colonists decided that Botany Bay lacked the resources necessary for a settlement. They investigated Port Jackson and chose Sydney Cove as the site for their base. The Aboriginal people of Sydney showed some interest in the newcomers and this encouraged Phillip in his hopes that permanent communication could be established. His orders from the King of England were to open free communication with the indigenous people of Australia to convince them that although their country was to be colonised, they would be treated well and would live in harmony with the colonists:

> You are to endeavour, by every possible means, to open an intercourse with the natives, and to conciliate their affections, enjoining all our subjects to live in amity and kindness with them. And if any of our subjects shall wantonly destroy them, or give them any unnecessary interruption in the exercise of their several occupations, it is our will and pleasure that you do cause such offenders to be brought to punishment according to the degree of the offence. You will endeavour to procure an account of the numbers inhabiting the neighbourhood of the intended settlement, and report our opinion to one of our Secretaries of State in what manner our intercourse with these people may be turned to the advantage of this colony. (George III 1787, 485)

The establishment of a common language, at least between the colonial administration and the local Aboriginal people, was thus a high priority for Phillip.

Aboriginal people in the Sydney area visited the settlement and elementary communication began to develop. Phillip's strategy involved the use of a short vocabulary of the Guugu Yimidhirr language collected by Captain James Cook's expedition in 1770 at the Endeavour River, northern Queensland. This language is completely different from the languages of the Sydney district and attempts to use the vocabulary were therefore singularly unsuccessful. One product of the experiment was that, for a while, Sydney Aboriginal people thought that the colonists' word for all animals except dogs was the word derived from Guugu Yimidhirr 'kangaroo'. Conversely, the colonists thought the area in which they settled had little fauna because the Aborigines called all animals 'kangaroo':

> We have never discovered that...they know any other beasts but the kangaroo and dog. Whatever animal is shewn them, a dog excepted, they call kangaroo: a strong presumption that the wild animals of the country are very few... Soon after our arrival at Port Jackson, I was walking out near a place where I observed a party of Indians, busily employed in looking at some sheep in an inclosure, and repeatedly crying out, Kangaroo, kangaroo! As this seemed to afford them pleasure, I was willing to increase it by pointing out the horses and cows, which were at no great distance. (Tench 1979, 51)

Much later, the colonists realised that they had inadvertently taught the local Aborigines a word from another Aboriginal language:

> Kanguroo, was a name unknown to them for any animal, until we introduced it. When I showed Colbee the cows brought out in the Gorgon, he asked me if they were kanguroos. (Tench 1979, 269)

In spite of the seemingly amiable start to cross-cultural relations, Aboriginal people very soon became offended by the presence of the colony. Phillip was unable to prevent colonists from stealing the possessions of Aboriginal people and physically attacking them, and the Aboriginal population retreated and refused to have anything to do with the settlement.

THE FIRST LINGUISTIC EXPERIMENT: THE CAPTURE AND TRAINING OF ARABANOO

Phillip was very disturbed by the breakdown in communication. He attempted to control acts of aggression towards Aboriginal people by severely punishing offenders. Aboriginal people also retaliated violently and Phillip feared a full-scale war.

The need to establish communication became urgent. As it seemed impossible to entice Aboriginal people into the settlement where linguistic interaction could be achieved naturally, Phillip decided to capture a number of people, force them to learn English and then use them as interpreters:

> It being remarked with concern, that the natives were becoming every day more troublesome and hostile, several people having been wounded, and others, who were

> necessarily employed in the woods, driven in and much alarmed by them, the governor determined on endeavouring to seize and bring into the settlement, one or two of those people, whose language it was become absolutely necessary to acquire, that they might learn to distinguish friends from enemies. (Collins 1975 vol 1, 40)

In December 1788 Phillip's plan succeeded and Arabanoo became the first Aboriginal captive of the British and thereby the first Aboriginal person to enter into prolonged communication with the colonists. He was described as a poor but willing learner. There is no detailed description of the processes used in teaching him English although it is certain all the administration participated in the endeavour. When he acquired a word, it was observed that he could extrapolate to other similar items. Arabanoo supplied information about Aboriginal society to the colonists and errors of understanding were corrected as communication became more effective.

The colonists began their experiments by exposing Arabanoo to their own culture and language and watching him for his reactions in order to understand something of his culture and language. They noted words he used in his own language that they supposed described his experiences:

> To prevent his escape, a handcuff with a rope attached to it, was fastened around his left wrist, which at first highly delighted him; he called it '*Ben-gàd-ee*' (or ornament), but his delight changed to rage and hatred when he discovered its use...seeing the smoke of fire lighted by his country men, he looked earnestly at it, and sighing deeply two or three times, uttered the word '*gweè-un*' (fire). (Tench 1979, 141)

Eliciting Arabanoo's name proved to be a great challenge and it took until February to solve the mystery:

> Many unsuccessful attempts were made to learn his name; the governor therefore called him Manly, from the cove in which he was captured: this cove had received its name from the manly undaunted behaviour of a party of natives seen there, on our taking possession of the country. (Tench 1979, 141)

Tench attributed their eventual success to Arabanoo's increased confidence:

> His reserve, from want of confidence in us, continued to wear away: he told us his name, and Manly gave place to Ar-ab-a-noo. (Tench 1979, 143)

The colonists' main objective was to teach Arabanoo English and 'he readily pronounced with tolerable accuracy the names of things which were taught him' (Tench 1979, 140). Pictures were also employed by the colonists in their sociolinguistic experiments with Arabanoo:

> When pictures were shewn to him, he knew directly those which represented the human figure: among others, a very large handsome print of her royal highness the Dutchess [sic] of Cumberland being produced, he called out, woman, a name by which we had just before taught him to call female convicts. Plates of birds and beasts were also laid before him and many people were led to believe, that such as he spoke about and pointed to were known to him. But this must have been an erroneous conjecture, for the elephant, rhinoceros, and several others, which we must have discovered did they exist in the country, were of the number. Again, on the other hand, those he did not point out, were equally unknown to him. (Tench 1979, 140)

Music was another medium employed in Arabanoo's enculturation: '...he had...shown pleasure and readiness in imitating our tunes'. (Tench 1979, 142)

Arabanoo came to be well-liked by the colonists for the 'gentleness and humanity of his disposition' (Tench 1979, 143). It was observed with approval that:

> ...when our children, stimulated by wanton curiosity, used to flock around him, he never failed to fondle them, and, if he were eating at the time, constantly offered them the choicest part of his fare. (Tench 1979, 143)

When Hunter met Arabanoo for the first time in May 1789 he commented on his excellent memory for names and his mild nature. He also commented on Arabanoo's use of an Aboriginal word for boat. This indicates that Arabanoo was mixing English and Aboriginal words when he knew the meaning would be understood:

> He very soon learnt the names of the different gentlemen who took notice of him, and when I was made acquainted with him, he learnt mine, which he never forgot, but expressed great desire to come on board my *nowee*; which is their expression for boat or other vessel upon the water... The day after I came in, the governor and his family did me the honour to dine on board, when I was also favoured with the company of *Ara-ba-noo*, whom I found to be a very good natured talkative fellow; he was about thirty years of age, and tolerably well looked. (Hunter 1968, 93)

Arabanoo's gradual enculturation was noted, particularly with regard to everyday matters:

> Bread he began to relish; and tea he drank with avidity: strong liquors he would never taste, turning from them with disgust and abhorrence. Our dogs and cats had ceased to be objects of fear, and were become his greatest pets, and constant companions at table. (Tench 1979, 143)

Similarly, the colonists were acquiring knowledge of Arabanoo's language and culture, which they would later use in dealing with other Aboriginal people:

> One of our chief amusements, after the cloth was removed [that is, after dinner], was to make him repeat the names of things in his language, which he never hesitated to do with the utmost alacrity, correcting our pronunciation when erroneous. Much information relating to the customs and manners of his country was also gained from him. (Tench 1979, 143)

The colonists began to make use of the Aboriginal language they learned from Arabanoo. An early example is found in Hunter's account of an expedition to Broken Bay on 6 June 1789. After pitching their tents for the night, at 'Pitt-Water', they found an Aboriginal woman hiding from them in the long wet grass, unable to run away because she was weak from what was thought to be smallpox:

> She was discovered by some person who having fired at and shot a hawk from a tree right over her, terrified her so much that she cried out and discovered herself...we all went to see this unhappy girl...she appeared to be about 17 or 18 years of age, and had covered her debilitated and naked body with the wet grass, having no other means of hiding herself; she was very much frightened on our approaching her, and shed many tears, with piteous lamentations: we understood none of her expressions, but felt much concern at the distress she seemed to suffer. We endeavoured all in our power to make her easy, and with the assistance of a few expressions which had been collected from poor Ara-ba-noo while he was alive, we soothed her distress a little. (Hunter 1968, 96)

In spite of the knowledge gained from Arabanoo, Phillip's experiment was regarded as a linguistic disappointment:

> He did not want docility; but either from the difficulty of acquiring our language, from the unskilfulness of his teachers, or from some natural defect, his progress in learning it was not equal to what we had expected. (Tench 1979, 150)

Phillip's hopes that Arabanoo would be their link with the Aboriginal population in general were finally dashed by his death on 18 May 1789 (Tench 1979, 149). Collins describes how Arabanoo cared for two Aboriginal children during what appeared to be a smallpox plague raging amongst the Aboriginal population. Arabanoo caught the disease and eventually succumbed:

> From the first hour of the introduction of the boy and girl into the settlement, it was feared that the native who had been so instrumental in bringing them in, and whose attention to them during their illness excited the admiration of every one that witnessed it, would be attacked by the same disorder; as on his person were found none of those traces of its ravages which are frequently left behind. It happened as the fears of every one predicted; he fell a victim to the disease in eight days after he was seized with it, to the great regret of every one who had witnessed how little of the savage was found in his manner, and how quickly he was substituting in its place a docile, affable, and truly amiable deportment. (Collins 1975 vol 1, 54)

The girl (named Boorong or Abaroo) and the boy (Nanberry) continued to live with the colonists. But they were not considered old enough to be influential, nor competent enough in either English or an Aboriginal language to explain Phillip's intentions to other Aboriginal people.

THE SECOND LINGUISTIC EXPERIMENT: BENNELONG'S COOPERATION

The ability to communicate fully with the Aborigines became an increasingly urgent concern for Phillip as attacks against lone colonists became frequent in 1789. Given the shyness of the Aborigines, official policy centred on training an Aboriginal captive to speak English:

> The want of one of the people of this country, who, from a habit of living amongst us, might have been the means of preventing much of this hostile disposition in them towards us, was much to be lamented. If poor Ara-ba-noo had lived, he would have acquired enough of our language to have understood whatever we wished him to communicate to his countrymen; he could have made them perfectly understand, that we wished to live with them on the most friendly footing, and that we wished to promote, as much as might be in our power, their comfort and happiness. (Hunter 1968, 114)

On 25 November 1789 Phillip detained two more men, Colbee and Bennelong. Colbee escaped almost immediately but Bennelong was caught in the act of following him. He was shackled and guarded by a convict and subjected to language lessons. Bennelong was judged to be a much better language learner than Arabanoo and he rapidly acquired enough English to communicate with the colonists:

> His powers of mind were certainly far above mediocrity. He acquired knowledge, both of our manners and language, faster than his predecessor had done. He willingly communicated information; sang, danced, and capered: told us all the customs of his country, and all the details of his family economy. (Tench 1979, 160)

He was described as an accomplished mimic:

> He is a very intelligent man, and much information may, no doubt, be procured from him when he can be well understood... He is very good-natured, being seldom angry at any jokes that may be passed upon him, and he readily imitates all the actions and gestures of every person in the governor's family. (Hunter 1968, 269)

As Tench mentions, he particularly liked imitating Phillip's French cook:

> ...whom he had constantly made the butt of his ridicule, by mimicking his voice, gait, and other peculiarities, all of which he again went through with his wonted exactness and drollery. (Tench 1979, 178)

Tench (1979, 176) noted that Bennelong spoke 'broken English' which suggests that at least an incipient pidgin language had developed through the colonists' communication with Arabanoo and then Bennelong.

Bennelong escaped from the settlement on 3 May 1790, returning many months later, but only after much enticing by Phillip. Bennelong was able to use his influence with both the Aboriginal people and the colonists to sustain interaction between the groups. Aboriginal people began to visit the settlement more often, and started to visit of their own accord unaccompanied by Bennelong. By November 1790, Tench was able to comment that:

> With the natives we are hand and glove. They throng the camp every day, and sometimes by their clamour and importunity for bread and meat (of which they now all eat greedily) are become very troublesome. God knows, we have little enough for ourselves! (Tench 1979, 192)

The social situation created by the influx of Aboriginal people into Sydney was conducive to the development of a pidgin language (see chapter 10 by Harris). Textual evidence of pidgin is scanty but Collins remarks that a mixed language had developed in the colony as a result of the regular communication between Aboriginal people and colonists:

> By slow degrees we began mutually to be pleased with, and to understand each other. Language, indeed, is out of the question; for at the time of writing this [September 1796] nothing but a barbarous mixture of English with the Port Jackson dialect is spoken by either party; and it must be added, that even in this the natives have the advantage, comprehending with much greater aptness than we can pretend to, every thing they hear us say. (Collins 1975 vol 1, 451)

Collins's comments strongly suggest the emergence of a stable pidgin language. His observation that Aboriginal people were the most proficient speakers of the language suggests that they were also its principal creators. Collins also confessed himself to be a user of the mixed language. The ethnographic data he was able to collect using the language allowed him to make a detailed comparison of Christian beliefs and those of the Aboriginal people familiar to him (Collins 1975 vol 1, 454–55). The mixed language must have been quite stable and must have had a substantial lexicon for Collins to have been able to converse at the necessary level.

INFORMAL CONTACTS

The records which remain from the period of Phillip's governorship are primarily official and there is little evidence of informal encounters between Aboriginal people and colonists aside from reports of attacks on convicts. Collins does report that within the first few days of settlement in a cove a 'family' of Aboriginal people was regularly visited:

> ...by large parties of the convicts of both sexes on those days in which they were not wanted for labour, where they danced and sang with apparent good humour. (Collins 1975 vol 1, 32)

Convicts formed the largest segment of the first colonial population and they were not overly confined. But their opportunities to mix with Aboriginal people were limited: they were compelled to work most of the day and they were subject to restrictions placed on them by Phillip. Phillip's desire to keep Aboriginal people and convicts apart was, nevertheless, very difficult to enforce given the sheer numbers of convicts relative to the Marine guards. At the very least, some informal linguistic interaction must have been taking place.

EXPERIENCES OF ABORIGINAL PEOPLE WITH THE ENGLISH LANGUAGE

Both Aboriginal people and colonists had difficulty with each other's languages:

> But if they sometimes put us to difficulty, many of our words were to them unutterable. The letters s and v they never could pronounce: the latter became invariably w, and the former mocked all their efforts...and a more unfortunate defect in learning our language could not easily be pointed out. (Tench 1979, 293)

> The S is a letter which they cannot pronounce, having no sound in their language similar to it. When bidden to pronounce sun, they always say *tun*; salt, *talt*; and so of all words wherein it occurs. (Tench 1979, 189)

Colonists acquired many Aboriginal words while interrogating Aboriginal people in their attempt to understand and describe their new country. Similarly, Aboriginal people interrogated colonists about their cultural artefacts and lifestyle. While colonists seem to have been content to use Aboriginal words for Aboriginal artefacts and many of the plants and animals new to them, Aboriginal people coined words from their own languages in addition to acquiring the English terms:

> Their translation of our words into their language is always apposite, comprehensive, and drawn from images familiar to them: a gun, for instance, they call *Gòroobeera*, that is — *a stick of fire*. Sometimes also, by a licence of language, they call those who carry guns by the same name. But the appellation by which they generally distinguished us was that of *Bèreewolgal*, meaning — *men come from afar*. (Tench 1979, 292)

> The first time Colbee saw a monkey, he called *Wùr-ra* (a rat); but on examining its paws, he exclaimed, with astonishment and affright, *Mùl-la* (a man). (Tench 1979, 270)

Arabanoo died before he re-established extended communication with other Aboriginal people and cannot be regarded as having contributed significantly to the early acquisition of knowledge about English by Aboriginal people. Bennelong, on the other hand, returned to live with his people after several months of captivity amongst the colonists. It is well-attested in the literature of the period that he was a major catalyst in disseminating knowledge about the colony and its official language. One fragment of English that he taught other Aboriginal people was that 'the King' was said in connection with wine drinking:

> A bottle was held up, and on his being asked what it was, in his own language, he answered, 'the King'; for as he had always heard his Majesty's health drank in the first glass after dinner at the governor's table, and had been made to repeat the word before he drank his own glass of wine, he supposed the liquor was named 'the King'; and though he afterwards knew it was called wine, yet he would frequently call it King. (Phillip 1789–91, 306–7)

Aborigines from Roma in Queensland still use 'king' as a generic for alcohol. (John Ward Watkins, personal communication)

OFFICERS OF THE MARINES AND ABORIGINAL LANGUAGES

Phillip strongly encouraged his officers to acquire an Aboriginal language and, most accounts of life in the colony written during Phillip's governorship include at least a short vocabulary and some grammatical comment about the Aboriginal languages encountered in and around Sydney. The officers grappled with ways to pronounce and transcribe the sounds they heard:

> Not only their combinations, but some of their simple sounds, were difficult of pronunciation to mouths purely English: diphthongs often occur: one of the most common is that of a e, or perhaps, a i, pronounced not unlike those letteres [sic] in the French verb *haïr*, to hate. The letter y frequently follows d in the same syllable: thus the word which signifies a woman is *Dyin*; although the structure of our language requires us to spell it *Dee-in*. (Tench 1979, 292–93)

For two years it was believed that there was only one Aboriginal language in the Sydney region. This fallacy was exposed when Phillip, in April 1791, explored forty miles (about sixty-four kilometres) west of Sydney to the Hawkesbury and discovered a group of Aboriginal people with a language that was different to that of the Port Jackson people:

> Though the tribe of Buruberongal, to which these men belonged, live chiefly by hunting, the women are employed in fishing, and our party were told that they caught large mullet in the river. Neither of these men had lost their front tooth, and the names they gave to several parts of the body

> were such as the natives about Sydney had never been heard to make use of. *Ga-dia* (the penis), they called *Cud-da; Go-rey* (the ear), they called *Ben-ne*; in the word *mi* (the eye), they pronounced the letter I as an E. And in many other instances their pronunciation varied, so that there is good reason to believe several different languages are spoken by the natives of this country, and this accounts for only one or two of those words given in Captain Cook's vocabulary having ever been heard amongst the natives who visited the settlement. (Phillip 1789–91, 347)

Several of the officers included in their published journals small comparative sets of vocabulary used by people and inland people, to indicate the differences. For example (Tench 1979, 231):

English	Name on the sea coast	Name at the Hawkesbury
The Moon	Yèn-ee-da	Con-dò-en
The Ear	Goo-reè	Bèn-na
The Forehead	Nùl-lo	Nar-ràn
The Belly	Bar-an\`g	Bin\`-dee
The Navel	Mùn-ee-ro	Boom-bon\`g
The Buttocks	Boong	Bay-leè
The Neck	Càl-ang	Gan-gà
The Thigh	Tàr-a	Dàr-a
The Hair	Deè-war-a	Keè-war-a

WILLIAM DAWES AND HIS RESEARCHES

The richest source of information about a Sydney language is a collection of three small notebooks which are held in the School of Oriental and African Studies in London. The first notebook is catalogued as SOAS Manuscript MS.4165 (a), and it is titled Grammatical Forms of the Language of N.S. Wales, in the Neighbourhood of Sydney, by Dawes, in the Year 1790. It contains verb paradigms and some textual examples as well as a few comments on grammatical aspects of the language. The second manuscript, bound with the first and catalogued as SOAS Manuscript MS.4165(b), is titled Vocabulary of the Language of N.S. Wales in the Neighbourhood of Sydney. Native and English, by Dawes. It begins with a table of the orthography chosen by Dawes for recording his data and is mainly a lexicon in roughly alphabetical order with longer and more numerous texts than in manuscript (a) and with further brief grammatical comments. Held with these notebooks is another notebook labelled SOAS Manuscript MS.4165 (c), titled

Vocabulary of the Language of N.S. Wales, in the Neighbourhood of Sydney. (Native and English, but not Alphabetical). It is mostly a lexical set with a few texts and grammatical comments.

The authorship of this notebook remains controversial, but a comparison of the two hands in the manuscript with those of other First Fleeters, suggests that it is at least in part written by Governor Phillip himself. The rough hand matches that of Phillip's rough hand exactly. Two First Fleet officers, David Collins and John Hunter, are also likely to have been contributors to the notebook. Evidence of their authorship is found in a comment by another officer, Philip Gidley King. King published a list of words in his journal, which he copied from a notebook used by Phillip, Hunter and Collins and lent to him by Collins. He wrote:

> I shall now add a vocabulary of the language, which I procured from Mr. Collins and governor Phillip, both of whom had been very assiduous in procuring words to compose it...the following vocabulary, which Mr. Collins permitted my to copy...was much enlarged by Captain Hunter. (King 1968, 270)

The list copied by King is very similar to the list in the anonymous notebook and the orthography used is the same. Minor differences in the lists can be attributed to King who 'rejected all doubtful words' so that the list could be 'depended upon to be correct' (King 1968, 270). Within the notebooks there is no name given to the language nor is there a word for language, but the word for people is given in several places as Iora, a name now often given to the language of Sydney.

Lieutenant William Dawes was a well-travelled and well-educated man of twenty-six years when he came to Australia with the First Fleet as the colony's astronomer at the suggestion of Joseph Banks. The other officers were also well-versed in the various humanitites and sciences of the eighteenth century, but Dawes:

> ...was the scholar of the expedition, man of letters and man of science, explorer, mapmaker, student of language, of anthropology, of astronomy, of botany, of surveying and of engineering, teacher and philanthropist. (Wood, quoted in McAfee 1981, 10)

Captain Watkin Tench testified to the excellence of Dawes' research from which he had hoped to benefit in his own publication:

> Of the language of New South Wales I once hoped to have subjoined to this work such an exposition, as should have attracted public notice; and have excited public esteem. But the abrupt departure of Mr Dawes, who, stimulated

> equally by curiosity and philanthropy, had hardly set foot on his native country, when he again quitted it, to encounter new perils, in the service of the Sierra Leona [sic] company, precludes me from executing this part of my original intention, in which he had promised to co-operate with me; and in which he had advanced his researches beyond the reach of competition. (Tench 1979, 291)

Dawes's notebooks reveal more than the grammatical and lexical features of the language he was studying. They are also a record of his interactions with Aboriginal people in Sydney and particularly with a young woman called Patyegaráng (or Patye as he usually called her), who was probably Dawes's main teacher. He included notes that demonstrate that he checked his queries about the language with her:

> On saying to the two girls to try if they would correct me *Ngyíne, Gonagulye, ngia, Nangadyíngun.* Patye did correct me and said *Bial Nangadyingun*; *Nangadyínye* Hence *Nangadyingun* is Dual We, and *Nangadyínye* is Plural We. (Dawes 1790–91b)

There is also evidence within the Dawes manuscripts that he was teaching Patye English. He wrote of his chagrin at her shyness in displaying her reading skills:

> *Wúrul. Wúrulbadyaóu* Bashful. I was ashamed. This was said to me by Patyegaráng after the departure of some strangers, before whom I could scarce prevail on her to read 2tthSeptr. 1791. (Dawes 1790–91b).

When Dawes asked Patye why she cooperated in his linguistic experiments, she frankly answered that he made her life easy:

> Dawes: *Minyin ngíni bial piabúni whiteman*? Why don't you (scorn to) speak like a whiteman? Patye: *Mangabuninga bial.* Not understanding this answer I asked her to explain it which she did very clearly, by giving me to understand it was because I gave her victuals, drink and every thing she wanted, without putting her to the trouble of asking for it. (Dawes 1790–91b)

Unfortunately, Dawes several times disobeyed orders given by Phillip (once in an attempt to mediate on behalf of the Aboriginal population) and was considered to be a hazard to discipline in the colony. His term of service was not renewed despite his desire to settle in New South Wales. He was sent home to England when Phillip was relieved in December 1791 and never returned to Australia.

LINGUISTIC EVIDENCE FOR LANGUAGE CONTACT IN SYDNEY

As noted above, the writings of First Fleeters contain some data that provide evidence for the development of contact language in Sydney. Data such as Dawes' notes on the Sydney language are an invaluable record of one colonist's attempts to grapple with the problems caused by the lack of a common language between himself and the Aboriginal people. His account of the Sydney language is excellent in its detail and fulsome enough to facilitate a reconstruction of the language by modern linguists (Osmond 1989; Troy 1992a; Wilkins forthcoming). However, within all the linguistic data and comments on language contact produced by the First Fleeters, there is enough evidence to suggest the early beginnings of New South Wales Pidgin (Troy 1990 and 1992a).

The early language contact provided Australian English with some of its core vocabulary. The following list contains words found in the Sydney language notebooks which are now used in Australian English and must have been very early borrowings. The words were also part of the core vocabulary of New South Wales Pidgin (Troy forthcoming).

Sydney	*Meaning*	*English*	*Meaning*
dingu	dog	dingo	Australian native dog
wuragal	large dog	warrigal	dingo, wild
bubuk	owl	boobook	boobook owl
warada	sceptre flower	waratah	waratah
wumarang	scimitar, sword	boomerang	boomerang
bumarit	scimitar, sword	boomerang	boomerang
gunya	house, hut	gunyah	temporary shelter
gawi	call to come	cooee	a call used in the bush
giba	stone, rock	gibber	stone, rocky outcrop
dyin	wife or woman	gin	Aboriginal woman/wife
manuwi	feet, leg	mundowie	foot, footstep
ngalangala	a war club	nulla-nulla	Aboriginal war club
wumara	spear throwing stick	woomera	spear thrower
bugi	swim, bathe	bogey	swim, bathe
yilimung	small parrying shield	hieleman	bark shield
garabara	dance	corroboree	Aboriginal dance ceremony
garradjun	bark fibre fishing line	kurrajong	kurrajong tree

The *wumarang* and *bumarit* were different kinds of sword-like weapons which could be used for fighting hand-to-hand or could be thrown (Troy 1992a). The Australian English word 'boomerang' is probably a combination of the two words which came into use in the early nineteeth century.

Aboriginal people borrowed words from English and coined new words in their own language to provide the new vocabulary needed to describe the colonists and their culture. The English words they borrowed were mostly for food and artefacts — biscuit, bread, breakfast, book, handkerchief, jacket, candle, potato, tea, sugar, window. They used both 'whiteman' and the Sydney language coinage *barawalgal* as words for the colonists. The following table lists the coinages that can be found in the Sydney language notebooks. Many of the borrowings and coinages also became part of New South Wales Pidgin.

Coinage	*Meaning*	*Derivation*
barawalgal	non-Aboriginal person	barawal 'very far', -gal 'people'
dalangyila	window glass	dalang 'tongue'
djarraba	musket	djarraba 'fire stick, giver of fire'
garadyigan	non-Aboriginal surgeon	garadyigan 'healer, clever man, sorcerer'
garani	biscuit	derivation unknown
garrangal	jacket	derivation unknown
gunya	house or hut	gunya 'artificially constructed shelter'
marri nuwi	the ship *Sirius*	marri 'big', nuwi 'canoe'
madyi	petticoat	derivation unknown
namuru	compass	na- 'see', maru 'path'
nananyila	reading glass	nana- 'very see'
nanyila	telescope	na- 'see'
narang nuwi	the ship *Supply*	narang 'little', nuwi 'canoe'
ngalawi	house	ngalawa- 'sit', -wi 'them'
ngunmal	palisade fence	derivation unknown
wanyuwa	horse	derivation unknown
wulgan	a pair of stays	derivation unknown

CONCLUSION

During the governorship of Arthur Phillip permanent social relations between Aboriginal people and colonists were established. Phillip's policy of developing communication between the indigenous and introduced populations of New South Wales provided the motivation for language contact. Although thwarted at first, Phillip persisted and subjected captive Aboriginal people to linguistic experiments. Eventually, through his own efforts and those of Bennelong, prolonged language contact was established. The settlement provided an environment in which a pidgin language could develop. It is well-established that a pidgin now known as New South Wales Pidgin had its origins in Sydney and was in regular use by the middle of the nineteenth century (Troy 1990). The beginnings of such a pidgin can be seen in the records of the First Fleet chroniclers.

FOR DISCUSSION

1. How did communication begin between colonists and Aboriginal people in early colonial New South Wales?

2. Who were the key people in the establishment of communication and why were they important?

3. What languages were used for communication between Aboriginal people and colonists in Sydney and what was the product of contact between those languages?

4. How did the social environment of early Sydney contribute to the development of contact language?

REFERENCES

Anon

nd Vocabulary of the Language of N.S. Wales, in the Neighbourhood of Sydney. (Native and English, but not Alphabetical), School of Oriental and African Studies manuscript MS.4165 (c).

Barton, G.

1889 *History of New South Wales from the Records: Volume 1 — Governor Phillip, 1783–1789*, Charles Potter, Sydney.

Collins, D.

1975 *An Account of the English Colony in New South Wales, with Remarks on the Dispositions, Customs, Manners, etc, of the Native Inhabitants of that Country by David Collins Late Judge-Advocate and Secretary of the Colony*, 2 vols, vol 1 originally published 1798, vol 2 originally published 1802. Edited by Brian H. Fletcher, A.H. & A.W. Reed, Sydney.

Dawes, W.

1790–91a Grammatical Forms of the Language of N.S. Wales, in the Neighbourhood of Sydney, by — Dawes, in the Year 1790. School of Oriental and African Studies manuscript MS.4165 (a).

1790–91b Vocabulary of the Language of N.S. Wales, in the Neighbourhood of Sydney. Native and English, by — Dawes. School of Oriental and African Studies manuscript MS.4165 (b).

George III

1787 Instructions for our Trusty and Well-Beloved Arthur Phillip... Quoted in Barton 1889, 481–87.

Hunter, J.

1968 [1793] *An Historical Journal of Events at Sydney and at Sea, 1787-1792, by Captain John Hunter, Commander H.M.S Sirius, with Further Accounts by Governor Arthur Phillip, Lieutenant P.G. King, and Lieutenant H.L. Ball.* Edited by J. Bach, Angus and Robertson, Sydney.

King, P.G.

1968 Lieutenant King's Journal. In Hunter 1968, 196–298.

McAfee, R.J.

1981 *Dawes's Meteorological Journal*, Department of Science and Technology, Bureau of Meteorology, Historical Note No 2, Australian Government Publishing Office, Canberra.

Osmond, M.

1989 A Reconstruction of the Phonology, Morphology, and Syntax of the Sydney Language as Recorded in the Notebooks of William Dawes, term paper, Department of Linguistics, Australian National University.

Phillip, A.

1789–1791 Journal of Governor Phillip, Quoted in Hunter 1968, 299–375.

Tench, W.

1979 *Sydney's First Four Years, Being a Reprint of 'A Narrative of the Expedition to Botany Bay' and 'A Complete Account of the Settlement at Port Jackson' by Captain Watkin Tench of the Marines*, introduction and annotations by L.F. Fitzhardinge. Library of Australian History, Sydney.

Troy, J.

1990 *Australian Aboriginal Contact with the English Language in New South Wales; 1788–1845*, Pacific Linguistics B–103, Canberra.

1992a *The Syddney Language*, J. Troy, Canberra.

1992b The Sydney Language Notebooks and Responses to Language Contract in Early Colonial NSW, *Australian Journal of Linguistics* 12, 145–70.

forth-coming Melakeuka: A History and Description of NSW Pidgin.

CHAPTER

TASMANIAN ABORIGINAL LANGUAGE: OLD AND NEW IDENTITIES

Terry Crowley

A lesson in history

The child sits at his desk
twiddling a pencil
idly staring out the window
the teacher announces
today we will learn
about the Tasmanian Aborigines
mind snaps back to the present
the child leans forward
attention eagerly given
the last Tasmanian Aborigine
died in 1876
hand goes up
but, teacher, I'm Aboriginal
how can you be
but teacher, I am, I am
Mum and Dad told me
no you are not
that's the end of it
mouth turns down
eyes glisten and slowly fill
yes, teacher
another lesson learnt
of historical inaccuracies
closed minds and white impassivity.

Karen Brown (Clark 1983, 53)

THE MYTH OF EXTINCTION

There is a widespread myth in Australia that the original inhabitants of the island state of Tasmania were driven to extinction by colonising Europeans, a myth which is expressed in *A Lesson in History*, the recent poem by Karen Brown, a Tasmanian Aborigine. N.J.B. Plomley (1977, 1), the well-known scholar of Aboriginal history, stated quite unambiguously that 'the Tasmanian Aborigines are an extinct people' and, furthermore, that the present-day hybrid people 'have no history'. The year 1876 is chosen as the end of the Tasmanian people because it was on 8 May of that year that Truganini died in Hobart, in her sixties.

In this chapter we will see that, sad as the circumstances of Truganini's death were, this did not mark the end of the Tasmanian people. For one thing, Rae-Ellis (1976, 129) reports that the last recorded full-blooded Tasmanian was in fact Sukey, who died twelve years after Truganini, in 1888, on Kangaroo Island off the coast of South Australia. Truganini's honour was simply to have been the last to die of the people who were rounded up by George Augustus Robinson in the period 1829–34 and exiled to the bleak and unhealthy settlement on Flinders Island.

Notwithstanding the death of the last full-blooded Tasmanians well before the turn of the century, there are today about 4,000 people of Aboriginal descent living throughout Tasmania and on the islands of Bass Strait (Clark 1983, 51). This figure represents about the same proportion of the total population of Tasmania as the Aboriginal proportion of the total mainland population. Recognisably non-European features can often be distinguished in the faces of these people. Moreover, they interact socially in ways that are different from Europeans, and they have a strong sense of their own history and of their own belonging to Tasmania, in particular to the Bass Strait islands. Most importantly, these people identify as Aborigines, and the world has come to hear of them in recent years through the words and actions of political activists such as Michael Mansell.

The history of the Tasmanian Aborigines is not, in fact, particularly unusual in Australian Aboriginal history at all. In all main respects, what happened to the Tasmanian Aborigines is the same as what happened to Aborigines in the more densely settled areas of the mainland. The only major difference is that nobody has tried to tell the Aboriginal people of Victoria, for example, that they no longer exist.

THE DISTANT PAST: THE ORIGINAL LANGUAGES

Archaeologists tell us that the first evidence of human occupation in Tasmania dates back to about 35,000 years ago when sea levels dropped and people were able to migrate across from the already long-populated mainland (Flood 1983, 103–10). As sea levels began rising again about 12,000 years ago, the land bridge between Tasmania and Australia was flooded, separating the people on the mainland from the Tasmanians, leaving them to develop culturally and adapt to their new and changing surroundings.

In appearance, the people of Tasmania were evidently somewhat different from the nearby mainlanders (though it should be pointed out that mainland Aborigines are not uniform in appearance either). The most noticeable difference involved the Melanesian-looking woolly hair of the Tasmanians, as against the relatively straight hair of the mainlanders. The beautiful watercolour portraits of Tasmanian Aborigines painted by Thomas Bock in the 1830s present facial features that are similar to those of people from some parts of Melanesia.

At around the time that Europeans first arrived in Tasmania, we know that there were at least nine separate communities ranging in size from 250 to 700 people, making a total population of about 4,000 (Ryan 1982, 13–44). Each of these groups was divided into smaller groups — or 'bands' — of probably between forty and fifty people each, which roamed over a range of land together in search of food, and were in periodic contact with other bands of the same group, and probably those of neighbouring groups as well.

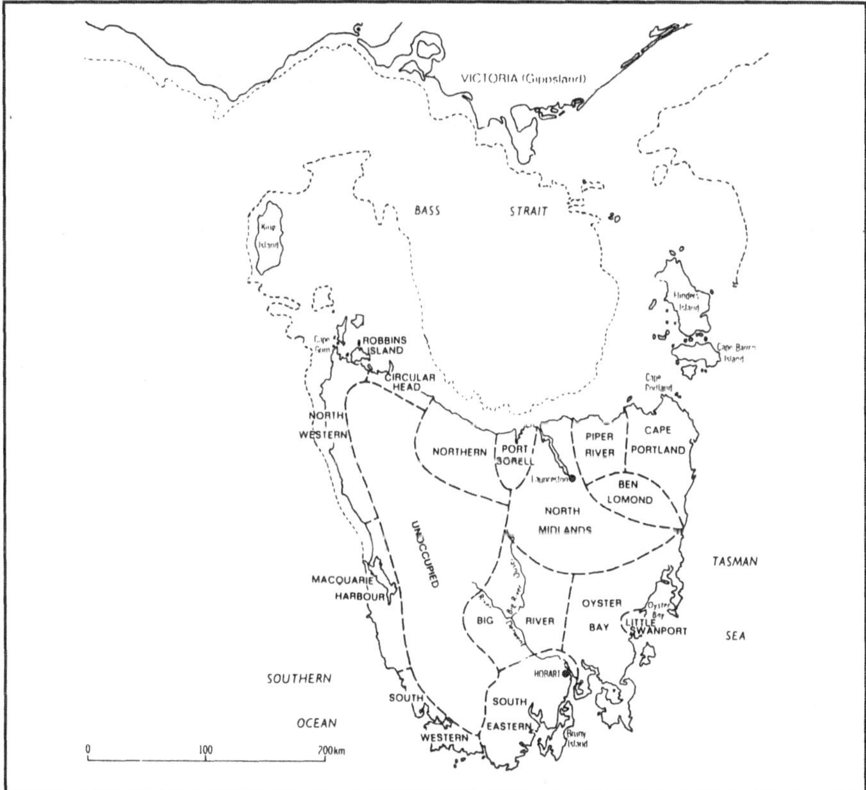

Map 6: Tasmania, showing the regions to which vocabularies have been assigned. Dotted line indicates earlier coastline linking Tasmania and mainland Australia (from Crowley and Dixon 1981, 394).

The members of those bands belonging to the same group would all have spoken basically the same kind of language, though some bands or groups of bands apparently spoke locally recognisable dialects of these languages. The language of each group would probably have been fairly distinct from that of the neighbouring group. Examining the vocabularies of the various bands for which we have written records, as well as paying attention to what observers from the time said about who could and who could not understand each other, it seems that there were probably at least eight separate languages, and possibly as many as a dozen (Crowley and Dixon 1981, 398–403), a conclusion that is roughly consistent with the earlier observation that there were nine distinct communities.

Unfortunately, it is impossible on purely linguistic grounds to be any more precise than this because the records of the speech of all areas are very poor in quality, and the records of some areas are fragmentary. Thus, it is almost impossible to say what the Tasmanian languages were like.

As an illustration of the difficulties we face in trying to interpret early written sources, we find that the word for 'emu' in the South Eastern language was recorded variously as (Plomley 1976, 147):

gon.nan.ner
gonanner
'ngunannah
nganana

(Thanks to the early European colonists, there are no longer any emus in Tasmania.) The word probably began with the [ŋ] sound — the sound heard at the end of English *hang* or *sing*. But this sound does not occur at the beginning of English words, and those who wrote 'g' at the beginning of this word probably failed to hear the pronunciation correctly. While we may be able to make an intelligent guess about the pronunciation of the word for 'emu' in the South Eastern language, other words are more difficult to reconstruct from the written record. For instance, the word for 'ear' from the North Western language was represented variously as follows (Plomley 1976, 113):

nin.ne.woon.er
hen.ne.wun.ner
un.ne.woo.ner

These words were all recorded by one person on different occasions, and exactly what was the shape of the first syllable is almost anybody's guess.

THE COLONIAL IMPACT

Despite occasional contacts between Tasmanian Aborigines and European sailors from as early as 1772, contacts between the two peoples did not commence in earnest until the early nineteenth century. In 1804 Lieutenant-Governor Collins arrived to set up a convict colony near what is now Hobart. Among his papers was an instruction similar to that given to Governor Phillip in New South Wales. He was to:

> endeavour by every means in your power to open an intercourse with the natives and to conciliate their goodwill, enjoining all persons under your Government to live in amity and kindness with them.... (quoted in Turnbull 1948, 20)

The European population of the colony grew rapidly, and quickly overtook the Aboriginal population. About half of the Europeans were convicts, while the remainder were military officers and free settlers who took up land and developed farms in the rural areas.

The early European settlers found life in the new colony much harsher than did the Aborigines, who had a superior knowledge of what the land had to offer. The Europeans came to rely heavily on kangaroo meat for sustenance, thereby encroaching on Aboriginal hunting areas to obtain their supplies (Turnbull 1948, 38). As the Aborigines came to be deprived of their own food by Europeans, incidents began to take place in which Europeans' houses were raided for flour (Turnbull 1948, 42).

The official policy of the administration, however, was to discourage hostility and to prevent the frequent instances of unprovoked cruelty that the Europeans often inflicted upon the Aborigines. In 1828 Governor Arthur had boards nailed to trees in the bush, depicting peace and happiness if the law was obeyed, and equal punishment for Aborigines and settlers if it was broken (see Plate 1).

As European settlement spread further into the rural areas, Aborigines were less and less able to avoid contacts with Europeans, and they found that their food resources were increasingly coming under pressure. As a result, the 1820s saw a significant increase in hostile contacts between the two peoples. The result was the decree of 1828 in which Arthur effectively stated his intention to impose a partition of Tasmania. Under the provisions of this proclamation, Aborigines were forbidden to enter into defined settled areas, except with special 'passports'. The perimeter of these areas was to be policed by a series of military posts (Turnbull 1948, 85).

Partition failed. Rural Aborigines, still for the most part speaking no English, did not understand the proclamation, and it was unenforceable in any

Plate 1: The pictures on the boards Governor Arthur ordered nailed to trees in 1828 (courtesy Tasmanian Museum and Art Gallery).

case. Conflicts continued, and Governor Arthur was forced to look to other solutions to his problems.

In 1830, he decreed that every male settler was to make himself available to his local magistrate and, in a vast military operation, the entire settled area of the colony was to be systematically scoured. A giant pincer movement was to force those Aborigines still remaining at large onto the Tasman Peninsula, which was attached to the mainland by the easily guarded narrow Eaglehawk Neck. This operation — the so-called 'Black Line' — was also a total failure. Only one old man and a boy were captured (Clark 1983, 40), at a cost of £35,000. Five or six soldiers died in accidents (Turnbull 1948, 199).

After this failure, conflicts between Aborigines and Europeans in settled areas continued to be reported. The colonial administration saw as the last hope the commissioning of George Augustus Robinson to directly contact those Aborigines living in the bush and to persuade them to relocate to an island in Bass Strait, where they would be cared for by the government. Between 1829 and 1834, Robinson was successful in gathering together all the remaining Aborigines and they were relocated ultimately to a settlement on Flinders Island where they were to be 'civilised' and Christianised.

By 1835, after three decades of conflict, the Aboriginal population had declined from about 4,000 to a couple of hundred. Severely reduced birth-rates, poor health as a result of loss of hunting grounds and introduced diseases, and murder were the main reasons for the sharp reduction in numbers. The total number of Europeans killed by Aborigines during the same period of conflict was 183 (Clark 1983, 41).

NON-PASTORAL CONTACTS: THE BEGINNINGS OF A NEW LANGUAGE

Appalling as the history of race relations described in the preceding section was, conflict was probably inevitable: the Aborigines needed the land for gathering and hunting, and the Europeans wanted it for pastoral purposes. But a very different pattern of race relations was evolving at the same time outside the pastoral sector of the economy and beyond the area of government control in the islands of Bass Strait.

Seals were abundant on the Bass Strait islands. Even before the establishment of the first government convict settlement near Hobart, sealing ships from as far afield as Sydney, the United States and the United Kingdom had been taking skins from Bass Strait (Ryan 1982, 66). A pattern of mutually beneficial contacts quickly emerged between these sealers and the local Aborigines on the adjacent mainland, with Aborigines exchanging seal and kangaroo skins for tobacco, flour and tea (Ryan 1982, 67).

It was a fact of Tasmanian Aboriginal culture that the men seldom learned to swim: when they needed to cross a body of water, they were often ferried across on rafts by the women, who were proficient swimmers. The Aboriginal men were therefore of limited use as labourers to the sealers, but the women proved to be invaluable. Ryan (1982, 67) reports that by 1810, local Aborigines had begun to gather along the northeast coast in anticipation of the seasonal arrival of the sealers, and a number of Aboriginal women would be offered for the season as labourers (and as sexual partners), for which the men were compensated with dogs (which were new to the Tasmanians), muttonbirds and flour.

A number of sealers — often convicts and ex-convicts — gradually settled permanently on various Bass Strait islands. None of these islands had a permanent Aboriginal population at the time of European contact, and far from representing a threat to the Aborigines on the adjacent mainland, the presence of these sealers was generally regarded in the early years as beneficial (though relationships deteriorated when the proportion of women in the population was reduced as a result of kidnapping and increased death rates among Aborigines). The sealers generally took numbers of Aboriginal women as labourers and wives (Ryan 1982, 67) and by 1820, there were about fifty European men and about a hundred Aboriginal women (and their mixed-race children) living on various islands throughout Bass Strait (Ryan 1982, 69).

Seal numbers declined and so, too, did the size of the sealing population. By 1830, there were seventy-four Aboriginal women living with the remaining European sealers in Bass Strait, twenty-eight of whom came from the North Eastern community, twenty-one from the North Western community, and the remainder from a variety of other eastern Tasmanian groups (Ryan 1982, 71). The Bass Strait community also included a few mainland Aborigines, and this ethnically mixed group became the nucleus of the surviving Aboriginal population in Tasmania today (Ryan 1982, 71). Eventually, because of the shortage of seals, the sealers who remained were forced to shift their economic activity to the seasonal gathering of muttonbirds, which were valuable for their oil.

In the preceding chapter, Jakelin Troy has described the emergence of a pidgin in early colonial Sydney. The Bass Strait sealing trade between about 1800 and the 1830s was another situation in which such a pidgin might have developed for use between the European sealers and the Aboriginal women. Those Aboriginal women, both from Tasmania and the mainland, who did not share common languages would have been able to use such a language amongst themselves as well. Ryan (1982, 150) and Plomley (1976, 59–60) both report that these women had indeed formed a new 'lingua franca', or contact language. From historical references, we can say very little about what this pidgin spoken in Bass Strait was like, other than that it comprised mostly English vocabulary — as we would predict — along with an admixture of local Aboriginal words, predominantly from the various languages of the numerically dominant eastern part of Tasmania.

From elsewhere in Tasmania at the same period, Rae-Ellis (1976, 22) reports that Truganini, then a sixteen-year-old, began to take a keen interest in the European men at a government timber cutting settlement on the mainland adjacent to her native Bruny Island in the southeast. She and her Bruny Island female friends were also frequently found consorting with European convicts, sealers and whalers when they called in at the area. What we would expect is that Truganini and her friends would also have ended up picking up a form of pidgin. Almost certainly the whalers they came into contact with would have spoken to them in what has come to be known as South Seas Jargon, which was the incipient pidgin widely spoken on whaling vessels around the Pacific at the time (and from which many later pidgins in the southwest Pacific ultimately evolved).

Truganini (see Plates 2 and 3) and her Bruny Island people also had close contact with Robinson from the time that he attempted to establish a government settlement on Bruny Island in 1829, and subsequently when Truganini accompanied him on his travels around Tasmania to round up the last groups of Aborigines still living in the bush. Robinson is often quoted as having spoken 'the Aboriginal language', a quality which he considered particularly qualified him for his role as 'conciliator'. Many sources (for example, Rae-Ellis 1988) also indicate that Robinson was a man of limited intellect — and even dishonesty — who tended to exaggerate his achievements. As Plomley (1976, 34) points out, while Robinson's diaries provide plentiful examples of Tasmanian vocabulary, there is no evidence that he acquired any real knowledge of the grammar of these languages.

For instance, in 1829 Robinson claimed that while on Bruny Island he 'preached to the Aborigines in their own tongue' (Plomley 1966, 61). Given that he had only been on the island for eight weeks at the time, this would seem to be a somewhat presumptuous claim. The extract from the relevant section of his journal reads as follows (Plomley 1966, 61):

> At 11 am performed divine service in the natives' hut. Four of the prisoners attended. Preached to the aborigines in their own tongue. Part of the sermon — MOTTI (one) NYRAE (good) PARLERDI (God) MOTTI (one) NOVILLY (bad) RAEGEWROPPER (devil). PARLERDI (God) NYRAE

Plate 2: *Truggernana* (1837), watercolour 29.2 x 22 (courtesy Tasmanian Museum and Art Gallery).

> (good). PARLERDI (God) MAGGERER (stop) WARRANGELLY (sky), RAEGEWROPPER (devil) MAGGERER (stop) TOOGENNER (below) UENEE (fire). NYRAE (good) PARLERWAR (native) LOGERNER (dead) TAGGERER (go) TEENY (road) LAWWAY (up) WARRANGELLY (sky) PARLERDI (God) NYRAE (good) RAEGE (whiteman) etc, etc. NOVILLY (bad) PARLEWAR (native) LOGGERNER (dead) TAGGERER (go) TEENNY (road) TOOGUNNER (below) RAEGEWROPPER (devil) UENEE (fire) MAGGERER (stop) UENEE (fire).

The text of his sermon contains words strung together in an order that is identical to English, but stripped of all grammatical markers such as suffixes and prepositions. What this text looks like, in fact, is a pidgin in which the English lexicon has been systematically replaced by vernacular words.

Thus Truganini would have been supplied with a variety of inputs from which she presumably worked out some form of communication that she could use with Europeans and with Aborigines from other areas. Exactly what was the nature of the 'English' that Truganini eventually learned is impossible to say. Despite various claims in Robinson's official reports that Truganini learned to speak English 'fluently' (Turnbull 1948, 203–5), he admitted in his private diaries that none of the Tasmanian Aborigines ever learned to speak English 'properly' (Rae-Ellis 1988, 127). For instance, Sir Charles Du Cane, a one-time governor of Tasmania and an acquaintance of Truganini in her late years, reported that:

> every now and then [she] paid us a visit of ceremony at Government House where she would laugh and chuckle...and occasionally savour us with a few words of English. On one occasion she eyed me intently...and said 'This fellow he too much jacket' meaning thereby that I had become stouter than comported with her notions of vice-regal dignity. (quoted in Rae-Ellis 1988, 46)

If this utterance was typical of Truganini's speech in her old age, and in the company of the Governor, presumably she used pidgin throughout her life in her dealings with all Europeans.

Contacts of a similar sort to Truganini's were repeated all over the settled areas of Tasmania between the beginning of European settlement and the 1820s. By 1822, there was one band of acculturated Aborigines in the Oyster Cove area known as the 'tame mob'. No longer dependent on the resources of the bush for their survival, they begged for food, tobacco and alcohol, and suffered from lack of hygiene and associated health problems (Turnbull 1948, 61–62). This band was headed by an Aboriginal convict from Sydney named Mosquito. Mosquito is

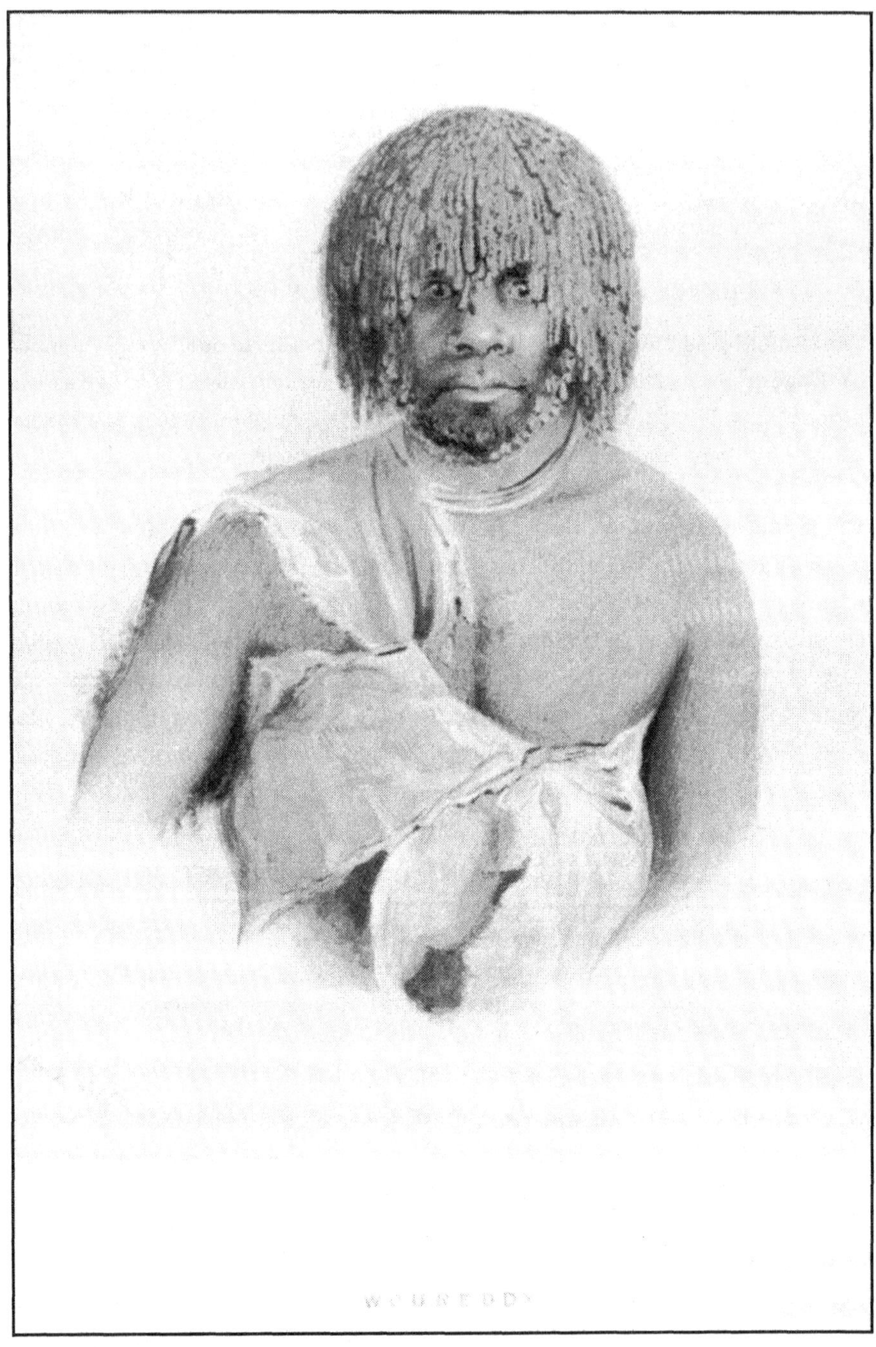

Plate 3: *Woureddy* (1837), watercolour by Thomas Bock, 29.5 x 22.3 (courtesy Tasmanian Museum and Art Gallery).

quoted in Turnbull (1948, 63) as having said:

> I stop wit white fellow, learn to like blankets, clothes, bakky, rum, bread all same white fellow: white fellow give'd me. By and by Gubernor send me catch bushranger – promise me plenty clothes and send me back Sydney, my own country: I catch him, Gubernor tell too much a lie, never send me. I knockit about camp, prisoner no liket me then, givet me nothing, call me bloody hangman nose. I knock one fellow down, give waddie, constable take me, I then walk away in bush. I get along wid mob, go all about beg some give it bread, blanket: some take't away my gin: that make a fight: mob rob the hut: some one tell Gubernor: all white fellow he never give, mob make a rush, stock-keeper shoot plenty, mob spear some. Dat de way me no come all same your house. Never like see Gubernor any more. White fellow soon kill all black fellow. You good fellow, mob no kill you.

A number of features of later Aboriginal or South Pacific Pidgins were already present in the speech of Mosquito, such as the use of 'stop' to mean 'stay', 'all same' to mean 'like', 'by and by' to mark the future tense, 'plenty' as a marker of the plural before nouns, the suffix '-it' as a marker of transitive verbs, and 'no' as a negative marker before verbs. Given that Mosquito was regarded as the leader of this 'tame mob', it is likely that other members of this community also spoke this pidgin by the 1820s.

THE GOVERNMENT-CONTROLLED COMMUNITY

Despite the mortal threat they were believed to pose in the settled areas, only 135 Aborigines from all parts of the colony remained in the bush to be rounded up by the early 1830s. They were removed from the mainland and settled ultimately into a single community on Flinders Island. Coming from all different areas, they spoke a variety of languages.

Given that a form of pidgin was probably already spreading among Tasmanian Aborigines in the 1820s, this set of circumstances would have been ripe for the further spread and development of this new contact language. Access to English on Flinders Island would have been less than in the sealer communities, where each working group included at least one European male. Thus, we might expect that any contact language that was used on Flinders Island would have contained a higher proportion of Aboriginal words than was the case with the sealers' women's pidgin. Some Aborigines, such as Truganini herself, arrived at Flinders Island with a fair knowledge of some form of pidgin already, and there was also some direct input from the pidgin spoken in Bass Strait as Robinson succeeded in forcing some of the sealers' women into the government settlement. There was also further contact with mainland varieties of Aboriginal Pidgin, as Robinson took thirteen Tasmanian Aborigines with him for a time when he was transferred to Port Phillip in what is now Victoria in 1839 (Rae-Ellis 1976, 34–38). Davies, a sailor, made several voyages to the Flinders Island settlement between 1832 and 1837, and he noted that:

> The Aborigines from the westward, and those from the eastward, did not at first understand each other, when brought to Flinders Island...but they afterwards, in common with the whites, used a kind of lingua franca. (quoted in Plomley 1976, 79)

Bonwick (1870, 153) also reports the catechist Clark on the island as saying: '...on my first joining them in 1834, I found them instructing each other to speak their respective tongues'. He also reports that in this settlement 'they had constructed, by force of circumstances, a sort of *lingua franca* — a common language' (Bonwick 1870, 153). Clark apparently learned to use the 'gibberish peculiar to the settlement', a fact which was condemned by Robinson (Rae-Ellis 1988, 174). A Board of Enquiry set up to investigate Robinson's administration of the Flinders Island settlement and his claim to have 'civilised' the Aborigines, and to have taught them English, reported finding Aborigines participating in church services only in what it called 'broken dialect' (Rae-Ellis 1988, 169–70). Dr Henry Jeanneret, a medical superintendent at Flinders Island, also reported that the people there spoke a '...barbarous English...replete with native words and pronounced with little regard to the distinctions of consonants...' (quoted in Rae-Ellis 1988, 113).

We will never know the exact nature of this language, though it is almost certain that it was a variant of the same pidgin that was in use in Bass Strait and which had previously been in use in various parts of rural Tasmania. Plomley (1976, 39) quotes a manuscript reference from the catechist Clark in 1837 which bears out the earlier prediction that it would have contained a substantial proportion of non-English vocabulary:

> Noemy, after some introductory observations in his native language, commenced speaking in the dialect of the settlement —
>
> God *narracoopa* [good]. He *coethee* [loves] us, you *coethee* God, *coethee* plenty a big one you *taplaldy* [go] *weethicallee* [heaven?]. God sent Jesus Christ to save us to *parraway* [chase away] the Devil, pother [if?] you *coethe* the Devil, *parraway coethe* God *coethe* Jesus Christ the son of God. You *taplady luthra* [hell?] you *coethe* you *norocoopa* God make you good man, go top *wiethienetta* [heaven?].

Another manuscript reference from Clark to Robinson in 1837 quotes the dying words of an Aborigine on Flinders Island, which reflect a similarly mixed lexicon:

> I said to Hector 'you are very sick?' Hector '*yes me plenty menaty*' [sick]. You coethee God? Hector '*yes me coethee plenty*'. You coethee Jesus Christ? '*Yes me coethee Jesus Christ the son of God*'. Do you pray to him? '*Yes me pray to him plenty, me pray last night our Father which art in heaven plenty*'. You very sick you krakabuka [die] by and bye? '*Yes me talbetee werthickathe [?] to God, me coethee*'. (quoted in Plomley 1976, 39–40)

Finally, Robinson quotes the words of an Aborigine in an official report explaining his absence from the settlement:

> Blackfellow no come back. Too much sickness at Flinders at Pea Jacket Point. Too much dead man. Blackman frightened like to crackenny [die] bust. (quoted in Rae-Ellis 1988, 128)

By the time that the Flinders Island settlement was established, the Aboriginal birthrate had dropped catastrophically. For example, one tribe, which had formerly numbered about 500 people, by 1830 consisted of just seventy-two men, six women and no children (Clark 1983, 44), and by 1832 the whole Flinders Island community consisted of twenty-six men, thirteen women, but only one child (Turnbull 1948, 145). This was due to a combination of circumstances, which presumably included the severe imbalance between males and females (largely a result of women being abducted by European sealers), stress, and health problems brought about by food shortages and introduced syphilis. Conditions on the Bass Strait settlements were so uniformly bad that the death rate among residents was phenomenal. Of the 135 people who had been relocated from the mainland to the Flinders Island settlement by 1834, only forty-seven survived by 1847. Most of the casualties succumbed to lung infections and other avoidable diseases. To replace those who had died during the same period there were only fourteen births (Turnbull 1948, 222).

Because of the appalling mortality rate, the government decided in 1847 to move the community back to the mainland, to a new settlement at Oyster Cove, south of Hobart (Turnbull 1948, 225). In their new location, the members of this sad little community continued to die one by one. William Lanney, the last of the men of this community, died in 1867, and Truganini was the last of the women to die, in Hobart, in 1876. After her burial, Truganini's body was exhumed and her bones were placed on public display in a glass case in the Tasmanian Museum. According to her final request, she was eventually buried at sea near her home of Bruny Island on the centenary of her death, in 1976 (Rae-Ellis 1988, 41).

THE LINGERING LANGUAGE

The Tasmanian languages were probably doomed well before Truganini's death. The nature of the linguistically fragmented Flinders Island settlement as far back as the 1830s was sufficient to ensure that the languages had no viable future, and the sealer communities could not ensure the survival of the languages either. Children born in the Flinders Island settlement, such as Fanny Cochrane Smith and William Lanney, probably acquired only a very limited knowledge of the language of their parents. Tasmanian Aboriginal Pidgin was probably the only commonly used language.

It is likely that if this community had been able to maintain itself for another generation, with full-blooded Tasmanians surviving into the twentieth century, these people would probably have ended up speaking English, just as Aborigines in many parts of Victoria and New South Wales today do. Although Robinson was trying to force people to give up their traditional songs and dances, he evidently did not try to force them to give up their languages. He did not *need* to, as the languages would have disappeared simply because of the nature of the social context into which the people had been forced.

Although Truganini and people like her spent their early years speaking nothing but their ancestral language, and did not learn some form of English until at least adolescence, the original languages did not disappear *completely* with the death of these 'old-timers'. Fanny Cochrane Smith was born in 1834 on Flinders Island from an Aboriginal mother and a European sealer father. She eventually married a European, and lived until 1905. In 1899, and again in 1903, the Royal Society of Tasmania recorded her singing Aboriginal songs, which she had learned as a child on Flinders Island (presumably in secret, given Robinson's attitude to Aboriginal songs). The technology of the time was so poor that these recordings sound like little more than a scratchy squawk. Fanny Cochrane Smith and others obviously did manage to learn some words and expressions of the languages of their parents because she and the generations that followed her were still able to transmit some linguistic remnants to their own children.

In 1908–10, Ernest Westlake interviewed about thirty people of Aboriginal descent in Tasmania and gathered around 100 words (Plomley 1976, 56–67). Fanny Cochrane Smith's daughter, Mary Jane Miller, was one of the people interviewed by Westlake, and she was interviewed again by Archibald Meston in 1941–42, when she was able to supply nineteen words that she had learned from her mother (Crowley and Dixon 1981, 397).

Other people of Tasmanian Aboriginal descent also retained some knowledge of remnants of the old languages. In the 1930s, the anthropologist N.B. Tindale interviewed descendants of Tasmanian women and European sealers on Kangaroo Island, from whom he recorded four phrases of Tasmanian language (Tindale 1937, 36). Tindale's 1939 journal from Cape Barren Island also included a few words and a single sentence, which were published for the first time in Crowley and Dixon (1981, 397).

In Tasmania in 1972, I interviewed Mrs Heffernan and Mrs Mundy, who are two of the granddaughters of Fanny Cochrane Smith. Mrs. Heffernan remembered begging her mother to tell her anything of the old language that she knew, though neither she nor her mother (nor probably even her grandmother) ever used the language for communicative purposes. The words that I recorded were all pronounced with normal Australian English phonology, and the word *langana* that she gave as the word for 'foot' was even given with the English plural suffix '-s'. Mrs Heffernan also remembered a whole sentence, which she pronounced with a fairly typical Australian English accent as if it were spelt as follows:

Tabbenty ning-ena moomera probbeby par-drooler.

This meant, she explained, 'Get a bit of wood and put it on the fire'. Finally, she also remembered a fragment of a song that she said was sung by her grandmother before an audience at Government House in Hobart. The meaning of the song is unknown, but it went as follows (Crowley and Dixon 1981, 398):

Kumeraynqo kunekuneli
Rrpa rrpa hiriyawa tachima tachima

Although the Tasmanian languages are now extinct, it is testimony to the power of the Tasmanian Aboriginal sense of identity that scraps such as these should have survived in people's memories for almost a century and-a-half.

MAINTAINING A LINGUISTIC IDENTITY

People who lose their original language by the force of circumstances beyond their control often maintain their distinct identity using the language of their oppressors. For instance, even when speaking English, Aboriginal people prefer indirect methods of seeking information, rather than the direct questioning approach of Europeans (compare comments on this in other chapters of this book, especially chapters 2 and 13 by Yallop and Eades respectively). The differences between an Aboriginal way of speaking and a European way of speaking in situations such as these may be lost on the average European unless they are carefully pointed out.

A separate Tasmanian Aboriginal linguistic identity did not disappear completely with the loss of the original languages, just as the Tasmanian Aborigines themselves did not disappear. Through the remainder of the nineteenth century and early twentieth century, the mixed-race descendants of the Bass Strait sealers continued to raise pigs and goats, grow wheat and potatoes, and catch kangaroos, seals and muttonbirds for their sustenance; and the women continued to make necklaces made of small shells (Clark 1983, 47). Although the government negotiated leases for the land they were occupying in the nineteenth century, there were problems over access to muttonbird rookeries, and an area was set aside for a single reserve on Cape Barren Island (Ryan 1982, 222–27). In 1951 this reserve was abolished on the grounds that the occupants were 'no longer Aborigines'. Throughout the latter half of the nineteenth century and into the twentieth century, these people often called themselves 'Islanders', but from the early 1970s they began to refer to themselves again proudly as Aboriginal Tasmanians (Ryan 1982, 253).

English was the language of this new Cape Barren Island Aboriginal community, though the people retained a knowledge of some words in the Aboriginal languages passed on to them by their mothers and their grandmothers. The descendants of these people still live today on Cape Barren Island and they still hunt muttonbirds. They still make shell necklaces, from the shells which they call 'mariners' — a word which is also recorded in the vocabularies of Tasmanian languages from a century-and-a-half ago (Plomley 1976, 326). West (1984, 15, 75) reports a number of other words in use in English among Bass Strait Aborigines which may also be of Aboriginal origin:

barilla	saltbush
bidgie-widgie	burr
kanie gan	pigface
boobyalla	baby food
ne na	amen

The English spoken by the Tasmanian Aboriginal residents of Cape Barren Island today is noticeably distinct from other varieties of Australian English. Sutton (1975, 65) notes that 'traces of early nineteenth-century or dialectal British English, and traces of Aboriginal foreign accent, are clearly discernible...in...Cape Barren English'. For instance, there are people on Cape Barren Island who pronounce 'follow' and 'swallow' as 'folly' and 'swally' respectively, which are also characteristic pronunciations in certain Scottish and southwestern English dialects of English (Sutton 1975, 69). Sutton (1975, 82) also notes that a certain amount of variation between sounds such as [v] and [b] in Cape Barren English may derive from the fact that the original Tasmanian Aboriginal languages did not make this distinction.

There are also English words that occur only on Cape Barren Island, or which occur elsewhere but have special uses among the people there. Sutton (1975, 90–95) notes that what most Australians call a 'house' is referred to there as a 'bungalow', and people use 'chains' as a measure of distance in addition to yards (or metres). 'Getting dark' is 'getting duskified'. What most Australians would call 'chooks' or 'chickens' are referred to there as 'fowls' (as is also widely found among mainland Aboriginal speakers of English).

Probably for as long as the Tasmanian Aborigines living on Cape Barren Island *feel* different from other people in Australia, they will continue to speak their own variety of English.

FOR DISCUSSION

1. Languages can die out in a number of different ways. What can you find out about how other languages have disappeared (or show signs that they may disappear)? How do these compare with what happened in Tasmania? Case studies that you could investigate include the following:

- Any mainland Aboriginal language (check some of the other chapters of this book)
- Hawaiian
- Moriori (formerly spoken on the Chatham Islands in New Zealand)
- Cornish or Manx

2. 'Languages generally don't die, they commit suicide.' What do you think this means? Did the Tasmanian languages commit suicide or were they murdered?

3. If you had been in Governor Arthur's position in 1830, what might you have done to ensure that the Tasmanian languages survived to the present? (check some of the other chapters of this book)

4. If you were doing research on your family history and you discovered that your great-great-great-grandmother was a Tasmanian Aborigine, would that make *you* an Aborigine?

REFERENCES

Bonwick, J.

1870 *Daily Life and Origins of the Tasmanians*, Sampson, Low, Son and Marston, London.

Clark, J.

1983 *The Aboriginal People of Tasmania*, Tasmanian Museum and Art Gallery, Hobart.

Crowley, T. and R.M.W. Dixon

1981 Tasmanian. In R.M.W. Dixon and B.J. Blake (eds), *Handbook of Australian Languages*, vol 2, Australian National University Press, Canberra, 394–421.

Eades, D.

1985 "You Gotta Know How to Talk"... Information Seeking in South-East Queensland Aboriginal Society. In J.B. Pride (ed), *Cross Cultural Encounters: Communication and Mis-Communication*, River Seine Publications, Melbourne, 91–109.

Elder, B.

1988 *Blood on the Wattle: Massacres and Maltreatment of Australian Aborigines since 1788*, Child and Associates, Frenchs Forest, New South Wales.

Flood, J.

1983 *Archaeology of the Dreamtime*, Collins Publishers, Sydney.

Plomley, N.J.B.

1966 *Friendly Mission: The Tasmanian Journals of George Augustus Robinson 1829–34*, Tasmanian Historical Research Association, Kingsgrove, New South Wales.

1976 *A Word-List of the Tasmanian Aboriginal Languages*, N.J.B. Plomley, Launceston.

1977 *The Tasmanian Aborigines: A Short Account of Some Aspects of Their Life*, Adult Education Division, Launceston.

Rae-Ellis, V.

1976 *Trucanini: Queen or Traitor?*, O.B.M. Publishing Company, Hobart.

1988 *Black Robinson: Protector of Aborigines*, Melbourne University Press, Melbourne.

Ryan, L.

1982 *The Aboriginal Tasmanians*, University of Queensland Press, St Lucia, Queensland.

Sutton, P.

1975 'Cape Barren English'. In J.V. Neustupny (ed), *Linguistic Communications* 13*: Working Papers of the Linguistic Society of Australia*, Monash University, Melbourne, 61–97.

Tindale, N.B.

1937 Tasmanian Aborigines on Kangaroo Island, South Australia, *Records of the South Australian Museum* 6, 29–37.

Turnbull, C.

1965 [1948] *Black War: The Extermination of the Tasmanian Aborigines*, Lansdowne Press, Melbourne.

West, I.
1984 *Pride Against Prejudice: Reminiscences of a Tasmanian Aborigine*, Australian Institute of Aboriginal Studies, Canberra.

NOTE

I would like to thank Diana Eades for helpful comments on earlier versions of this paper. All responsibility for interpretation is, of course, my own.

CHAPTER

5 BUNDJALUNG: TEACHING A DISAPPEARING LANGUAGE

Margaret Sharpe

INTRODUCTION

Bundjalung is the name given to the language spoken in the area shown in the map (Map 7). We spell it Bundjalung so that the average English speaker will read and pronounce it correctly, as desired by Bundjalung people. In some publications for linguistically trained readers, the name is spelt Bandjalang, but the *a* is meant to indicate a vowel like that of English *bun* or *lung* rather than that of *ban* or *Lang*.

As Map 7 shows, there were various dialects of Bundjalung. Most of these had names which the speakers themselves or their neighbours used to identify some characteristic of the dialect. For example, the Minyangbal people are those who use the word *minyang* (meaning 'what?'), whereas the Nyangbal people are those who say *nyang* for 'what?'. Similarly, names like Wiyabal, Wuyehbal, Wahlubal and so on, are based on different words for 'you (singular)', all of them carrying the suffix *-bal* meaning 'those who say'.

My own experience of Bundjalung began in 1965 when I went to Woodenbong in northern New South Wales to record information on the Yugambeh dialect of Bundjalung from a man who was considered to be the last person with significant knowledge of this dialect. At that time there was a big drive in Australia to record 'dying' languages and dialects. There was also great concern to get 'pure' language, not 'contaminated' with English, and to carefully record differences in neighbouring dialects. Two members of the Summer Institute of Linguistics, Brian and Helen Geytenbeek, were living at Woodenbong at the time, with the aim of translating the Bible into the Gidhabal dialect. There were then a number of fluent speakers of that dialect at Woodenbong. The Geytenbeeks later spent some time at Tabulam, where it appeared that a greater number of younger people spoke some Bundjalung. But they eventually came to the conclusion that a simplified English Bible translation would be far more use to the Woodenbong and Tabulam people than a Bundjalung one would be. All people spoke English, and younger people did not know much Bundjalung.

There are still a few people who can speak the language fluently and who use it with each other, though for a restricted range of functions. A good number of people of all ages (including children) use some Bundjalung words in their English (for such things as turtle, echidna, witchetty grubs, bodily functions,

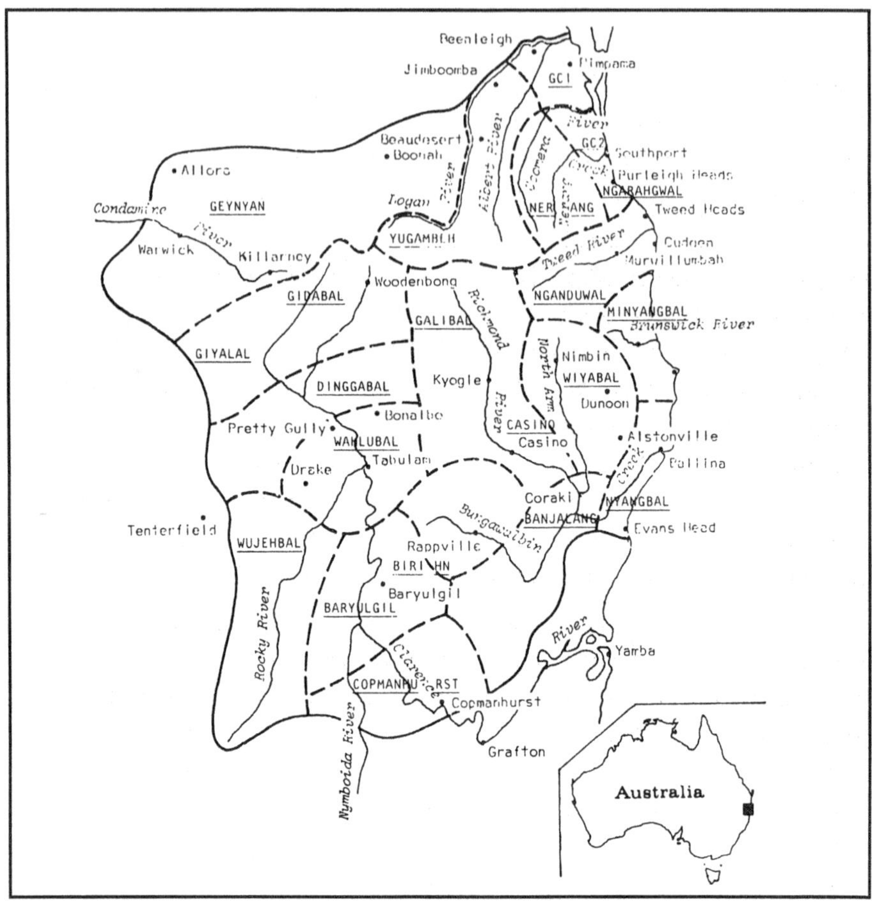

Map 7: Approximate location of the Bundjalung–Yugam dialects. The broken line encloses the approximate dialect ranges of the language. The unbroken line encloses the Bundjalung dialects (taken with permission from Sharpe et al 1985, xviii).

food and cigarettes), and a number (particularly at Baryulgil) use some Bundjalung phrases within English. There have also been school language programs and courses in Bundjalung held not only in northern New South Wales, but also in southern Queensland and in Victoria. Bundjalung people and some non-Aboriginal people have been keen to know more about the language: some courses have been instigated by Bundjalung people; others by non-Bundjalung Aboriginal people; and some by non-Aboriginal people, including school staff and others. In these courses constant issues for organisers and students are: what is the 'correct' word or phrase to teach, the 'correct' pronunciation; why are there variant forms; and which of the variant forms should be used?

THE SPECIAL PLACE OF BUNDJALUNG

Bundjalung is unusual in New South Wales, and indeed in Australia, for two reasons. The first is that it has been studied for a relatively long time; the second, that there are still some people living who learned it as their first language, even in one of the most densely populated rural areas of Australia.

There are word lists in Curr (1886–87), and a useful if brief grammar of the Minyang (Brunswick River) dialect published in 1892. A grammar and vocabulary of the Wangerriburra clan of the Beaudesert area was published in 1913, co-authored by a Wangerriburra man (Bulam or John Allen) who had used the language as a child, and a white colleague. A grammar of another dialect, presumably spoken around Casino, was written in the 1940s by a medical doctor (Smythe 1978 [c 1942 or 1948]); and grammars have been published from the late 1960s onwards in Yugambeh (Cunningham 1969), Gidhabal (Geytenbeek 1971), Wiyabal/Wuyehbal of Lismore/Coraki (Holmer 1971), Wahlubal and Wehlubal (Crowley 1978), and Manandjali or Yugambeh (Holmer 1983).

Attitudes towards 'sharing' the language with whites have varied from community to community. One community, near Coraki, has generally been antagonistic to whites — unless, understandably, they were trusted friends with an understanding of the culture. Others, both as individuals and as groups, have been keen for the language — and some cultural activities also — to be preserved, and to be taught to any interested person, irrespective of race. Notable advocates have included Joe Culham, Lyle Roberts the younger, and the Kombumerri Aboriginal Corporation. In 1965 and 1966 I recorded data from Joe Culham. Lyle Roberts the younger (a nephew of an older Lyle Roberts) lived in Lismore and died some years ago: over many years he passed on information to the late Marjorie Oakes, and he encouraged children to learn dances, with no restrictions on whether they were of Aboriginal descent or not. The Kombumerri Aboriginal Corporation of southern Brisbane and the Gold Coast (places traditionally within their dialect area) obtained funding for courses in the language in 1988, 1989 and 1990, and welcomed a number of non-Aboriginal participants. The reluctance of the Coraki group to share knowledge with whites seems to have several causes: the Coraki people may have assumed that academic writers have gained financially from their published books (which is generally not the case, although there is little doubt the writers have gained in academic status by their work); they have also felt whites have taken so much from them, and it is a matter of pride and dignity to retain something of their own, and to maintain sufficient separateness in language use to allow privacy.

It has also been proposed (Calley 1960, Crowley 1978) that the Bundjalung were survivors of a long campaign to maintain their cultural separateness from certain nearby Aboriginal groups, and were therefore better equipped to continue their fight for autonomy when the white invasion came upon them. Such cultural barriers seemed strongest towards groups to the south. On the other hand, it is known that Bundjalung people were among the tribes or clans that made trips to the Bunya Mountains in Queensland every few years when the bunya pines bore heavily. In these seasons the owners of that territory invited others to a great time of feasting, from which, early white records tell us, the people of the Northern Rivers area of New South Wales returned looking sleek and well nourished. Cultural barriers to the south and inland, however, were not impenetrable: there is a Bundjalung song about travelling down the main road through New England to the Moonbis; and another Bundjalung song, about the Dunoon 'boxer' and playing two-up, was recorded down the south coast of New South Wales, where it had presumably been transmitted or traded. It would help in understanding the cultural ties and barriers if we could be certain of the route Bundjalung people followed to the Bunya Mountains (that is, was it a coastal route, or was it inland west of the Brisbane tribe?), and of the route this gambler's song took in its transmission to the south coast. While (as Calley 1959 points out) we cannot assume that cultural barriers and alliances were immutable over time, both these songs were post-contact songs, possibly not dating back beyond this century, and so alliances and barriers probably differed little from those we have recorded.

SOME FEATURES OF BUNDJALUNG

As has already been mentioned, Bundjalung is unusual in its survival in a relatively densely settled area of Australia. Apart from that, there are some features of the language itself which are not typical of Australian languages.

In pronunciation, Bundjalung is more similar to English in the way in which stressed syllables are pronounced with considerable prominence and unstressed syllables markedly reduced or 'slurred'. Most Australian Aboriginal languages do not show this kind of stress-timed rhythm. Bundjalung is also unusual — though not unique — in the way in which plosive consonants, such as *b* and *g*, may be pronounced as fricative sounds, similar to English *v* and *h*. (More precisely, Bundjalung here resembles Spanish, in which plosives like *b* and *g* may be pronounced as fricatives [β] and [γ] in certain positions.)

In its grammar, Bundjalung is unusual among Pama-Nyungan languages in its gender system. The language distinguishes four genders: masculine, feminine, arboreal (for trees) and neuter (for anything else). In at least some of the dialects, adjectives carried a suffix showing agreement with the gender of the noun. Note in the following examples how the adjective *gama(y)* 'big' takes different suffixes depending on the gender of the preceding noun:

baygal gamaygali
man big (masc)
'big man'

dubay gamaynyahgan
woman big (fem)
'big woman'

jali gamaynyahn
tree big (arbor)
'big tree'

balun gamagay
river big (neuter)
'big river'

The masculine/feminine distinction can also be seen in the words for 'she' (*nyahngan* or *nyulagan*, depending on the dialect) and 'he' (*nyula, nyule* or *nyuuli*, depending on the dialect). Most Pama-Nyungan languages make no distinction between pronouns 'he' and 'she'.

Bundjalung has the ergative case marking that is typical of Pama-Nyungan languages (with a suffix to mark the agent of transitive verbs such as 'see', 'hit', 'bite', and so on). Less typically, Bundjalung also has an accusative suffix on some nouns to mark the goal or object of a transitive verb. This accusative marking seems to have applied to human nouns, nouns referring to larger animals and birds, and to pronouns and demonstratives.

DIFFERENCES AMONG THE DIALECTS OF BUNDJALUNG

What are the differences among the dialects? It is reasonable to guess there were some global differences in quality of voice and style of delivery, which may well have interfered with intelligibility across dialects. Unfortunately, our recorded materials are not comprehensive enough to define these differences; but there were sufficient differences for some Kombumerri people to feel that a southern speaker, Michael Walker, did not sound like the speakers they remembered, although others could name relations he sounded like. Old written accounts indicate that some people had little difficulty in understanding different dialects (like McQuilty, who spoke the Lismore dialect fluently, see Rankin 1900), while others found problems (Bray 1899).

There are more specific differences in pronunciation, for example in the vowels in various words. Variation in the pronunciation of 'he' has already been mentioned: southern speakers seems to have said *nyula*, while northern speakers said either *nyuuli* or *nyule*. A similar difference is observable in the final vowel of other words such as *gala* (or *gali* or *gale*) meaning 'this'.

A difference between western dialects (Gidhabal, Wahlubal, et cetera) and northern and eastern dialects (Yugambeh, Wiyabal, et cetera) is that the former sometimes have the vowel *a* where the latter have *u*. The word for 'no', for instance, is *yagam* in the west and *yugam* elsewhere.

In general, vocabulary differed among the dialects, as is common in Australia. The difference between *minyang* and *nyang* ('what?') has already been mentioned as the basis of the names of the Minyangbal and Nyangbal dialects. Crowley (1978) comments on quite substantial lexical differences between the original northernmost and southernmost dialects.

WHY DO PEOPLE LEARN BUNDJALUNG?

Bundjalung is going out of everyday use. Why then have people shown an interest in learning it?

In the first place, a sizeable number of Aboriginal people of Bundjalung ancestry want to know more about this part of their inheritance. Some of them remember the days when use of the language was strongly discouraged by white disfavour and by the perceptions of their older relatives that it was to their advantage to use English. Many people recently have come to the realisation that it should not be a thing of shame to use their old language. A groundswell of desire by many people worldwide to find their roots has also affected Aboriginal people as well as non-Aboriginal people. Now those who remember only snatches of the language want to revive it and learn more.

Secondly, many non-Aboriginal residents of the Northern Rivers area and the Gold Coast and southern Brisbane had and have a genuine interest in the language as one of the features of the area. There are many place names of recognisable form and meaning in Bundjalung — some traditional, a few bestowed in recent times. For such people also, there is far more scope to pursue this interest than in places where less is known of the old languages.

A third source of interest is in Victoria, where Eve Fesl from Monash University, whose ancestral affiliation is to Gabi Gabi, north of Bundjalung, wished to teach an Aboriginal language in Victorian schools to Koori (Aboriginal) children. She wanted to use a language that was known in some depth, which excluded Victorian languages. In her search for a language which was spoken in as similar an environment as possible to that of the Victorian languages, she ruled out well-known and widely spoken desert languages such as Pitjantjatjara, and chose

Bundjalung as the most suitable. She also expressed the hope that this very choice might inspire Bundjalung people to take a greater interest in the survival of their language. Some years ago, from her initiative, a unit in Bundjalung was introduced at Associate Diploma level at Churchill College (now Monash University College, Gippsland).

ISSUES IN TEACHING A DISAPPEARING LANGUAGE

In teaching any language, decisions must be made about such matters as which dialects to cover, what materials to use, and so on. Decisions of this kind may be particularly difficult in the teaching of a language with no available large body of speakers.

The diversity of Bundjalung dialects has presented some challenge to teachers. When I taught a Bundjalung course in Lismore in 1977, we confined our interest to the Lismore dialect, Wiyabal. We had as helper the late Lyle Roberts Jnr, who spoke this dialect. In Armidale, when I taught some Bundjalung to external students attending residential schools for the Associate Diploma in Aboriginal Studies, the choice was less clear. The course was being offered outside the Bundjalung area to an Aboriginal group who knew little or nothing of traditional Aboriginal languages. But we had in the group two with Bundjalung ancestry — from different dialect areas. We had good information on both of these areas (Tabulam/Baryulgil and Beaudesert) and we used common vocabulary as far as possible.

In Queensland, after the first series of language afternoons in 1988, when some teaching was done in a southern Bundjalung dialect and some in the northern dialect of Yugambeh, the Kombumerri Aboriginal Corporation insisted that only their dialect be taught in future courses. Even this decision was not simple to implement. In fact, our information on this dialect is comparatively sketchy: only some 500 words are well attested, and some holes in the grammar cannot be filled. We decided to fill in the missing portions with material extrapolated from better known dialects. It is reasonably certain, for example, that Yugambeh had the same range of demonstratives as Gidhabal — where we had examples, they fitted the same pattern; so, gaps were filled from other dialects.

In Victoria, for the unit taught at Monash University College, Gippsland, the first choice was to continue to teach the dialect that had been taught at Lismore in 1977. But it was also agreed that if a Bundjalung speaker came to help, the teaching would have to adjust towards that speaker's dialect.

So far as the material to be taught is concerned, it must be remembered that those who are learning Bundjalung today will not be blending into a community where the language is actively spoken, with the exception of a small minority of people at Woodenbong. If there is any community, they must make one themselves. A group like the Kombumerri Corporation is already a cohesive group, with extensive family ties, and some words and phrases that have been passed down. The choice as to how they will use the language is theirs. Will it be used for greetings and leave-takings, for complaining about weather (rain, heat, cold), for talking about traditional activities, for use in a bush setting, or for shopping? Will it be used primarily orally, or will some want to concentrate on written stories from earlier speakers? Will their learning be basically to sensitise themselves to their ancestral roots, to another way of viewing the world, or to the structures of traditional Aboriginal languages; or will they want to have an in-group language to talk about private matters, or to mark their own group? There is reasonable flexibility to do any of these things. Bundjalung has survived long enough to incorporate words and expressions so that its users can talk about non-traditional artefacts (for example, lights, cars, glasses, tea, butter, grog and money). But to be realistic, it is unlikely that Bundjalung will take over functions which English already performs well for them.

The question of what weight to give to spoken language or written forms is also important. We all learn to listen and speak before we read or write, of course, and in any language course I teach I insist on a spoken input. After perhaps some initial mood-setting music, I often have a session I call 'language wash', where I (or someone else) say a number of sentences. After that I get the group to repeat many of these as best they can, concentrating on fluency and intonation, even if some sounds are wrongly pronounced. Somewhere in the process I attach translations to some of the phrases, and at some stage (but not initially) I provide written transcripts. At the end of the session it is also advisable to have another 'language wash', with students listening, not viewing their printed sheets. Students can practise hearing the words and phrases in their heads, using the written form to remind them, rather than thinking of only reading them.

The written mode is also important. Some worksheets can be designed where words must be matched with pictures, again reinforcing the association of objects and actions with Bundjalung words.

There are also a good number of Bundjalung texts in various dialects which have been transcribed from spoken originals. These texts give an insight into fluent discourse, in a way that is now impossible to do with live speakers. The texts also illustrate differences from dialect to dialect, and they contain samples of humour, cultural customs, accounts of recent happenings, and traditional stories.

Ideally, of course, the role model in teaching should be a fluent native speaker of the language and dialect being taught, but in the case of Bundjalung this is becoming an increasingly difficult requirement to meet. In addition, so much of what we have in recorded material in the language (on tape and cassette tape) was recorded under poor conditions with background noise, flies buzzing near the microphone at times, bird calls, and interruptions and asides, mostly in English.

I have, with some reluctance, used my own speech as role model, and would expect that another teacher-learner of the language would do the same. I also remind learners that they are a new Bundjalung group, and it will be up to them to set their own norms and become their own role models. If they gain reasonable fluency, even with 'defective' pronunciation, they will, after a little tuning in on both sides, be able to understand and communicate with native speakers. My aim in courses I teach is to build up fluency, even if the repertoire is small. With that fluency, which also helps to internalise structural patterns of the language, the learners have a chance of extending their knowledge more efficiently than if they needed to construct what they said or wrote word by word or with frequent checking of dictionary and grammar book.

Transcribed texts must also serve as role models, especially for more advanced knowledge. A few of the post-contact songs which have been fully transcribed provide a model, which helps to reinforce grammar and vocabulary.

A further question is how much colloquial detail to cover. Different groups among the Bundjalung people have developed different greeting and leave-taking phrases. Almost certainly many of these were not traditional, but have been modelled on English greetings and leave-takings. Examples are: *bugalbeh* (literally 'good indeed') in Gidhabal; *giŋgala wahlu* ('how doing you') in Baryulgil. If we can extrapolate from other Aboriginal communities where the language is reasonably viable, we can assume that verbal greeting or acknowledgement of an arrival or imminent departure was not always required. When there was a verbal exchange, sentences such as 'you have come', 'where have you come from?', 'where are you going?', 'I'm going', 'off you go', were far more common.

Geytenbeek (1971) includes some colloquial and idiomatic expressions which are also given in Sharpe et al (1988, 17–19). I find it useful to show such a list to students quite early in their learning. They should not be expected to memorise them, but they illustrate the imaginative thinking of speakers of another language. What description beats *jalayn giyuhmbiyn* (throat [is] sandstone) for a sore throat? Or *nyuladhahŋ* (he-very) for self-important? Students should be encouraged to pick out and use phrases that appeal to them or are pertinent for describing situations and friends significant to them.

One other matter that should be considered is the place of Aboriginal English. One form of Aboriginal English is Baryulgil Square Talk (Fraser-Knowles 1985), which takes its name from the settlement known as The Square. It includes words and phrases from Bundjalung (for example, *giŋgala wuja*,'how are you?'; that's *ŋanyahz*,'that's mine'), Aussie-English contractions of these (for example, *nyagz*, from *nyaguhŋ* 'money'), and strongly variant forms of English which are sometimes modelled on Bundjalung constructions (for example, *mal* got me, 'I'm hungry'; *shordi-gandi* got me, 'I'm puffed').

CONCLUSION

Many of the general issues discussed in this chapter apply to the learning of any language. However, there are special problems — and sometimes opportunities — in the teaching or learning of a language which is going out of use. There is, I feel, much to be gained from studying a language such as Bundjalung, in what it reveals about traditional Aboriginal language patterns, and about traditional lifestyles in what was and still is a fertile and densely populated rural area of Australia, where issues of land tenure and preservation of sacred mythological sites are very much alive. The relatively extensive information we have on the language and culture of this area make such study a worthwhile exercise, despite the lack of native speakers as teachers.

FOR DISCUSSION

1. Babies have language washing over them for perhaps over a year (including time in the womb) before they start using any. What does this suggest about how we should teach languages?

2. Spoken language is not primarily linked to marks on paper; it is linked with gesture and body language, intonation and voice quality. If we don't have information on these things in a disappearing or dead language, what choices should we make?

3. If you were given the task of designing a course to sensitise people in your district to Aboriginal languages, what choices would you make of language and technique of teaching/learning, and why?

REFERENCES

Allen, J. and J. Lane

1913 Grammar, Vocabulary, and Notes of the Wangerriburra Tribe, Queensland Parliamentary Papers 3, 1034–51. In Annual Report of the Chief Protector of Aborigines for the Year 1913, Brisbane, 22–34.

On the Yugambeh dialect. John Allen was a native speaker; however, he had not used the language actively for some 40–60 years when this was written.

Bray, J.

1899 On Dialects and Place Names, *Science* 21 November.

An article quoting Bray and others, comments (mainly negative) on Aborigines, and short word list.

Calley, M.J.C.

1960 Bandjalang Social Organisation, PhD thesis, University of Sydney.

Crowley, T.

1978 *The Middle Clarence Dialects of Bandjalang*, Australian Institute of Aboriginal Studies, Canberra.

A detailed grammar of the Wahlubal/Wehlubal dialects of Tabulam and Baryulgil. It includes as an appendix Smythe's grammar of Bundjalung.

Cunningham, M.C.

1969 *A Description of the Yugumbir Dialect of Bandjalang*, University of Queensland Arts Series 1, 8, 69–122.

A description of the Beaudesert dialect.

Curr, E.M.

1886-87 *The Australian Race: Its Origin, Languages, Customs, Place of Landing in Australia, and the Routes by Which it Spread Itself over the Continent*, 4 vols, J. Ferres, Government Printer, Melbourne.

Fraser-Knowles, J.

1985 A New Bundjalung Language: Baryulgil Square Talk. In M.C. Sharpe et al 1988, 174–201.

A description of the Bundjalung-laced English of the Baryulgil people.

Geytenbeek, B. and H. Geytenbeek

1971 *Gidabal Grammar and Dictionary*, Australian Institute of Aboriginal Studies, Canberra.

A detailed grammar of the Gidhabal dialect of Bundjalung, spoken around Woodenbong.

Holmer, N.M.

1971 *Notes on the Bandjalang Dialect: Spoken at Coraki and Bungawalbin Creek, New South Wales*, Australian Institute of Aboriginal Studies, Canberra.

Grammar, texts and vocabulary of Wiyabal/Wuyehbal, but note Holmer does not consistently mark vowel length.

1983 *Linguistic Survey of South-Eastern Queensland*, Pacific Linguistics, D–54, Canberra.

This covers material in neighbouring languages to Bundjalung, as well as the Yugambeh dialect.

Rankin, T.

1900 Aboriginal Place Names and Other Words, with Their Meaning, Peculiar to the Richmond and Tweed River Districts, *Science* 22 September 1900, 132–34.

Rankin was a district surveyor. Word list with pronunciation guide.

Sharpe, M.C. et al

1985 *An Introduction to the Bundjalung Language and Its Dialects* (revised), ACAE Publications, Armidale.

A relatively non-technical description of the language and its dialectal variants. Includes a chapter on Baryulgil Square Talk, the distinctive Bundjalung-laced English in domestic use among Baryulgil people.

Sharpe, M.C.

1991 A Bundjalung Language Course, prepared for Monash University College, Gippsland.

Sharpe, M.C. (ed)

1992 *Dictionary of Western Bundjalung, including Gidhabal and Tabulam Bundjalung*, Margaret Sharpe, University of New England, Armidale.

Smythe, W.E.

1978 [c 1942 or 1948] Bandjalang Grammar. In Terry Crowley 1978, 247–478.

CHAPTER 6

LANGUAGE AND CULTURE: SOCIALISATION IN A WARLPIRI COMMUNITY

Edith Bavin

This chapter discusses the context in which children acquire Warlpiri as a first language. Children learn not only the forms and structures of the language, but also what is appropriate in different situations. In discussing how children acquire a language and how they learn about appropriate behaviour in society, researchers often talk about language acquisition as one topic and socialisation as another. This assumes that the two are separate, but other researchers do not support this view. They argue that language is acquired through socialisation; the two are integral aspects of child development. This paper demonstrates the closeness of this linkage for one Aboriginal language, Warlpiri, but we can assume that it has been widespread throughout Aboriginal Australia and continues today.

THE WARLPIRI LANGUAGE

Warlpiri is a Pama-Nyungan language spoken in the centre of Australia by about 3,000 speakers. There are several places in which the language is the community language, namely Yuendumu, Willowra and Lajamanu. In addition, Warlpiri is spoken in other places including Tennant Creek and Alice Springs. The discussion below is based on observations made in Yuendumu, which is 300 kilometres northwest of Alice Springs. There are about 800 Warlpiri people living in the community. While the people have access to packaged food in the two shops, they still like to hunt and gather bush food. The people live in extended families and prefer to live and sleep outside even though some housing is available in the community. Television reception and telephone contact have been available since the end of 1987. Before that, radio telephone was used to make contact with other communities.

The following sentence, consisting of three words, could be spoken in six different orders. The only requirement is that the *lpa* (an auxiliary, which signals that the action is not complete) is attached to the first word in the sentence. The actual order of words depends on the perspective of the speaker: instead of the verb, the word for 'woman' could be first or the word for 'dog'. The *ngku* on *karnta* is the ergative suffix which shows that the woman is the person who is looking.

Nyangulpa	maliki	karntangku
was looking	dog	woman

'The woman was looking at the dog.'

While English uses word order primarily to determine who is doing what to whom, Warlpiri uses case suffixes to show what function each noun has.

Some more examples of simple Warlpiri utterances are given below. Note that, compared with English, Warlpiri can omit pronouns and nouns in many circumstances. The suffix *-pala*, which is here attached to the verb, indicates that the subject is dual; it is sufficient to indicate that two people or things are performing the action, even when no pronoun or noun is included. If *palangu* is used instead of *pala*, this signals that the two entities are now the objects or goals of the action rather than the performers or agents. Note also that, like most other Pama-Nyungan languages, Warlpiri follows the ergative pattern: the *-rlu* attached to *kurdujarra* ('two children') is another form of the ergative suffix (an alternative to the *-ngku* used in the previous example).

Nyangupala maliki
saw dog
'They two saw the dog.'

Nyangupala kurdujarrarlu
saw two children
'The two children saw something/someone.'

Nyangupalangu
saw
'Someone/something saw them two.'

Nyangupalangu kurdujarra
saw two children
'Someone/something saw the two children.'

This small sample of Warlpiri should give an indication that Warlpiri and English are quite different, not just in the words used, but also in structure. There are, of course, many other grammatical structures that the Warlpiri child must acquire. But it is not only in grammar that Warlpiri and English differ; there are also differences in the way in which adults and children interact.

SOCIALISATION AND LEARNING

Not all cultures have the same expectations of children. For example, in white middle-class society, preverbal children are generally considered to be potential conversation partners and a care-giver carries on 'conversations' with a child. When the child starts producing words, the care-giver often points to things and asks the child to name the object or picture. Or the care-giver helps the child to develop communicative skills by telling the child what to say to a third person. However, in other cultures, children are not necessarily encouraged to speak until they have some knowledge to give, and question-answer routines are not part of the adult-child interaction.

Warlpiri adults give a great deal of love and attention to young babies but they do not assume that children are attempting to communicate or talk when they make their first sounds. A baby is carried around for a few months on a curved wooden carrier (*parraja*) supported on the mother's hip. Older babies and infants are carried around on an adult's hip or shoulders. A baby is fed at any time, and woken up at any time, often by older children who take delight in pinching the baby's cheeks, hoping to make the baby smile. A baby is passed around to any willing holder.

Warlpiri adults do not generally modify situations to suit the child, or generally structure the child's learning experience in stages, as is a common pattern in Western societies. The child learns through direct observation and real-life experience, the responsibility for learning being on the child. Similar patterns prevail in other Aboriginal communities (Harris 1981). A Warlpiri adult assumes that children learn by being with adults, watching what they do and listening to what they say. When an adult does initiate talk with a young child, it is to name others or to use an imperative to get the child to do something. The question-answer routine found in some other societies is not part of the interaction between a Warlpiri mother and her child. Such routines tend to be limited to societies with books and pictures, and books are not found in Warlpiri camps.

Children are encouraged to be independent and are not protected from potential danger in the way that many white middle-class children are. Warlpiri adults will protect children from serious dangers such as snakes, but they do not normally stop children from playing with a knife or piece of broken glass. When a baby cries the mother provides milk, but when infants cry or scream for attention they are likely to be left alone and not fussed over, unless a real reason for the crying is determined.

The children learn language by exposure to it in real situations. They learn the names of animals, trees and berries by being with the adults when they hunt and gather. They learn names and kin terms by being told the names of people in the immediate environment. Although the learning environment is not modified and graded, there is some control over the knowledge the child is exposed to. For example, a child would not be allowed to participate in all types of ceremony. There is also some modification in the words used with young children, which will be discussed a little later.

SKIN NAMES

To function as a member of the society, a Warlpiri person requires a name known as a skin or section name. Systems of skin names are in operation in many Australian Aboriginal groups. In the Warlpiri system there are eight skin groups, each of which has a male and a female name. A child's name is determined by the names of the father and mother, according to a fixed pattern of descent. For example, a *Japaljarri* man should marry a *Nakamarra* woman and their children will be *Jungarrayi* (if male) and *Nungarrayi* (if female). The sister of a *Japaljarri* man will be *Napaljarri*: she should marry a *Jakamarra* man (possibly, but not necessarily, her brother's wife's brother) and their children will be *Jupurrula*.

The full system can be summarised in a diagram (see Figure 1). The horizontal lines in the centre link marriage partners, while the vertical lines at the sides link fathers and sons. Male skin names (all beginning with *J*) are listed immediately above or below their female counterparts (all of which begin with *N*). Note the regularity in the system: for example, a boy will have the same skin name as his paternal grandfather.

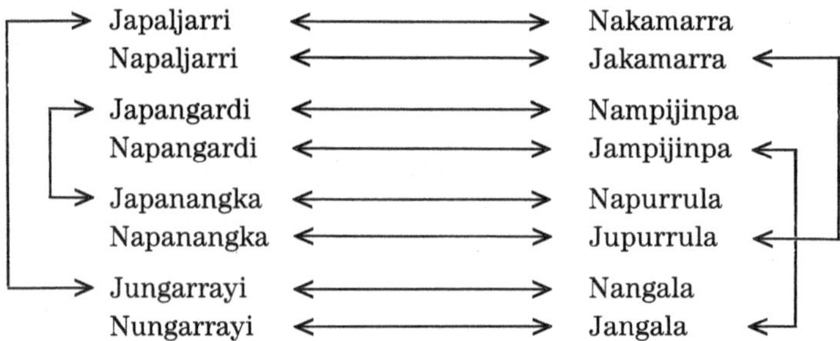

Figure 1: The Warlpiri skin names.

All members of the community must have a skin name so that they can fit into the social structure. Different land, stories and ritual are associated with each group: people choose marriage partners on the basis of the skin names; and people have obligations to others depending on their skin relationships. Children must acquire knowledge about the system and must learn the names of individuals, so that they know how to relate to them. For example, if a child's mother is named *Napaljarri*, any *Napaljarri* has a classificatory mother relation to the child and can be called *ngati* 'mother' by the child.

When someone approaches a baby, the skin name for that person is spoken, as is the baby's skin name. Thus, there is a type of introduction. Even though the baby will not be able to process or remember the names, the behaviour indicates the importance of knowing who other people are. The baby is socialised right away to one important aspect of Warlpiri society.

The cultural significance of the skin name is reinforced in many ways as the baby grows up. For example, children attend ceremonies with their mothers and other female kin and see the designs on the dancers' bodies and the dances that are associated with the different skin groups. When young people start participating in ceremonies, they watch as the older people paint them; through experience they become aware of their own skin group designs.

Of great importance is the relationship of Aboriginal people to their land. When families go out from Yuendumu to gather food or to stay at outstations, the adults point out who 'owns' the land which is being driven through, for example, *Jakamarra-Jupurrula* land. This indicates the historical significance of that land for *Jakamarra* and *Jupurrula* people and shows that they are responsible for the land. The children are also told about significant sites on the land. For example, the old people will point out rock holes, and perhaps sing a traditional song that is related to the place. This is all part of the socialisation of the child; the exposure to the skin names in relation to land ownership helps to reinforce their importance, and the names themselves are learned through the socialisation process.

BABY TALK

As noted earlier, Warlpiri children learn in real-life situations and not through structured situations graded in difficulty, nor do they experience the question-answer routines that are typical of adult-child interaction in many English-speaking homes. Adults do, however, make some modifications in the language which they use to babies. In this baby-talk style, the modifications include changing some of the sounds in words and dropping some initial consonants. In addition, some baby words, particularly animal and kin terms, are used, many of which are borrowings from English. For example, *mamiyi* (from 'Mummy') is used for *ngati* 'mother', and *jiji* (from 'gee-gee') is used for *nantuwu* 'horse'. There is also a special baby word for food. While adult Warlpiri divides food into three types, namely *kuyu* 'meat', *miyi* 'vegetable food' and *pama* 'honey and nectar', the form *nyanya* 'food' is used with babies, an acknowledgement that children do not have the experience to categorise food types under different labels.

This modified baby talk attempts to imitate the forms that the youngsters first use when they start articulating words (Laughren 1984). Whereas an adult would say *nyampu* for 'here' or 'this', a baby says *ampu*, leaving off the initial consonant *ny*. In playing with young children or teasing them, adults and older children might use *ampu*. This teasing puts responsibility on the child to learn the adult form, and by the age of four the children have mastered most of the phonology of the language, although some words continue to be said in the baby form for many years, for example, *pawu* for *pardu* 'diminutive'.

Older siblings as well as adults use baby talk when playing with a Warlpiri baby. Warlpiri children of four tease their baby siblings, indicating that they are socialised by that age to use different language forms in different contexts. The following example is taken from an interaction between a four-year-old child (4;11) and her two-year-old sister (2;8). The younger sister does pronounce initial consonants but her sister uses baby talk back to her, leaving off the initial consonant from *nganayi*, *nyampu* and *jayi*; she also substitutes *w* for *ng* in *ngula*. The teasing style is also marked by a relatively high pitched voice.

J: (=2;8)	ngula	nganayijayi	
	that one	do what's it	
	That one is doing something.'		
S: (=4;11)	wula	anayi-ayi	ampu
	that one	do what's it	here
	'That one's doing something here.'		

From the age of three-and-a-half, children are able to take turns in conversation, and they talk more often about events in the past. That is, children talk about events that their conversation partner may not have experienced: they contribute information. Thus, in addition to having acquired many of the grammatical structures in the language, Warlpiri children have acquired basic conversational skills by the middle of their fourth year. This is the age when they show some independence by wandering away from the immediate camp environment with other children. They go off looking for food or entertainment usually with another child of a similar age, or with older children who look out for them. They find sticks and dig into holes, as do their mothers when hunting for *wardapi* 'goanna', they reach for *yakajirri* berries on low shrubs, and they throw stones at birds in the trees. These provide experiences which they can recall on later occasions.

Once they have developed basic conversational skills, the children start manipulating the language as in the teasing routines mentioned above. In other cultures also, children tease and role-play by imitating features of the language of others, and they do this from an early age (Schieffelin and Ochs 1986).

KIN TERMINOLOGY

The kinship systems of Warlpiri and English are quite different. In English we have a single term 'grandmother' whereas Warlpiri distinguishes between *yaparla* (father's mother) and *jaja* (mother's mother). But there is a further difference here: *yaparla* refers not only to father's mother but also to her brothers and sisters; likewise *jaja* also refers to mother's mother's brothers and sisters. Where English has the word 'aunt', Warlpiri has *pimirdi* (father's sister); mother's sister is treated as mother and referred to as *ngati* (mother).

Although Warlpiri adults do not generally grade learning situations, they do simplify kin terms when they speak directly to young children between the ages of two and three. Adults neutralise the basic opposition between male and female by using *papa* to refer to father, father's brother and father's sister, and *mamiyi* to refer to mother, mother's sister and mother's brother (Laughren 1984). Later, when the child is about three or four, sex is distinguished; *papa* is distinguished from *pimiyi* (=*pimirdi*) 'father's sister', and *mamiyi* is distinguished from *aminyi* (=*ngamirni*) 'mother's brother'. The age difference between siblings is also neutralised, so that *kakiyi* 'brother' replaces both *papardi* 'older brother' and *kukurnu* 'younger brother', while *yayi* 'sister' replaces both *kapirdi* 'older sister' and *ngawurru* 'younger sister'. This simplification is in addition to phonetic modifications which give forms such as *wayingiyi* for *warringiyi* (father's father), and *yaparli* is used often instead of *yaparla* (father's mother).

So, there is some acknowledgement that a child needs to be introduced to forms gradually. The basic opposition between father's kin and mother's kin is deemed more important for the child than sex distinctions within that opposition.

Since adults reduce the number of oppositions in the kin system when talking directly to young children, we might assume that this modification assists the child in learning the terms and the system. Understanding of the kin system and the terms used to label relations nevertheless takes many years to master. At first, children use kin terms as names for individuals; for example, *jaja* 'mother's mother' is a particular individual. The realisation that any person with a particular skin name has a particular classificatory kin relationship does not come immediately, just as English-speaking children may take some time to grasp that even adults have aunts and uncles. The focus of the Warlpiri modifications is to provide the child with a basic distinction between father's and mother's kin, a distinction that is crucial in the social organisation of the community. The concern is more with socialising the child to this distinction than with teaching the child the language for naming.

The kin terminology is large and the full range of terms is not acquired until adulthood. Before the age of five, the children can use appropriate terms to distinguish between own and other generations, but they can make few generalisations. They can identify particular individuals but the system is not understood. They often make the mistake of taking a parent's perspective, assuming that because a parent can identify a particular skin group as *ngati* 'mother', for example, that skin group is appropriate as their own *ngati*. Between the ages of six and eleven knowledge of the connections between skin names and particular kin relations increases. Those for at least one grandparent and mother are known first, while those for children and spouse are acquired later. This suggests that the child learns the system gradually, based on what is relevant in the child's experience. Other evidence supporting this view is that children without an actual example of a particular relation (for example, *pimirdi* 'father's sister') tend not to know which skin group fills this relationship as early as children who do have such a relation.

The kin domain is an interesting area to observe the acquisition of a language when the group is in contact with another language. For most children, the general terms *kakiyi* 'brother' and *yayi* 'sister' are used, although some children between six and ten can make the distinction between older and younger siblings, using the appropriate terms. This may reflect some change going on in the language, with the age distinction being lost. In Warlpiri, actual siblings as well as the children of father's brother and mother's sister are classified as a person's brothers and sisters. While the Warlpiri children often use English words to label kin, some of them maintain the Warlpiri system by using 'sister' and 'brother' for relations that would be classified as cousins in English.

EARLY UTTERANCES

By the age of two, Warlpiri children produce connected utterances that contain recognisable forms. A few words are said in isolation before that age, baby-talk words such as *jiji* 'horse' and *nyanya* 'food'. The adult shows pronounced pride with the knowledge gained by the child, and teases the child, repeating the words as they are pronounced. When the child produces longer utterances, utterances using suffixes on nouns and verbs, Warlpiri adults do not attempt to interpret what is not easily recognisable. In fact, adults may be quite dismissive: one Warlpiri speaker is quoted as saying:

> Witawita kujakalu jaajaawangka, kulalpalu Warlpiriji wangkayarla
> 'Little ones who talk like crows, they are not speaking Warlpiri.'

The following is from a two-year-old. The forms are recognisable despite the modified pronunciation of *naka* for *nyanka* 'look', *nanuwu* for *nantuwu* 'horse' and *ajuku* for *ngajuku* 'for me'. But even though the forms can be identified, the child's communicative intentions are not easy to determine. The listener needs to guess, and this adults do not choose to do.

mamiyi,	kuku	naka	warna
mummy	evil spirit	look	snake

mamiyi	nanuwu
mummy	horse

mamiyi	punku-lu	aju-ku
mummy	bad-they	me-DAT

When children are recognised as talking, they are assumed to have knowledge and will be answered by the adult. Their maturity is measured in knowledge gained rather than in years of age. When adults talk to children who they do recognise as speaking Warlpiri, talk is not modified to help the child in the task of acquiring the language structures. The language produced is fast and repetitive, as in discourse style among adults themselves. Imperatives are frequent: the child is told to do things such as take, give, come, or leave something. The adult expects appropriate behavioural responses, but is not upset if the child does not respond as expected. It is assumed that children will eventually take responsibility for their own actions.

There is considerable phonetic variation in the speech of the young Warlpiri child. A word may have the correct initial consonant in one utterance but not in the next. Of particular interest is the play on sounds, even in the speech of two-year-olds. Consider the following example from a two-year-old child. Long strings like this are often sung by children. (Below the forms uttered by the child are possible corresponding adult words.)

ala	tutu	tutu	lala	tu	atu
Nangala	jarntu	jarntu	Nangala	jarntu	ngaju
Nangala	dog	dog	Nangala	dog	me

ati	pupu	ampu	ampuku	ata	ataku
?	?	nyampu	nyampuku	ngaju	ngajuku
?	?	here/this	for this	me	for me

Another example of word play is with *wita* 'small' which may be pronounced in several ways in one utterance: *wita, tita, pita* and *wuta*. One two-year-old produced the following. The suffixes on *wita* may correspond to the adult diminutive suffix *-pardu*.

witapu	tita	tu
witapardu	wita-pardu	
tiny	tiny	

An awareness of different speech styles and sounds also seems to be apparent in the use of the fricative [s] with pretend baby talk. Warlpiri does not have fricatives. Yet a four-year-old uttered a series of six nonsense words, all with initial [s]. An adult Warlpiri claimed that she was imitating English and that is the way children imitate English speakers; they are aware of the [s] sound as a marker of the language of the non-Aboriginal people in the community.

THE CURRENT SITUATION

The Warlpiri lifestyle is not as it was before white settlement. It has changed as other cultures have changed. The community at Yuendumu has a school in which children are taught in classroom settings. This means that there are discontinuities between traditional learning and school teaching situations. The children learn literacy skills, something their grandparents did not do. Food is available in the shops, and the acquisition of skills necessary for food gathering is not as crucial as it once was. The children are now able to watch television and see other lifestyles as depicted through the programs.

In spite of these changes, the community still maintains traditional values. Warlpiri children learn about social relations through naming, and they acquire skills for gathering and preparing bush food as well as other skills and the language that they involve by observing and imitating their elders. I have seen children of two using twigs to make the digging motions they have observed from adults, motions they will need to dig for food when they are older. Knowledge increases through adulthood with experience, and continues to develop. I have seen a woman of sixteen catching, gutting and cooking a lizard with great confidence, a woman of thirty painting ritual body designs for the first time, checking her knowledge with older women sitting close by; and another woman in her late thirties checking with an older woman about interpreting tracks in the sand. Knowledge is acquired over many years.

Like children from other language groups, Warlpiri children first talk about the here and now, and the hearer must rely on the immediate context for interpretation. Talk about the remote develops as the child masters the necessary grammatical forms in the language and the experiences to draw upon. Like other children, the Warlpiri first use simple clause utterances before linking clauses together to establish sequential and causal relations. Narrative skills take longer to acquire.

Although there have been changes in the lifestyle of the Warlpiri people, a strong sense of appropriate behaviour persists and is evident in the interactions between adults and children. Through these interactions children are socialised into the culture, and in their socialisation children acquire language and its appropriate use.

FOR DISCUSSION

1. Observe for about twenty minutes a mother (or other care-giver) with a baby of about one year of age. Note the language forms the mother uses, and what function these have. For example:

- Does she try to direct the child's attentions to objects or people? If so, does she do this by pointing or by verbal expressions or both?
- Does she ask questions of the baby?
- Does she offer explanations to the baby?
- Does she interpret the baby's cries as attempts to communicate? That is, does she articulate what she thinks the baby is trying to say? If so, is she confident that her first guess correctly identifies the baby's intentions or does she try to work out some other interpretation?

2. Observe an older sibling with a baby (under one year old). What voice modifications, if any, does the sibling make when directly addressing the baby? Can you detect any systematic differences between the sibling's talk to the baby and the mother's in terms of (a) what they talk about, (b) how they interpret what the baby is communicating, and (c) modifications in voice or words used?

3. Listen to some speech from a two-year-old child. Write down what the child is trying to communicate. How easy is it to interpret the words used? Discuss any difficulties. Does the child use gesture to accompany speech?

4. Calculate what percentage of the day a particular baby spends alone, how much time adults talk directly to the child, and how much time the child is exposed to speech that is not directly addressed to the child. Compare your findings with others in your group.

5. Discuss what you perceive are the major differences between the early experience for a Warlpiri child and the early experience of a baby such as the one you observed for question (1).

6. Use Figure 1 to work out the skin names of relations: choose a name for yourself, then work out the skin name of your relatives, including mother, father, (potential) mother-in-law, father's father, and so on.

REFERENCES

Harris, S.

1981 *Culture and Learning: Tradition and Education in North East Arnhem Land*, Australian Institute of Aboriginal Studies, Canberra.

Laughren, M.

1984 Warlpiri Baby Talk, *Australian Journal of Linguistics* 4(1), 73–88.

Schieffelin, B.B. and E. Ochs (eds)

1986 *Language Socialization across Cultures*, Cambridge University Press, Cambridge.

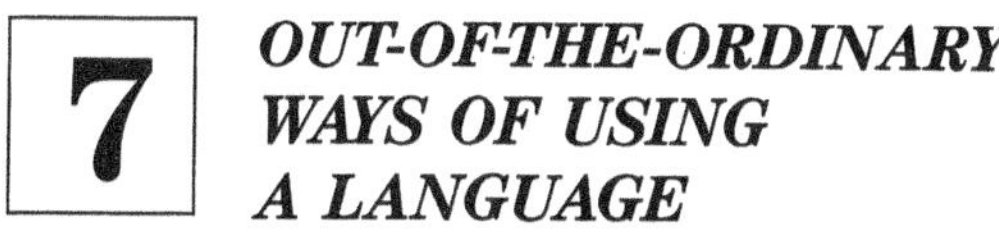

CHAPTER

7 OUT-OF-THE-ORDINARY WAYS OF USING A LANGUAGE

Barry Alpher

REGISTERS

Australian Aborigines often speak fluently more than one Aboriginal language, more than one regional variety of the same Aboriginal language, and one or more varieties of English. If they live in a traditional community, they are also likely to have available different varieties of their own regional dialect, which they use for different purposes and with persons of different social categories. These speech varieties include forms of the language used with or about relatives with whom people maintain relations of respect or avoidance (for example, mothers-in-law and certain kinds of cousins); forms used with relatives with whom people maintain relations of jesting familiarity; forms used with very young children ('baby talk'); forms learned by young men in the course of their initiation and used only in that context; and sign language, in which gestures made with the hands are used instead of spoken words.

The use of the same language in different varieties for different social purposes is perfectly familiar to speakers of English. Consider the difference between saying 'Harry needs a car' and 'Mr Fanshaw requires an automobile'. A car is the same thing as an automobile, needing is the same thing as requiring, and — let us say — 'Harry' and 'Mr Fanshaw' refer to the same person. The difference is one of appropriateness in certain situations and with certain people. A term often used for speech varieties of this sort is 'register'. Registers in English tend to be characterised by differences in vocabulary, as in the examples just given, and by differences in grammar and sometimes in pronunciation as well.

RESPECT REGISTERS

The term 'register' seems an appropriate one for spoken varieties of Aboriginal languages of the types mentioned above. The special 'respect' speech variety used by a man (in some parts of Australia) in talking about his mother-in-law, for example, is used only in certain situations and with persons of certain categories, and it differs from 'ordinary' speech largely in the use of different vocabulary items. So, for example, in the Uw-Oykangand language of southwestern Cape York Peninsula the ordinary term for 'foot' is *ebmal*, but a man speaking to a person who stands in the kinship relation of potential mother-in-law to him will refer to the foot as *arrmbun*. The respect register, the form of speech that makes use of the term *arrmbun* for 'foot', is known in Uw-Oykangand as Olkel-Ilmbanhthi.

In explaining how whole sentences are put together in a respect register like Olkel-Ilmbanhthi, it is useful to distinguish between 'content words' and 'function words'. This distinction can be made for any language. Content words in English include all the nouns, verbs, and adjectives while function words are conjunctions ('and', 'or', 'but', 'if', 'when', et cetera), prepositions ('to', 'by', 'on', et cetera) and pronouns ('you', 'she', 'it', 'they', et cetera). Function words tend to signal relationships among words and clauses and they are very limited in number though frequent in occurrence. In certain (but by no means all) Aboriginal languages, all of the content words in a proper respect register sentence belong to the respect vocabulary rather than the ordinary vocabulary. Uw-Oykangand is one such language. An example is the two ways to say 'I have a sore foot':

ORDINARY	Ebmal	ijam	ilg	ay.
RESPECT	Arrmbun	obmben	ilg	ay.
English	foot	sore	with	I

Here the respect-vocabulary word *arrmbun* 'foot' corresponds to the ordinary content word *ebmal*, a noun, and the respect-vocabulary word *obmben* 'sore' corresponds to the content word *ijam*, an adjective (in Uw-Oykangand a kind of noun). But the function words *ilg* 'with' and *ay* 'I' remain the same in both ways of speaking.

In a language like Uw-Oykangand (or English), the list of 'function' elements includes not only whole words, but also parts of words. Examples of such parts in Uw-Oykangand are the endings that signal the tense of verbs and those that signal the case of nouns. These are expressed with the same forms in respect-register speech as in ordinary speech, as the following examples, which mean 'I speared it with a spear', illustrate:

ORDINARY	Alka-nhdh	idu-rr	ay.
RESPECT	Udnga-nhdh	yanganunyja-rr	ay.
English	spear-INSTRUM	spear-PAST	I

Here the content words for 'spear' (the nouns *alka-* and *udnga-*) and 'to spear' (the verbs *idu-* and *yanganunyja-*) differ from one register to the other, but the instrumental case-ending *-nhdh* ('with' a spear) and the past tense-ending *-rr*, like the function word *ay* 'I', remain constant.

Not all Aboriginal respect languages are as thorough as Olkel-Ilmbanhthi in replacing content words. For example, in the Yir-Yoront language — spoken by Uw-Oykangand's neighbour to the northwest — inclusion of the function word *wangal* in a sentence, preceding the verb, characterises the sentence as respectful (*wangal* also occurs as a content word meaning 'hand' in the respect register). The Yir-Yoront respect register also makes use of special content words, but in nowhere near as consistent or thoroughgoing a way as Uw-Oykangand.

Respect-register vocabulary is in a sense an 'add-on' to the ordinary vocabulary of a language. It is created in a number of ways; some of these are more favoured in some regions than in others. There are, to start with, certain words which occur in the respect vocabularies of a number of not-very-closely related languages in a single region. For example, the Yir-Yoront respect word for 'tree, stick', *yulh*, is cognate with the respect word for 'tree, stick' in a number of languages spoken to the north. Then there are respect words derived from ordinary words on the basis of some trope: the ordinary Yir-Yoront word *thorrchn* means 'hair', and its derivative *thorrchonh* means 'dog' or '(hairy) yam'. Respect words can, for example, be derived from ordinary words: the Yir-Yoront respect word for 'go', *larr-ma*, is compounded of the ordinary words for 'ground', *larr*, and 'tread on', *ma*. And, in a number of regions, there is a practice of using certain ordinary words from a neighbouring dialect or language as respect words in one's own.

Although the function words in Aboriginal respect registers are normally the same as those in the ordinary register, they are in certain cases used differently. One typical case is the pronouns for 'you'. In ordinary Uw-Oykangand, 'you' (one person) is *inang*, 'you two' is *ubal*, and 'you' (more than two persons) is *urr*. But in Olkel-Ilmbanhthi, any person or persons addressed, even if only one, are addressed with the plural pronoun *urr*. The use of the plural in respectful speech is a feature of many languages right across the world, with no historical connection to each other. Those readers who have studied French will recognise it in the different usage of the pronouns *tu* (singular) and *vous* (plural), both meaning 'you', but the latter used where respect or deference is intended.

Another common feature of respectful speech is a certain amount of intentional vagueness. It is as if the message of the utterance becomes to an extent less important than the nature of the social relationship that the speaker is trying to maintain or establish with the person spoken to. In the respect registers of Aboriginal languages such vagueness is implicit in the use of a single respect-register word to substitute for any of a number of ordinary-register words that are related to each other in one way or another. Most usually, this relation is one of membership in the same class based on similarity of meaning. It is as if, in English, there were a respect register in which the word 'vehicle' was always used whenever one wanted to refer to a car, a bus, or a truck. An Aboriginal respect register may, for example, refer to any of the different kinds of shark and stingray, each with its own name in the ordinary register, by a single term. It is still possible to be precise in a respect register. One can, if necessary, always use the respect word for 'shark-or-ray' and qualify it as, say, 'the one with spots and a long tail'. It is rather that the normal purpose of respect register is not so much to make precise commentary as to negotiate difficult relationships.

Classifying things according to their family-like relations, or taxonomic class inclusion, is by no means the only principle on which Aboriginal respect registers use a single term as a substitute for more than one ordinary term. Olkel-Ilmbanhthi, for example, uses *elngamb* instead of ordinary Uw-Oykangand *ew* 'mouth' and *ow* 'nose' (perhaps because of their proximity on the face, but possibly also because of the phonetic similarity of the words), and *unhunh* for the ordinary words *ef* 'tongue' and *ukan* 'grass' (presumably having in mind the similarity in shape).

RESPECT VOCABULARY AND CLASSIFICATION

Where a respect register, like Olkel-Ilmbanhthi, has the feature that all content words must have a special equivalent word in the respect vocabulary, it is typically taxonomic class inclusion that is the major principle on which many ordinary-register words are equated with a single word in the respect register. Here the respect register becomes a handy means for investigating the taxonomic classes that a language recognises. People are sometimes rather vague about these things: is a bicycle a kind of vehicle? What about a train? An aeroplane? But in the relation between an ordinary vocabulary and a respect vocabulary with a replacement term for every content word, such questions have been answered, in a sense, in advance. The most extensively described language of this type is Dyirbal, spoken in the rainforest region of southeast Cape York Peninsula. Its respect register is known as Dyalnguy and its ordinary register as Guwal.

In studying the correspondence between Guwal and Dyalnguy, Dixon (1971) asked speakers of Dyirbal to do two things: first, for every ordinary (Guwal) word, he asked a speaker what its respect vocabulary (Dyalnguy) equivalent was. Usually, each Guwal word corresponded to just one Dyalnguy word, but often each Dyalnguy word corresponded to several Guwal words. Second, for each Dyalnguy word, he asked what its Guwal equivalent was. With great consistency, Dyirbal speakers cited not all of the corresponding Guwal words, but just one of them. For example, for each of the Guwal words *buwanyu* 'tell', *jinkanyu* 'tell a particular piece of news', *gindimban* 'warn', and *ngarran* 'tell someone one does not have a certain thing, for example food, when one has', the Dyalnguy equivalent is *wuyuban*. When asked what the ordinary word was for *wuyuban*, Dyirbal speakers answered that it was *buwanyu*, that is, 'to tell', purely and simply. So, not only do the correspondences of Guwal to Dyalnguy vocabulary amount to an objective form of evidence for speakers' feelings about the similarities in meaning between words, but they suggest that some of these meanings are more fundamental than others. In Dixon's terminology, verbs like *buwanyu* 'tell' are nuclear verbs, and the other 'tell' verbs, *jinkanyu*, *gindimban*, and *ngarran*, are non-nuclear verbs. On these taxonomic groups and on the nuclear/non-nuclear distinction, an extensive analysis of the meanings of Dyirbal words can be built.

THE NATURE OF RESPECT

The study of respect registers helps in the understanding of many other areas of Aboriginal life besides the meanings of words; one such area is that of the nature of respect itself, and of the particular social relations of which respect is a feature. Most Aboriginal languages have a respect register, but the particular relatives with whom, or about whom, one uses the respect register differ from one group to the next. In some groups, the relative is only the mother-in-law, or any person who is related in such a way as to be appropriate as a mother-in-law. In most Aboriginal groups, a woman and a man related as mother-in-law and son-in-law take great care never to be anywhere near each other; often the man will use respect register when he talks about his mother-in-law. In some communities a man is allowed to be in the presence of a potential mother-in-law (a woman to whose daughter he is neither married nor betrothed), but if he addresses her he will use respect register, and more usually he will speak to her using a third person as an intermediary. Sometimes this third person will just stand there and maintain the fiction of being an intermediary; sometimes the conversation is carried on through an imaginary third person. In various communities of Cape York, including the Yir-Yoront and the Wik-Ngathana community not far to the north, the list of relatives with whom one uses respect register is a longer one: a man speaking to (or sometimes about) his daughter, a man speaking with his wife's brother or with his mother's brother or with certain of his grandparents. The list and the details of how and when the respect register is used vary from one community to the next.

People can manipulate relationships by failing to use respect register where it is appropriate, or using it where it is not. Storytellers can create irony when they have a character use respect register but fail to follow through with other appropriate actions: so it is that a personage in a Yir-Yoront story who is notorious for his outrageous behaviour correctly addresses his mother-in-law's father (a kind of grandfather) in respect register, informing his grandfather that he is keeping for himself the wallaby that the grandfather has killed. According to proper etiquette, he should be giving food to his grandfather rather than taking it from him.

INITIATION REGISTERS

The detailed study of the use of respect registers can reveal endless subtleties in social behaviour. But the Aboriginal repertoire of speech varieties is by no means limited to these. Another sort of register in Aboriginal languages that has received a great deal of attention from scholars is that which older men teach to younger men as part of their advanced initiation. Of these registers it can in general be said that they are brilliant creations in which a very small stock of special words is made to do all the work of framing any proposition that a speaker wants to express. Because details of initiation practices are sacred and are kept as secrets among initiated men, it is not in general ethical to discuss them in scholarly publications.

But in one case, that of the initiation register (known as Demin or Damin) of the Lardil people of Mornington Island in Queensland, the initiated men themselves have released details to the general public. They have done this because, on the one hand, they are no longer performing initiations — having been prevented from doing so in the past by the mission authorities in charge of their settlement — and, on the other hand, they feel that they have in Demin a creation worthy of the world's admiration. Demin uses some 150 basic elements to substitute for all the words of regular Lardil. Demin words differ from those of ordinary Lardil in one very conspicuous way: the sound-system according to which they are pronounced is radically unlike that of ordinary Lardil or of any other Australian Aboriginal language. This system includes in its inventory of sounds several nasalised clicks and an ingressive lateral (an [l] sound made by drawing the breath into the lungs). Without going into the details of how all these sounds are produced, it should nonetheless be clear to readers that words in Demin have and are intended to have a bizarre sound. Speakers find them both funny and fun to make.

The extremely small number of basic elements in Demin forces speakers to make very judicious use of them in allocating them to the various concepts expressed by single words in ordinary Lardil. It also forces speakers to draw extensively on their knowledge of complex sentence constructions in Lardil, in order to express distinctions at a level of fineness not possible by naming a thing with a single basic element. It seems also that there is in Demin no use of overgeneral reference to things to produce a deferential mode of speech. Rather, what seems to be asked of the young initiands is that they demonstrate verbal proficiency, just as they are asked to demonstrate proficiency in other aspects of adult life. In Lardil tradition, the invention of Demin is ascribed to a single person, Kalthad (or Yellow Trevally, as he would be known in English). Here, there is no mistaking the linkage of Demin with exceptional personal competence.

SIGN LANGUAGE

A phenomenon of a rather different kind from the spoken registers is sign language. Not a register, it is a different medium of communication — in somewhat the same sense as written language is. In sign language, the 'words' are hand motions. For example, the sign in the Warlpiri language (north-central Northern Territory) for 'old man' is the hand with fingers spread apart but slightly flexed, held with palm towards the face and moved a short distance forwards and back; the corresponding spoken word is *purlka*. Sign language is used by various persons in various situations, although some of the situations in which it might be thought to be most useful, such as between men who must be quiet while they are stalking game, are not in fact the occasions when it is most highly developed. The most highly elaborated sign language is used by mature women in Aboriginal communities where a woman, upon the death of her husband, must avoid speaking during an extended period of mourning. In these communities, most of which are located in the north-central desert region of the Northern Territory, mature women become proficient enough in sign language to express anything that can be expressed in the spoken language.

Any number of features of sign language are worthy of extensive discussion; here it will have to suffice to mention just three. The first is that a highly developed sign language like that of the Warlpiri is modelled closely on the spoken language, with signs corresponding to all the content words and also to some of the function words and affixes. There is little one-to-many correspondence of sign language words to spoken words; sign language is specific.

The second feature is that sign language omits signs for elements of the spoken language that indicate the grammatical relation of the parts of a sentence (who did what to whom) and the relative time at which the action is said to have occurred (the tense of the verbs). So, for example, the spoken Warlpiri sentence that means 'two men are carrying firewood' is:

Wati-jarra-rlu	ka-pala	warlu	ka-nyi.
two men	they two	wood	carry

where the ergative suffix *-rlu* signals that the men are the agents of the action, the auxiliary element *kapala* signals that the time is the present and that the subject of the sentence is dual, and the suffix *-nyi* signals that the time of the action is not in the past. The same sentence rendered in sign language contains the signs for 'men', 'two', '(fire)wood', and 'carry', in that order, and omits the rest.

The third feature is that sign language 'words', when they are extended to cover the meanings of more than one spoken word, sometimes do so, not on the basis of shared features of meaning, but on the basis of shared features of sound. So, for example, the Warlpiri sign corresponding to the spoken word *winpiri* 'spearwood' (a species of tree) is used also for the spoken words *wina* 'winner', *wiki* 'week', *wiki* 'whisky', *Winjiyi* 'Wednesday', and *Winiyi* 'Winnie'. The basis for the association is the shared syllable *wi*. It is of interest here that the first languages ever to be written, Sumerian and Egyptian, some 5,000 years ago, used signs which were pictures of what they represented but which also represented words that sounded similar. In so doing the writers of these languages made the first steps towards a representation of the sounds of language rather than of the meaningful units as wholes. Aboriginal sign language is a linguistic medium, and it appears to be evolving along similar lines to that other non-spoken medium, writing.

CONCLUSION

This discussion of non-ordinary forms of Aboriginal languages has, of course, barely scratched the surface. Much more can be said about each of the language varieties considered above, and numerous other varieties have not been mentioned at all. What is worth mentioning in closing is that all of these forms of communication represent not just intricate patterns of communication and social interaction, but intellectual achievements that involve conscious creative acts by their users.

FURTHER READING

Much of the information in this chapter comes from the readings mentioned below. Those who are interested in further study of this subject might wish to begin by consulting them.

The notion of 'register' is explained in Halliday and Hasan (1976). Interesting explorations of the subtleties of respect registers are contained in the articles by McConvell, Merlan, Rumsey and Sutton in Heath, Merlan, and Rumsey (1982). In the same collection is an introduction by Kenneth Hale to the initiation register of Lardil. The Dyirbal respect register is discussed in Dixon (1971). A discussion of the Yir-Yoront respect vocabulary and of the various origins of the words in it can be found in Alpher (1991). An excellent and thorough discussion of Aboriginal sign language is Kendon (1988).

FOR DISCUSSION

1. Consider some examples of what would count as respectful or disrespectful utterances in English. Try to relate such examples to real situations and avoid artificially elaborate utterances that are unlikely to be genuinely used (such as 'I wonder whether you would graciously consent to lending me a dollar'). You might consider such situations as writing a letter to apply for a job or introducing yourself to a new neighbour or to a new colleague at work, or speaking to someone who has just been to a funeral.

2. Why do you think many languages use a plural 'you' to show respect? What other ways are there of avoiding a direct 'you'? In Parliament, for example, it is conventional to speak of 'the member for Southtown' rather than to address the person directly: can you add other examples of this kind?

3. How would you set about designing a sign language? How would you represent words like 'true' and 'honest'? How, if at all, could you distinguish between 'fall' and 'fell' or between 'tomorrow' and 'today'?

REFERENCES

Alpher, B.
1991 *Yir-Yoront Lexicon: Sketch and Dictionary of an Australian Language*, Mouton de Gruyter, Berlin.

Dixon, R.M.W.
1971 A Method of Semantic Description. In D.D. Steinberg and L.A. Jakobovits (eds), *Semantics: An Interdisciplinary Reader in Philosophy, Linguistics and Psychology*, Cambridge University Press, Cambridge.

Hale, K.
1982 The Logic of Damin Kinship Terminology. In J. Heath, F. Merlan, and A. Rumsey (eds), *Languages of Kinship in Aboriginal Australia*, Oceania Linguistic Monographs 24, University of Sydney, Sydney, 31–37.

Halliday, M.A.K. and R. Hasan
1976 *Cohesion in English*, Longman, London.

Haviland, J.B.
1979a Guugu-Yimidhirr Brother-in-Law Language, *Language in Society* 8,365–93.

1979b How to Talk to Your Brother-in-Law in Guugu-Yimidhirr. In T. Shopen (ed), *Languages and Their Speakers*, Winthrop, Cambridge MA, 160–239.

Kendon, A.

1988 *Sign Languages of Aboriginal Australia: Cultural, Semiotic and Communicative Perspectives*, Cambridge University Press, Cambridge.

McConvell, P.

1982 Neutralisation and Degrees of Respect in Gurindji. In J. Heath, F. Merlan, and A. Rumsey (eds), *Languages of Kinship in Aboriginal Australia*, Oceania Linguistic Monographs 24, University of Sydney, Sydney, 86–106.

Merlan, F.

1982 'Egocentric' and 'Altercentric' Usage of Kin Terms in Mangarayi. In J. Heath, F. Merlan, and A. Rumsey (eds), *Languages of Kinship in Aboriginal Australia*, Oceania Linguistic Monographs 24, University of Sydney, Sydney, 107–24.

Rumsey, A.

1982 Gun-Gunma: An Aboriginal Avoidance Language and Its Social Functions. In J. Heath, F. Merlan, and A. Rumsey (eds), *Languages of Kinship in Aboriginal Australia*, Oceania Linguistic Monographs 24, University of Sydney, Sydney, 160–81.

Sutton, P.

1982 Personal Power, Kin Classification and Speech Etiquette in Aboriginal Australia. In J. Heath, F. Merlan, and A. Rumsey (eds), *Languages of Kinship in Aboriginal Australia*, Oceania Linguistic Monographs 24, University of Sydney, Sydney, 182–200.

CHAPTER

8 CLASSIFYING THE WORLD IN AN ABORIGINAL LANGUAGE

Michael Walsh

INTRODUCTION

In every language there is an attempt to classify the world. While speakers are often unaware of it, a little reflection will show that it must be so. One of the more important functions of language is to transmit one person's impressions of the world to another. Given that each person's impressions are a product of their own individual experience, there must be some process of generalising from these highly individual impressions so as to communicate to others. Even as banal a pronouncement as 'I saw a cat' involves a number of choices about the classification of the world: self versus other ('I' versus 'you, she, they' et cetera); some kind of generalised visual perception: 'see' versus 'notice, glance at, caught sight of' et cetera; and some notion of 'catness' that sets that specific object off from 'other' objects in the world ('dogs, trees, people' et cetera) and at the same time relates that object to other objects of the 'same' kind (other cats). The very process of viewing some objects in the world as 'same' and some as 'other' is a matter of classification. Without this process language would become unworkable: a separate word for each 'catlike object' one ever encounters? Even then those separate words would separate one speaker from another. For language to work it must be based on a communally accepted classification of the world.

While every language classifies the world in some way, some languages oblige their speakers to assign objects in the world to a relatively small number of classes. In French, for example, each noun is assigned to one of just two classes, referred to as 'masculine' and 'feminine':

masculine	feminine
cadeau 'gift'	cloche 'bell'
chou 'cabbage'	craie 'chalk'
doigt 'finger'	dent 'tooth'
fromage 'cheese'	foule 'crowd'
pied 'foot'	patte 'paw'

Membership in a noun class has grammatical consequences: a 'masculine' noun like *cadeau* 'gift' will appear as *le cadeau* for 'the gift' and *un cadeau* 'a gift' while a 'feminine' noun like *cloche* 'bell' will appear as *la cloche* for 'the bell' and *une cloche* 'a bell'. A speaker of French cannot decide to reclassify 'cheese' and say **la fromage*. Whatever the basis of the classification, it is fixed.

In much the same way in German there are just three classes — masculine, feminine and neuter:

masculine	feminine	neuter
Wein 'wine'	Limonade 'lemonade'	Bier 'beer'
Tee 'tea'	Milch 'milk'	Wasser 'water'

This classification can suggest something of the way the speakers see the world. In Swahili there are as many as eighteen classes: one class refers to long, thin objects like 'wall', 'sword', 'river' and 'tongue', another includes most names of animals and kinship terms while another has words for abstract qualities like 'peace', 'evil' and 'beauty'. Among Australian Aboriginal languages are some languages, like Nunggubuyu (Heath 1984), which seem to behave like French in that there is no obvious reason why a noun should belong to one class rather than another; and there are many other languages which pattern more like Swahili, in that there is a fairly clear motivation for class membership. One such language is Murrinh-Patha, spoken by around 1,500 people on the west coast of the Northern Territory.

In Murrinh-Patha each noun can be associated with a 'noun class marker' (abbreviated as NC). The noun class marker appears before the noun but differs in function from the French forms *le* versus *la* ('the') or *un* versus *une* ('a'), mentioned above. Membership in noun classes is semantically based (Stanner 1964; Street 1987, 41–44; Walsh forthcoming), for example:

(ku) baybaye
NC kangaroo

(thu) kuragadha
NC boomerang

(mi) lawam
NC flour

Members of the *ku*-class include animals, birds, fish, et cetera and their products (honey, eggs, meat et cetera), the *thu*-class refers to offensive weapons and the *mi*-class relates to fruit and vegetable food.

In all, around ten noun classes might be distinguished for Murrinh-Patha. Street (1987, 41–44) sets up ten noun classes which are semantically based.

The list below follows Street but is supplemented by examples of my own.

1. kardu Aboriginal people and human classification (including human spirits)

kardu thipmam	'black person [that is, Aboriginal]'
kardu pule	'old man; husband; boss'
kardu ngepan	'spirit/soul of a living person'
kardu warnangkal	'clever man; "witch doctor"'
kardu kawu	'mother's mother'

2. ku Non-Aboriginal people and all other animates and their products.

ku thipmam	'black person [non-Aboriginal]'
ku pule	'old man; husband; boss [non-Aboriginal]'
ku warnangkal	'clever man; doctor [non-Aboriginal]'
ku kulerrkkurrk	'brolga'
ku lawarnka	'wallaby'
ku murl	'fly'
ku thitay	'(wild) honey, sugarbag'

3. kura Fresh water and associated concepts, as potable fluids (except 'milk' which is in Class 5), and different collective terms for fresh water like 'rain' or 'river'.

kura thurrulk	'beer (= foam water)'
kura ngipilinh	'creek, river'
kura yelyel	'rain'

4. mi Flowers and fruits of plants and any vegetable foods. Also faeces.

mi thathangadhay	'flower of certain trees'
mi marrarl	'fruit of native tree (*Terminalia ferdinandiana*)'
mi lawam	'flour'
mi ngukin	'faeces'

5. nanthi Essentially a residue category, in that a noun can usually be assigned to the *nanthi*-class if it does not obviously fit into any of the other nine classes which are relatively well-defined. This class includes most inanimate objects, implements and natural phenomena of all kinds.

nanthi thelput	'house'
nanthi wirrirr	'wind'
nanthi thay	'stick'

6. thamul Spears.

thamul nguni	'short light spear'
thamul menek	'ironwood spear'
thamul waya	'fishing spear; "fish wire"'

7. thu Offensive weapons (defensive weapons like shields predictably go into the *nanthi*-class). Thunder and lightning. Playing cards.

thu kuragadha	'boomerang'
thu paku	'large club'
thu malarntath	'thunder; lightning'
thu kat	'playing cards'

8. thungku Fire and things associated with fire.

thungku thay	'firestick; firewood'
thungku len	'hot coals'
thungku methith	'matches

9. da Time and space: names for localities, seasons et cetera.

da pemanhay	'sandhill'
da therri	'"dry grass time"; latter part of the dry season'
da yidiyi	'Yidiyi (place name)'

10. murrinh Speech and language and associated concepts such as news, songs, school.

murrinh mamay	'baby talk; children's talk'
murrinh thelerrdhe	'news'
murrinh school	'school'

MULTIPLE MEMBERSHIP IN NOUN CLASSES

A particular noun may occur in a number of noun classes according to its function or according to the way it is viewed in the culture. When a boomerang is considered merely as an object and not as an offensive weapon, it will be assigned to the *nanthi*-class. So *nanthi kuragadha* might be said of a boomerang employed as a doorstop or as an improvised back-scratcher. Although *lawam* 'flour' can be assigned to the *mi*-class because it is a foodstuff derived from plants, *nanthi lawam* is used to refer to flour bought in a shop. The examples given above show some human classification terms turning up in the *kardu*-class as well as the *ku*-class. In mythological texts the transformation of culture heroes, who are regarded as human beings, into birds or animals is signalled by a switch from one noun class to another: so *kardu kulerrkkurrk* 'Brolga[-man]' becomes *ku kulerrkkurrk* 'brolga'.

Often a semantic domain will be captured by a singular noun class marker. Most body parts, for instance, belong to the *nanthi*-class. One category of body products is assigned to the *mi*-class: *mi ngukin* '(solid) faeces'; *mi yilulul* 'liquid faeces'. Presumably the association is between food and that body product which is itself the product of food (*mi* can be used generically to refer to 'food'). All other body products, whether blood, sputum or urine, are assigned to the *nanthi*-class.

For some body parts it is possible to switch noun classes with an attendant change in meaning:

nanthi kamarl	'eye/face'
kura kamarl	'water-hole'
kardu kamarl	'sweetheart'
mi kamarl	'seed'
nanthi ngi	'penis'
ku ngi	'death adder'
nanthi nginipunh	'body'
murrinh nginipunh	'skin(-name)'
nanthi pangkin	'back'
da pangkin	'ridge'

In these sets of expressions it is certainly the body-part meaning which is basic. When a term in one of these sets occurs without a noun class marker, the usual meaning for that term is the body-part sense. In addition, native speakers spontaneously volunteer glosses for the 'other' meanings in a way that suggests that the body-part sense is seen as being basic: 'the seed is round like your eye'; 'that snake looks like that ''man-thing'''.

Each noun will have a <u>norm</u> association with a particular noun class marker. The word *yirrthip* 'cat', for instance, has the norm association with the particular noun class marker, *ku*, but may be reassigned to other classes because of a marked usage:

ku yirrthip
NC cat
'cat-as-cat'

thu yirrthip
NC cat
'cat-as-offensive-weapon'

nanthi yirrthip
NC cat
'cat-as-object'

In the first instance, *ku yirrthip*, has its ordinary, expected meaning of a cat as we usually expect a cat to be — according to its inherent nature. The other two usages put the inherent characteristics of the cat to the background and focus on functional characteristics. If one were to pick up a cat by its hind leg and hit someone with it, the cat has become *thu yirrthip* — it is a cat being used as an offensive weapon. If a cat is used as an object, for example, as a foot-warmer or a doorstop, then it becomes *nanthi yirrthip* because of this change of function.

Another example is provided by *tumtum* 'egg':

ku tumtum
NC egg
'egg-as-egg'

thu tumtum
NC egg
'egg-as-offensive weapon'

nanthi tumtum
NC egg
'egg-as-object'

In the first usage *tumtum* is in the *ku*-class because it is the product of creatures such as *ku thikin* 'chicken', *ku kananganthan* 'emu' or *ku ngupu* 'loggerhead (large saltwater) turtle', which by their inherent characteristics naturally fit into the *ku*-class. But an egg used as a missile predictably becomes *thu tumtum* because functionally it has become an offensive weapon. Finally, an egg used as a paperweight or some such must be assigned to the *nanthi*-class.

When a noun occurs in its most basic or normal sense, more often than not the noun class marker is omitted.

PROTOTYPICAL CHARACTERISATION

The contents of noun classes are often superficially heterogeneous but can be characterised in terms of certain central notions. Dixon (1968) provides an example of this in the four-class system of Dyirbal, and Lakoff (1986) shows how more general characterisations of the Dyirbal noun classes can be expressed in terms of prototypes. Here, something of the same sort is applied to Murrinh-Patha. I repeat the earlier examples, slightly rearranging the categories so as to put the *nanthi*-class, which is the most general, at the end.

1. kardu Higher animates.

kardu thipmam	'black person [that is, Aboriginal]
kardu pule	'old man; ''husband''; boss'
kardu ngepan	'spirit/soul of a living person'
kardu warnangkal	'clever man; ''witch doctor'''
kardu kawu	'mother's mother'

2. ku Other animates.

ku thipmam	'black person [non-Aboriginal]'
ku pule	'old man; ''husband''; boss [non-Aboriginal]'
ku warnangkal	'clever man; doctor [non-Aboriginal]'
ku kulerrkkurrk	'brolga'
ku lawarnka	'wallaby'
ku murl	'fly'
ku thitay	'(wild) honey, sugarbag'

3. kura Fresh water.

kura thurrulk	'beer (= foam water)'
kura ngipilinh	'creek, river'
kura yelyel	'rain'

4. mi Food.

mi thathangadhay	'flower of certain trees'
mi marrarl	'fruit of native tree (*Terminalia ferdinandiana*)'
mi lawam	'flour'
mi ngukin	'faeces'

5. thamul Spears.

thamul nguni	'short light spear'
thamul menek	'ironwood spear'
thamul waya	'fishing spear; ''fish wire'''

6. thu Strikers.

thu kuragadha	'boomerang'
thu paku	'large club'
thu malarntath	'thunder; lightning'
thu kat	'playing cards'

7. thungku Fire.

thungku thay	'firestick; firewood'
thungku len	'hot coals'
thungku methith	'matches'

8. da Time and space.

da pemanhay	'sandhill'
da therri	'"dry grass time"; latter part of the dry season'
da yidiyi	'Yidiyi (place name)'

9. murrinh Speech and language.

murrinh mamay	'baby talk; children's talk'
murrinh thelerrdhe	'news'
murrinh school	'school'

10. nanthi Everything else.

nanthi thelput	'house'
nanthi wirrirr	'wind'
nanthi thay	'stick'

DISCUSSION

Class 1. *kardu* Higher animates. As in English the category of 'higher animates' is culturally conceived. In Murrinh-Patha the category of 'higher animates' is often thought of as just involving Aboriginal people while non-Aboriginal people are classified along with other animates like snakes, birds and fish. In English the grammar of the language distinguishes between higher animates and everything else through the use of personal pronouns:

higher animates	other
he/she	it
his/her	its

People are almost always assigned to the higher animate class in English, although a baby is sometimes referred to as 'it' when the sex is not known. But some animals are also assigned to this class, especially pets:

She has distemper/fleas; let's take her to the vet.
His coat has become matted.
We're having him speyed.

Speakers of English vary as to which nouns fall into this implicit class of higher animates: some think of cats as almost human and would always assign them to the class of higher animates while other speakers regard cats with indifference or even as something of a nuisance and assign them to the other class.

The border between higher animates and others is not sharply defined in either English or Murrinh-Patha. Even so most nouns can be assigned to one class or the other without hesitation.

Class 2. *ku* Other animates. This class includes not only animals, birds, insects, fish, and marine life but can include the products of these animates such as 'bird's nest', 'eggs' and 'honey'. Interestingly, the general term for 'money' in Murrinh-Patha is *ku* which also translates as 'meat'. The latter meaning is fairly predictable since meat is the product of most of the nouns classified in the *ku*-class. The sense of *ku* as 'money' presumably derives from the Murrinh-Patha view that 'money' is a product of non-Aboriginal people whom they assign to the *ku*-class.

Class 3. *kura* Fresh water. That this is a separate class suggests that fresh water holds a prominent place in the culture of the Murrinh-Patha.

Class 4. *mi* Food. The *mi*-class is a little problematic to characterise simply. We cannot call it the class which refers to plants because plants-as-plants for the most part are assigned to the *nanthi*-class – for example *nanthi were* 'thorny bush'. It is only plants-as-food that belong to the *mi*-class and something like *nanthi were* 'thorny bush' is not regarded as having much potential as food. I suspect, though, that if one were reduced to using *nanthi were* 'thorny bush' for food, then it would be reassigned to the *mi*-class.

What of 'faeces'? Two explanations spring to mind. The most straightforward is that, from a Murrinh-Patha perspective, faeces is seen as the product of objects from the *mi*-class (things like *mi lawam* 'flour', *mi yidingurr* 'tamarind fruit', *mi kugalng* 'Kurrajong fruit (*Brachychiton diversifolium*)', *mi palathi* 'fruit of Billy goat plum tree (*Planchonia careya*)', to mention just a few). One might then wonder about food from the *ku*-class which would contribute to this 'product', so why not call it **ku ngukin*? The second explanation may throw some light on this problem: when tracking animals, Aboriginal people look out for droppings as well as footprints. Often these droppings have the appearance of being the product of items from the *mi*-class. Kangaroo droppings, for instance, are sometimes likened to dried grass. Given that it is culturally salient to look closely at samples of *ngukin* from such animals, it seems reasonable that *ngukin* would be associated with the *mi*-class.

Class 5. *thamul* Spears. This class suggests that spears hold a prominent place in the culture of the Murrinh-Patha.

Class 6. *thu* Strikers. In this class are brought together those things which can be thought of as striking something else. The earlier characterisation as 'offensive weapons' is partly right in that such weapons are used to strike someone, in contrast to defensive weapons which are more involved in blocking an impact. But this view does not account for playing cards or thunder and lightning. Playing cards are thrown into the centre of the card-playing group and strike the ground, so they fit readily into this class. Similarly, it is easy enough to conceive of thunder and lightning as something which strikes something else.

Class 7. *thungku* Fire. This class suggests that fire holds a prominent place in the culture of the Murrinh-Patha.

Class 8. *da* Time and space. In this noun-class time and place are linked. This is not surprising given that many cultures make such linkages and reflect that linkage in the language.

Class 9. *murrinh* Speech and language. This class suggests that speech and language hold a prominent place in the culture of the Murrinh-Patha.

Class 10. *nanthi* Everything else. The *nanthi*-class is certainly the most heterogeneous: it includes all those items which do not obviously fit into any of the other nine categories. In an approximate way the *nanthi*-class in Murrinh-Patha serves the same function as 'things' in English. That is to say, it is a residue category which one uses when some entity fits into no other positively defined category. Not surprisingly, most introduced items from English-speaking Australia are assigned to the *nanthi*-class, for example:

nanthi kum 'bottle'
nanthi cassette 'tape recorder'

CLASSIFYING THE WORLD IN ENGLISH

Let us now return to something more familiar: how do we classify the world in English? This is far too big a subject to go into in any detail here but a few issues can be raised.

One way in which speakers of English classify the world is in the use of collective nouns. As with Murrinh-Patha it will not always be obvious to anyone, let alone the native speakers, what the motivation is for grouping certain things together. Consider collective nouns like 'flock', 'pack' or 'swarm'. We refer to a flock of galahs and a flock of sheep, a pack of cards and a pack of dogs, a swarm of bees and a swarm of locusts. Two questions arise: what kinds of nouns can be subsumed under a given collective noun? and to what extent can one reassign a given noun to a different collective? The first question makes us wonder what it is, if anything, that galahs and sheep, cards and dogs, or bees and locusts have in common. The second question considers whether we can sensibly refer to a pack of galahs or a swarm of galahs, to a flock of cards or a swarm of cards, or to a flock of locusts or a pack of locusts. Some collective terms are no longer in familiar usage so that speakers will use different collective terms to group together the same entities. Whales, for example, can be grouped as a 'pod of whales', although many speakers would be more likely to refer to them as a 'school of whales' generalising from 'school of fish' and thereby implicitly treating whales and fish as entities of the same kind. This raises questions about the currency and utility of some of the collective terms.

Another area of English which involves an implicit classification of nouns is to be found in the use of pronouns. Earlier it was shown that there is a basic distinction in pronouns between higher animates and everything else. It therefore becomes strange to use the distinctive higher animate personal pronouns with certain creatures:

?Look at that amoeba (under the microscope), isn't he pretty?
?Watch out for that slug, you almost stepped on him/her.

It is not a matter of needing to know the sex of what is being referred to for a speaker to use the higher animate personal pronouns: speakers will describe a cat as 'he' when they have no idea of what sex it is while other speakers will relentlessly describe a cat as an 'it' despite its ginger coat and prominent 'equipment'. In the same way a bull or a cow may be described as an 'it'. Moreover, it may happen that a speaker is only distantly aware of the sexual identification of the creature concerned:

Look at that peacock. Doesn't it have a magnificent tail?

The speaker can be reminded that it is only the male that has this prominent display of plumage and that the very word 'peacock' (versus 'peahen') indicates maleness. But for many speakers 'it' is used to describe a peacock, a peahen and any other kind of bird.

CLASSIFYING THE WORLD IN OTHER ABORIGINAL LANGUAGES

Although a range of Aboriginal languages have noun classification systems, most of these are not well-documented. A notable exception is Dyirbal, a language traditionally spoken in northern Queensland, described by R.M.W. Dixon (1982). In Dyirbal before each noun there must appear one of four forms (or variants of these four forms): *bayi*, *balan*, *balam*, *bala*. Here is a summary of the kinds of nouns that must be assigned to the four classes (Lakoff 1987, 92–3):

I. *Bayi*: men, kangaroos, possums, bats, most snakes, most fishes, some birds, most insects, the moon, storms, rainbows, boomerangs, some spears, et cetera.

II. *Balan*: women, bandicoots, dogs, platypus, echidna, some snakes, some fishes, most birds, fireflies, scorpions, crickets, the hairy mary grub, anything connected with water or fire, sun and stars, shields, some spears, some trees, et cetera.

III. *Balam*: all edible fruit and the plants that bear them, tubers, ferns, honey, cigarettes, wine, cake.

IV. *Bala*: parts of the body, meat, bees, wind, yamsticks, some spears, most trees, grass, mud, stones, noises and language, et cetera.

As with Murrinh-Patha an initial examination of the contents of these classes makes one wonder how Dyirbal people categorise things. Why, for instance, are spears distributed across three classes? Why do most trees appear in Class IV but some trees in Classes I and II? Even more surprising is the occurrence of the moon in one class but the sun and stars in another. But Dixon is able to give a more general characterisation of the classes (1968, 1982):

I. *Bayi*: (human) males; animals

II. *Balan*: (human) females; water; fire; fighting

III. *Balam*: non-flesh food

IV. *Bala*: everything not in the other classes

If this were the whole explanation, it would open up as many questions as it answers. Class I does contain many animals but there are also animals in Class II; most trees end up in the residue class (IV) but some trees appear in Classes I, II and III. Part of the explanation lies in associations between certain nouns (as it did in Murrinh-Patha). Spears used for fishing appear in Class I because that is where fish naturally belong; but spears used for fighting appear in Class II, the class associated with fighting, while other spears are relegated to Class IV. Stars and fireflies appear in Class II, the class which has associations with fire.

Most of the remaining nouns which are hard to account for can be handled by two explanatory principles developed by Dixon. One reason concerns traditional Dyirbal myth or belief. In traditional stories the moon and the sun were thought of as husband and wife, and so the moon is assigned to Class I because it can be thought of as a human male while the sun is in Class II because it is a human female. Most birds are in Class II, rather than Class I as we might expect, because in Dyirbal belief birds were seen as the spirits of dead human females. But some birds like Willie wagtails were thought to be men in myth and are therefore in Class I. The other explanatory principle involves some nouns having a special property which sets them off from other like nouns. Most fish, for instance, are in Class I with other animates, as one would expect, but the stonefish and the garfish have a special property — they are both harmful — and are assigned to a different class from the other fish. Hawks are also regarded as harmful and appear in Class I rather than in Class II with the other birds (appearing there because of their mythical associations).

Using all these principles, most loan concepts can be accounted for. Flour, cake and wine all appear in Class III as one would expect: flour is derived from plants; in turn, cake employs flour and may contain fruit; wine is derived from grapes, a kind of edible plant. Cigarettes are also in this class, being thought of as derived from leaves (of tobacco). Pipes and matches appear in Class II being associated with fire. Predictably the Dyirbal word for white woman, *mijiji* (derived from the English word 'missus'), is assigned to Class II.

A small number of nouns seem to resist explanation in terms of these explanatory principles. The loan concept, money, appears unpredictably in Class I when one might have thought it would appear in Class IV. There is no explanation given by Dixon for the appearance of bandicoot, dog, echidna and platypus in Class II when general principles would have them in Class I with other animates. It is easy enough to speculate about an explanation for some of these apparent exceptions: dogs have the special property among animals of being domesticated by Aboriginal people; and in the tradition of Western science the echidna and platypus are regarded as being animals with special properties (egg-laying mammals), so perhaps Aboriginal people also regard them as having special properties and have reflected that in their own system of classification.

It needs to be stressed that these suggestions must remain speculative. Even Dyirbal people may not be — or may no longer be — conscious of the principles underlying their classification system. Whatever their origins, the systems of categorisation presented in a brief form here for Dyirbal, English and Murrinh-Patha throw some light on the range of ways that people classify the world.

Linguists and others have pondered the effect of differing classification systems from different cultures. In part, this is a 'chicken-and-egg' question. Does the language you grow up using influence the way you perceive the world because of its inbuilt perceptual and conceptual grid? Or is it that the culture (and even the environment) shapes the perceptual and conceptual grid which has developed in the language? There is no short answer to these questions, intriguing as they might be. But we can confidently say that different languages have quite distinct ways of presenting the world. By looking at some features of classification in Aboriginal languages we can gain some insight into another way of looking at the world. In turn, this can help us to reflect on the way we see the world ourselves.

ACKNOWLEDGEMENTS, NOTES AND BACKGROUND

1. A quite accessible account of noun classification in Swahili can be found in Hinnebusch (1979).

2. The data on Murrinh-Patha are drawn from my own fieldwork and from the very extensive knowledge of Chester Street of the Summer Institute of Linguistics, Australian Aborigines Branch. I have relied heavily on Street's detailed knowledge of the lexicon of Murrinh-Patha which is partly documented in Street's (1983) dictionary (see also Street 1987). Otherwise, I owe a debt to my Murrinh-Patha language instructors, especially Kevin Bunduck and the late Harry Kulampurrurt and the late Jumbo Dala. The fieldwork was supported by grants from the Australian Institute of Aboriginal Studies: my thanks go to this body for making the fieldwork possible and to its staff for their considerable assistance. A fuller account of nominal classification is provided in Walsh (forthcoming).

3. The orthography adopted here is identical to that developed by the Summer Institute of Linguistics literacy team, Chester and Lyn Street, and now in use by the literate speakers of Murrinh-Patha. Stops are as follows: p, b; t, d; and k, g are essentially as in English; rt, rd are voiceless and voiced retroflex; th is voiceless and laminal, being dental before /a, u/ and palatal before /i, e/; dh is voiced and laminal, realised as a voiced laminointerdental fricative before /a, u/ and as a voiced laminopalatal stop before /i, e/. Nasals are bilabial m, laminal nh (dental before /a, u/ and palatal before /i, e/), alveolar n, retroflex rn and velar ng. Laterals are alveolar l and retroflex rl. Rhotics are semi-retroflex continuant r and alveolar flap/trill rr. There are four vowels: i, e, a, u.

4. The distinction between 'inherent nature' and 'functional characteristics' has been raised by a number of commentators on classification. See Allan (1977), Denny (1976), Dixon (1986) and Lee (1988).

5. I am grateful to Nick Reid for suggesting the term 'strikers' in reference to the noun classification system of a neighbouring language, Ngan'gikurrunggurr. I also thank Patrick McConvell for drawing my attention to the possible relationship between dried grass and animal droppings.

FOR DISCUSSION

1. In Murrinh-Patha a word for 'sand' is *darrimun* and this term is extended to refer to the foodstuff introduced by whites: 'sugar'. Why was the same word used for 'sand' and 'sugar'? What noun class is *darrimun* 'sand' assigned to? What noun class is *darrimun* 'sugar' assigned to? Why?

2. We have already seen the expression *thungku methith* 'matches'. What does *thu methith* refer to?

3. The noun, *were*, is usually assigned to the *ku*-class, where it refers to 'dog', but it may also appear in the *nanthi*-class, where it refers to a kind of 'thorny bush'. Is there a semantic connection or is it merely chance? How would you go about finding out? What would *kardu were* refer to?

4. The expression, *thamul menek*, translates as 'ironwood spear'. What would you expect *nanthi menek* to mean?

5. The term, *muthingka*, can be assigned to the *ku*-class to mean 'old woman (non-Aboriginal)' as well as to the *kardu*-class to indicate 'old woman (Aboriginal)'. What does *thu muthingka* refer to?

6. Consider the following Murrinh-Patha nouns:

karrak 'kookaburra'
wakal 'baby'
putek 'earth'
mayiyin 'dragon fly'
mulurn 'leaf'
dara 'mangrove'
birlmalu 'policeman'
ngakumarl 'totem'
thigath 'urine'

What would you expect to be the normal or basic noun class for each word. Why? Construct a context to put each noun into another noun class.

7. *mayiyin* 'dragon fly' is also used for the new concept 'helicopter'. Why? What noun class would *mayiyin* be assigned to in its meaning of 'helicopter'?

8. Considering the Dyirbal noun class system and noting that some of these nouns might be assigned to more than one class depending on the perspective taken, how would one expect the following nouns to be assigned? Why?

cigarette-lighter	spear
shark	meat pie
toy	cassowary

REFERENCES

Allan, K.

1977 Classifiers, *Language* 53 (2), 284–310.

Craig, C. (ed)

1986 *Noun Classes and Categorization*, John Benjamins, Amsterdam.

Denny, J.P.

1976 What are Noun Classifiers Good For? In *Proceedings of the Twelfth Regional Meeting of the Chicago Linguistic Society.*

Dixon, R.M.W.

1968 Noun Classes, *Lingua* XXI, 104–25 [also published in Dixon 1982].

1982 Classifiers in Yidiny. In R.M.W. Dixon (ed), *Where Have All the Adjectives Gone?*, Mouton, Berlin.

1986 Noun Classes and Noun Classification in Typological Perspective. In Colette Craig (ed).

Heath, J.

1984 *A Functional Grammar of Nunggubuyu*, Australian Institute of Aboriginal Studies, Canberra.

Hinnebusch, T.

1979 Swahili. In T. Shopen (ed), *Languages and Their Status*, Winthrop, Cambridge, MA.

Lakoff, G.

1986 Classifiers as a Reflection of Mind. In Colette Craig (ed) 1986.

1987 *Women, Fire and Dangerous Things*, University of Chicago Press, Chicago.

Lee, M.

1988 Language, Perception and the World. In J. Hawkins (ed) *Explaining Language Universals*, Basil Blackwell, Oxford.

Stanner, W.E.H.

1964 *On Aboriginal Religion*, Oceania Monographs, Sydney.

Street, C.

1983 *English–Murrinh-Patha Dictionary*, Wadeye Press, Port Keats, NT.

1987 *An Introduction to the Language and Culture of the Murrinh-Patha*, Summer Institute of Linguistics, Australian Aborigines Branch, Darwin.

Walsh, M.

forthcoming Nominal Classification in Murrinh-Patha. In M. Harvey and N. Reid (eds), *Nominal Classification in Australian Languages*, Pacific Linguistics, Canberra.

CHAPTER 9 MAKING DICTIONARIES

Jane Simpson

One of the questions commonly asked about Aboriginal languages is: how many words do they have? In this chapter we explore the answers to this apparently simple question. In doing so, we have to consider how many words there can be in *any* language. In turn, we examine the ways in which the words of a language can be documented and the purposes for which this task are undertaken. In short — making dictionaries.

HOW MANY WORDS ARE THERE IN A LANGUAGE?

People often try to compare languages in terms of the numbers of words the languages have. They may even do so by comparing the sizes of the largest dictionaries available for the two languages. The *OED (Oxford English Dictionary: A New English Dictionary on Historical Principles*, second edition) is, in twenty fat volumes, much bigger than the sixty-three page vocabulary of the Adelaide language in Teichelmann and Schürmann (1840).

This is clearly not a fair comparison, for many reasons. But the main reason is the basis for such a comparison. How do we measure the number of words in a language? First, what is a word? For instance, should the compound 'firehose' be treated as a single word different from 'fire' and 'hose'? Languages differ widely as to what is considered a word. Second, are we talking about all words ever used by any speakers of that language? Or about all words used currently? Or about all the words used by an individual speaker and, presumably, stored somehow in that speaker's mind? Or about all the words ever recorded of the language? These questions show how hard it is to compare languages with respect to the number of words in them.

ASSEMBLAGES OF WORDS

Let us look at the terms which the English language has developed for assemblages of words. Many of these, unfortunately, overlap in meaning. Thus, the total of words in a language is sometimes called the lexicon or vocabulary of the language ('lexicon' from the Greek *lexis* speech, word, phrase; 'vocabulary' from the Latin *voca:bulum*, a name). Now, if the language is taken to consist of all the words ever *uttered* by speakers of that language, it is not possible to have a complete record of the vocabulary of the language. Many words are never recorded because they have such a short life span, and hence never make it into dictionaries. But it is possible to gather a lexicon of most of the words ever *recorded* as being part of a particular language. Dictionaries like the *OED* which are organised along historical principles have this as a goal. A language which has a long history of writing will have dictionaries containing more words than languages which have a short history of writing. But such dictionaries will contain many obsolete or archaic words, not used by present-day speakers.

Another way of looking at the lexicon of a language is to narrow it down to the words known by present-day speakers. Dictionaries described as 'Contemporary English' are of this type. Different speakers know different words, resulting from their different specialisations. So the number of words known by any of the community of present-day English speakers is much greater than the number of words known by any one speaker of English. We have in effect a linguistic division of labour; we divide among ourselves the labour of knowing the meanings of different words, or knowing the meanings to different degrees of precision. For example, I know that a grebe is a kind of water-bird and I assume that ornithologists know more precisely what a grebe is, and can say 'This bird is a grebe; that bird is not a grebe'. Many of the words in a dictionary of contemporary English I do not know, but I assume that among the community of present-day English speakers are some people who use these words because they know what they mean.

When we talk of someone's ability to use words, we sometimes say she/he has a wide vocabulary. The words known by a speaker are sometimes also called the speaker's mental lexicon. They range over a continuum. At one end are those that we know actively (we understand and use them). At the other end are those that we know passively (we understand them, but would never use them). Allowing for individual variation, and for the fact that what counts as a word differs from language to language, the number of words used by the average speaker (her or his active vocabulary) probably does not differ significantly across languages.

The word 'vocabulary', however, can mean something different: language-teaching textbooks often contain texts accompanied by lists of the words in the text with explanations. Such a list is often called a vocabulary or a glossary (glossary from the Latin *glo:ssa* 'word that needs explanation'). A glossary consists of a list of words and glosses (explanations of the meanings of the words).

Notice that with these meanings of 'glossary' and 'vocabulary', we are introducing another type of word assemblage — written collections of words. Written language provides a way of preserving older stages of a language. Spoken language changes as each generation learns it, while written language preserves older words and older pronunciations.

When texts of written language are highly valued in a culture, such as the Chinese Classics (written from the eighth century BC onwards), younger people may be expected to learn to understand the older texts, even though the language is unfamiliar to them. And so commentaries on the texts may be made, explaining unfamiliar ideas, references to people and places, and including glossaries of unfamiliar words. This glossary may lead on to the preparation of a full-scale reference book containing an explanatory list of words, that is, a word-book, dictionary (from the Latin *dictio* 'choice and use of words'), or thesaurus (from the Latin *the:saurus*, 'treasure'). Thus, by AD 100 there was a dictionary of Chinese which helped the current generation read and pronounce the language used in the Classics. This was an early monolingual dictionary, a dictionary in which the words of one language are explained in the language itself.

Dictionary is the general cover-term for such a reference book. However, sometimes dictionaries are contrasted with word-books, word-lists and thesauri in different ways. Dictionaries contrast with ordinary word-lists and word-books by having complex entries (that is, the explanatory material associated with a word). Making dictionaries has become a specialised trade, known as lexicography, while dictionary-makers are called lexicographers.

A specialised kind of monolingual dictionary, a special purpose dictionary, arises when a society with a written language develops areas of specialisation, such as trades, which have their own specialised vocabulary. Learning the trade becomes in part learning the terms of the trade, and so dictionaries of these terms are useful in helping this process. In 1527 one of the earliest English special purpose dictionaries, a glossary of law terms, was published.

Another kind of dictionary, a bilingual dictionary, is needed when writers of one language are learning to write another language. For example, some of the earliest Babylonian texts (seventh century BC) are word-lists, showing Sumerian pronunciations and Akkadian equivalents, thus enabling translation from the spoken language (Akkadian) into the language used for writing (Sumerian), and perhaps acting as a spelling guide. Until very recently, all dictionaries of Aboriginal languages have been bilingual dictionaries, the language of explanation being English in most cases (exceptions include the Diyari–German dictionary of J.G. Reuther, and the Arrernte–German dictionary of Carl Strehlow). But with Aborigines learning to read and write their own languages, some have started to prepare monolingual dictionaries.

WORD STORAGE IN AN ORAL CULTURE

Traditional Aboriginal societies had no large-scale writing systems, and so had oral cultures. Dictionaries are products of written cultures. Nevertheless, some of the functions of dictionaries have to be carried out in oral cultures too — learning words from other languages, explaining words from older stages of a language, explaining specialised terms. The first function, learning other languages, can be done orally, with little formal instruction. Traditional Aboriginal societies are, and were, multilingual societies. People learn other languages through having to talk to speakers of other languages, because of marriage, because of visiting for long periods in other people's country, and because of a widespread convention of politeness that requires one to speak the language of the country one is visiting.

But the second two functions require greater efforts of memory and of social cooperation. Archaic language may be preserved in songs, and this is certainly true of the language of important song cycles of Aboriginal Australia. Young people learning the songs may be instructed by their teachers as to what the songs mean. In doing so they learn the older words preserved in the songs. Specialised terms of a trade will be learned by an apprentice from a master, as part of learning the trade. In Aboriginal Australia, this may include terms used in ceremonies, or even an entire respect language of the kind described by Alpher earlier (in chapter 7).

For words from older stages of the language or specialised terms of trade to be passed on, teachers must preserve information in their memories, while learners must train their memories, in order to learn. Socially accepted conventions of teacher–pupil relations develop so as to pass on information, while, in the society as a whole, there may be a division of labour as to who remembers what, and also as to how to keep a check on this.

The division of memory labour and of keeping check on memories has been achieved in many Australian Aboriginal societies by efficient social structures. In many areas, responsibility for knowing the songs, myths and ceremonies for different tracts of land is divided among people according to their family relationships. Sisters and brothers have responsibility for remembering information about both their mother's country and their father's country. A man must pass on to his children the knowledge of his father's country, and his sister passes on to her brother's children the knowledge of her father's country. A brother and sister's responsibility for their mother's country requires them to check that the knowledge about that country is being correctly passed on to those whose father's country it is (their mother's brother's children, for example). Likewise, some of their other cousins (father's sister's children) will check that the sister and brother are correctly passing on information about the country belonging to their common grandfather (father of both the cousins' mother and the brother and sister's father).

Concern with ensuring correct transmission of information has apparently been a part of Aboriginal societies for a long time. It is perhaps not surprising, then, that many traditional Aboriginal people have been interested in writing as a means of recording information, as a way of ensuring transmission of information, not simply to Europeans, but to their own grandchildren. Likewise, they have often enthusiastically taken part in dictionary-making, or made their own dictionaries, as a way of recording words and the associated concepts, artefacts, animals, plants, which they feel would otherwise be lost.

THE FIRST WORD-LISTS OF ABORIGINAL LANGUAGES

Word-lists of Aboriginal languages go back to Cook's voyage to Australia, during which Joseph Banks recorded some words of Guugu Yimidhirr, spoken near Cooktown. Banks's purpose was scientific, to record a sample of the language spoken by the people they met, just as he recorded the plants and animals they encountered. As Troy describes (in chapter 3), the people from the First Fleet tried to use Banks's list for communication, and were surprised to find that the words recorded by Banks were not always understood by the local people.

Most of the best early vocabularies of Aboriginal languages come from missionaries. One of the earliest was that of Lancelot Threlkeld, who was sent in 1825 by the London Missionary Society to start work at Lake Macquarie, 110 kilometres north of Sydney. The Society encouraged their missionaries to learn the native languages in order to translate the scriptures into those languages and preach the gospel more effectively. As a result of learning Awaba, the local language, Threlkeld published in 1834 *An Australian Grammar* (Threlkeld 1834), which included the first extensive word-list of an Australian Aboriginal language to be published.

Threlkeld's reason for publishing was partly scientific, and partly educational. He wanted to show the colonists that the Aborigines were human. As he writes:

> it was maintained by many in the colony that the Blacks had no language at all but were only a race of the monkey tribe! This was a convenient assumption, for if it could be proved that the Aborigines of New South Wales were only a species of wild beast, there could be no guilt attached to those who shot them off or poisoned them as cumberers of the earth. (p 46)

Threlkeld decided not to use English spelling principles to write the Aboriginal language, because of the ambiguity and redundancy of the English spelling system. Instead, he adopted the spelling system that had been used by missionaries in the South Pacific. As a result he had to give an explicit pronunciation key, which makes his renderings of Awaba words less liable to mispronunciation.

Words in the word-list are listed (or ordered) in groups. These groups consist of lists of words on a particular topic. Topics include names of persons, names of places, parts of the body. As well, some groups consist of words with the same grammatical category (part of speech), such as common nouns. Within these groups, words are listed more or less according to alphabetic order. The entries are not complex, but do contain occasional ethnographic comments (see below for an example). Hence I have called it a word-list, rather than a dictionary.

Head word	*English Gloss*	*Comment (ethnographic and occasionally etymological)*
Ko-ro-wa-tul-lun,	The Cuttle fish,	literally, wave tongue.
Be-ra-buk-kán,	Sperm whale,	which is not eaten, only the black whale.

INTEREST IN THE HISTORY OF LANGUAGES

When Threlkeld was preparing his vocabulary, scientific interest in classifying languages had reached new heights in Europe. This was because several scholars had realised that languages were related to each other, and some could be thought of as forming families stemming from a common ancestor, or proto-language. Historical linguistics (the study of the history of languages) was getting underway. In 1822 Jakob Grimm put forward the hypothesis that German, Sanskrit, Greek, Latin and German all had their beginning as dialects of a single proto-language, Indo-European. The hypothesis received widespread publicity among scholars. Soon attention turned to Australia. Did the Australian Aboriginal languages all stem from one proto-language? Threlkeld noted that, although people living 100 miles or so apart were not able to understand each other at first glance, yet they were able to understand each other within a short space of time. He argued that this meant the languages could not be radically different, and tentatively suggested that Australian languages might all belong to one language family.

Perhaps the most influential spreading of this hypothesis among people working on Australian languages was by Captain George Grey, later Governor of South Australia. A few years after Threlkeld produced his *An Australian Grammar*, Grey went exploring around the southern part of Western Australia. On his travels he met Aborigines in different parts and tried to find out what he could about their languages. In doing so, he realised that much of what had been recorded on Aboriginal languages was quite unreliable. With the help of a friend he compiled his material into a book, published in 1840 and followed by a second edition. Like Threlkeld, Grey was struck by the correspondences among Australian Aboriginal languages. He noted that the word for water was *kawi* in Western Australia and *kapi* in Adelaide. He argued that this could not be coincidence — there must have been a language which was ancestor to the languages of southwestern Australia and the Adelaide language, and which contained a similar word for 'water'.

Grey realised that reliable dictionaries were needed to check these correspondences. Being appointed Governor of South Australia in 1842 gave him the opportunity to do something about this, namely to act as patron and encourager of other people to prepare *accurate* word-lists and dictionaries. Previous work on the Adelaide language had been undertaken by people with little knowledge of the language, starting with the collection of a word-list on a French scientific expedition (Gaimard 1830–1835). After the establishment of the Adelaide colony in 1836, communication with Aborigines assumed more importance. Most colonists appear to have wanted them to learn English. However, there were moves to find out more about the language of the inhabitants of the Adelaide Plains. The second Protector of Aborigines in South Australia, William Wyatt, wrote a small account of the language, manners and customs of the Aborigines, mainly in order to instruct the population (reprinted as Wyatt 1879). Word-lists and phrases thought to be useful for conversing with Aborigines were published in the local newspaper in 1839 (Williams 1839). These word-lists of the Adelaide language all have simple structures, follow English spelling, and are often hard to interpret.

A DICTIONARY OF THE ADELAIDE LANGUAGE

A much deeper knowledge of the languages in South Australia was gained by several German missionaries, including Clamor Schürmann and Christian Teichelmann. Their arrival had been organised by a prominent English non-conformist Baptist, George Fife Angas, who was concerned about the welfare of the Aborigines, and who wanted the missionaries to help:

1. to preserve the native language;
2. to give the Aborigines a writing system and translations of the New Testament;
3. to teach the Aborigines to read.

Teichelmann and Schürmann were encouraged by George Grey and the then Governor, George Gawler, to publish their material, which they did in 1840 (see Plate 4). In the prefact they gave a number of reasons for publishing it: to help other Europeans learn the language, so as to be able to talk with Aborigines, and:

OUTLINES OF A GRAMMAR

VOCABULARY,

AND PHRASEOLOGY,

OF THE

ABORIGINAL LANGUAGE

OF

SOUTH AUSTRALIA,

SPOKEN BY THE NATIVES IN AND FOR SOME DISTANCE AROUND
ADELAIDE.

BY C. G. TEICHELMANN,
C. W. SCHÜRMANN,

OF THE LUTHERAN MISSIONARY SOCIETY, DRESDEN.

ADELAIDE:
PUBLISHED BY THE AUTHORS,
AT THE NATIVE LOCATION.

1840.

Plate 4: The frontispiece from Teichelmann and Schürmann's study of the South Australian language (Teichelmann and Schürmann 1840).

> to enliven the hopes of those who wish the christianization and civilization of their colored fellow-men, showing them that a race of human beings possessing a language so regular in its formation and construction as that of the South Australian natives, cannot be incapable of either; and to refute premature and unjust detractions concerning the mental capabilities of the Aborigines of Australia.

A third reason is scientific: 'to render a small contribution or inducement to a general study of the manners, customs, and origin of these people'.

The book contains about 1,900 words, ordered alphabetically, and 160 or so illustrative sentences, both in the vocabulary and in the remainder of the book. The words are written using a version of Threlkeld's orthography. The vocabulary contains words in almost every domain — material culture, ritual practices, kinship, bereavement, naming practices, plant names, animal names, meteorology, et cetera. The entries are more complex than Threlkeld's, and are structured as follows (the italics indicate parts of the entry that are italicised to set them off from the rest of the entry). The entries in Teichelmann and Schürmann follow this pattern:

Head word (capitalised), *part of speech*. gloss/definition. *example*, translation of example. Comment; includes ethnographic, etymological, *new term* [that is, the word is a term for a new item introduced by the European invaders], some *derived forms* and cross-reference.

> Kundo, *s.* chest; breast. *kundo punggondi*, to hurt one's feelings
>
> Kundobakkurta, *s.* ornamental dots on the chest
>
> Kundomanka, *s.* ornamental stripes on the chest
>
> Kundomuka, *s.* the breast of the male
>
> kundopungorendi, *vn.* to long; linger; languish; to be uneasy; anxious

Unlike the previous word-lists, parts of speech are recorded for each word: *s.* 'substantive' = noun, *vn.* 'intransitive verb'. Notice also that, while the first four words are clearly related, there is no attempt to bring out this relatedness in the structure of the dictionary entry. The fifth word, *kundopungorendi*, is probably related, since *kundo* seems to have two senses — one, the actual chest, and the other, the seat of emotions. But again, this relationship is not made explicit.

Exactly which words are included in such word-lists is usually dictated by the interest and circumstances of the dictionary-maker, and in the case of Aboriginal languages, of the people teaching the dictionary-maker. Dictionaries produced by people who are not native speakers of a language at the start of their work tend to focus on concrete things (words for plants, animals, food, artefacts, topography). Only with a much deeper knowledge of the language do words for complex emotions, sensations, thought and judgement appear. However, early word-lists and dictionaries often include words for concepts which were of contemporary concern. Detailed entries for terms for land ownership sometimes appear, suggesting that some colonists had scruples about their dispossession of Aboriginal people. Here is part of an entry from Teichelmann and Schürmann's dictionary.

> *Pangkarra, s.* a district or tract of country belonging to an individual, which he inherits from his father. *Ngarraitya paru aityo pangkarrila*, there is abundance of game in my country. As each *pankarra* [*sic*] has its peculiar name, many of the owners take that as their proper name, with the addition of the term *burka*; for instance, *Mulleakiburka* (Tam O'Shanter), *Mullawirraburka* (King John), *Kalyoburka, Karkulyaburka, Tindoburka* &c. [...]

In fact, most dictionaries of Aboriginal languages contain only a small fraction of the number of words in the languages. This is partly because, until recently, they have all been prepared by people who were not native speakers of the languages, and partly because the dictionary-makers have not had the time, resources and the source material available to some makers of English dictionaries.

In Teichelmann and Schürmann's dictionary there is no English to Adelaide-language word-list. In fact, most of the early word-lists and dictionaries tend to be lists of vernacular words with explanations in English, much as if the dictionary-makers recorded the words they heard, and then compiled the results into lists. In terms of communication, it suggests that people wanted to know the meanings of words in Aboriginal languages that they heard, rather than wanting to know how to express meanings in that Aboriginal language. But the lack of such reverse lists must have reduced the usefulness of the vocabulary for colonists who wanted to use the book to help them learn the language.

Under Grey's auspices, three more dictionaries of South Australian languages were published (Meyer 1843; Schürmann 1844; Moorhouse 1846). In 1857 Grey, who by then had moved to South Africa to be Governor of Cape Town, wrote to Threlkeld and Teichelmann asking for copies of their more recent material. They both sent him material, and noted that the languages were dying. Threlkeld wrote 'I think a memorial of a language passing out of existence ought to be preserved for posterity ...'

Teichelmann sent a manuscript dictionary of the Adelaide language. It is a very impressive piece of work which contains about 2,500 words (including both head words and sub-entries). The words are more fully glossed than in the

1840 dictionary, and (except for concrete terms) usually include at least one illustrative sentence. It has some unusual words, which indicate his familiarity with the language and speakers. But perhaps the major innovation in Teichelmann's manuscript dictionary is the structure of the entry. A good example of this is the word *kundo*. In the 1840 dictionary no attempt was made to show the fact that *kundo* has several senses, or that words could be derived from it. In the 1857 manuscript, however, three senses are given, and derived forms are listed under the senses:

> Kundo, the chest, whereas ngammi the female breast;
> 2. anything projecting similar as the chest
> 3. as the seat of several passions, as
> kundo wilta, 'brave, bold; fearless';
> kundo punggondi, to dislike, hate; [...]
> kundo punggorendi, to be concerned about; to be sorry;
> kundo punggorendaii ngaityo yungakko, 'I am concerned about, or long for my elder brother.' [...]

The hierarchical structure of this entry, indicated in the manuscript by indenting, contrasts with the flat structure of entries in the published dictionary.

The head word is capitalised. Senses are numbered. Some derived forms are still given under the head word entry, but many are given separate, although indented, sub-entries, with lower-case initial. Sub-entries can in turn have several senses, and even sub-entries of their own. Comparisons are made with lexemes that are clearly related. This more complicated structure makes for entries that capture the complexities of meaning better.

The dictionary has never been published. After the burst of dictionary publishing encouraged by Grey in the 1840s, interest in publishing dictionaries declined — such a burst was not seen again until the 1960s. Other large dictionaries compiled in the nineteenth century were either never published, or not published until long after their compilation. Such was the fate of James Günther's grammar and dictionary of Wiradjuri (Wiradhuri), compiled in 1840 on a mission station in the Wellington Valley, but not published until 1892. Late in the century, other German missionaries produced some large dictionaries, perhaps the most impressive being J.G. Reuther's unpublished manuscript A Diari Dictionary, originally written in German, and used at the mission at Lakes Kopperamanna and Killalpaninna in northern South Australia. Again, because it was unpublished, and because it was not translated into English until late this century, it had little influence on non-Aboriginal Australians. Some Diyari people learned to read and write their own language. But, like Awaba, Wiradjuri and the Adelaide language, Diyari has not survived, and these dictionaries remain important records of the languages.

COMPILATIONS OF WORD-LISTS FROM DIFFERENT LANGUAGES

In the late nineteenth century, attention turned to collecting small word-lists from many different languages, and comparing them. In 1876 R. Brough Smyth published *The Aborigines of Victoria: With Notes Relating to the Habits of the Natives of Other Parts of Australia and Tasmania*. This contained a variety of word-lists, some comparative (tables comparing the same concept — for example, 'crow' — in several Aboriginal languages), some organised by semantic domain. Over thirty of them were the result of sending lists of English words to people in different parts of Victoria and asking them to give the corresponding words in the local Aboriginal languages. It also contains lists of placenames and their meanings, something that has intrigued Australians for a long time. In 1886 E.M. Curr published *The Australian Race: Its Origin, Languages, Customs, Place of Landing in Australia, and the Routes by which It Spread Itself over That Continent*, which contained 300 word-lists of approximately 125 words, again the results of sending out English word-lists to people all over the country and asking for translations. The lists in Brough Smyth and Curr vary greatly in quality and reliability, but very often are the most important record we now have of the languages concerned.

While Brough Smyth and Curr were careful to record where the word-list came from, whether by named group (for example, the Karnathun group) or place (for example, Colac), the early part of the twentieth century saw the start of a pernicious practice which has done a great deal to hinder the recognition of Aboriginal languages. It probably stemmed from the fact that urban Australians were becoming less aware of Aborigines, and of the differences between Aboriginal societies. This was the spread of the 'Aboriginal word books'.

In 1930 Justine Kenyon published *An Aboriginal Word Book* which has been reprinted many times since. It consists of lists of meanings for 'Aboriginal words' and 'Aboriginal placenames'. The words come from many different languages, but there is no proper recognition of this. Several other books containing word-lists followed: H.M. Cooper's *Australian Aboriginal Words and Their Meanings*, R. Praite and J.C. Tolley's *Place Names of South Australia*, and perhaps the most popular of all, A.H. and A.W. Reed's *Aboriginal Words of Australia*. The problem with these books is that, whether their authors intended this or not, they give the impression either that there is only one Aboriginal language, or that the differences between Aboriginal languages are quite unimportant. Furthermore, because they give no language sources for a particular meaning, it is very hard to check whether they are right or not. Finally, in instances where the meanings can be checked, they are often misleading or even wrong.

THE DEMANDS FOR MODERN DICTIONARIES

In the last fifty years, work on dictionaries of Aboriginal languages has grown enormously. Some excellent large dictionaries have appeared, mostly because the reading public for dictionaries has changed. In the nineteenth century the main audience for dictionaries of Aboriginal languages was non-Aboriginal people, those who wanted to learn the local Aboriginal languages, and those who were generally interested in Aboriginal languages. But in the last thirty years or so, bilingual education programs have become more widespread in schools on Aboriginal communities. Aboriginal people are learning to read and write in their own languages. So there is a need for learner's dictionaries of Aboriginal languages, both monolingual and bilingual. Goddard's dictionary of Pitjantjatjara/Yankunytjatjara (Goddard 1987) is an excellent example. There is also a continuing need for reference dictionaries of Aboriginal languages.

Because the audience for dictionaries of Aboriginal languages has changed, the need for different kinds of dictionaries is emerging. Adults require different dictionaries from children. People who have learned to read and write in English use dictionaries in different ways from people who have never learned to read and write. People whose first language is an Aboriginal language might use a monolingual dictionary in preference to a bilingual dictionary. On the other hand, people whose first language is English could find the English explanations of a bilingual dictionary quite helpful.

What do they use dictionaries for? Native speakers may use them for checking the spelling of words, or for learning the basic principles of spelling their own language, or for finding out the meaning of an unfamiliar word. For people who are learning to read and write, a dictionary is a useful tool which frees them from complete dependence on their teacher for checking spelling. Furthermore, listing normal English words with synonyms helps people literate in English to increase their English vocabulary.

The language to be included in a dictionary clearly depends on its intended audience. A learner's dictionary would not include difficult words that are rarely used. A reference dictionary might include these words, but might exclude some slang words which people find offensive.

A more intractable problem is often what dialect is to be used in a dictionary. We face this problem with English dictionaries, since over time the English language has diverged widely in different places. Similarly, certain Aboriginal languages have dialects, as Sharpe describes for Bundjalung (chapter 5).

One way of representing these differences is to have different dictionaries for each dialect. In effect, this is what has happened with the group of dialects known as the Western Desert Language. Yankunytjatjara, Ngaanyatjarra, Pintupi can all be considered dialects of this language, but they each have their own dictionary. For school use, it is important to keep dialects distinct.

However, it is also useful to see what is common among dialects. And so another way of handling dialect differences is to have a single dictionary in which each head word is marked as to which dialect it comes from. By having a dictionary of many dialects of a language put together, one can see the circulation of words, and understand shades of meaning and extension of vocabulary. Such a dictionary would be David Zorc's *Yolngu Matha Dictionary*. Perhaps the largest attempt to cover dialect variation is the on-going Arrernte dictionary project, which is providing dictionaries for a number of Arandic languages and dialects.

Once the lexicographer has decided what language to record in the dictionary, the next task is to decide what should be included in the dictionary entry for each word, and how it should be structured. We have seen how Teichelmann and Schürmann structured entries in their dictionaries. What information should be included is an interesting question. For instance, Teichelmann and Schürmann include information about the part of speech, thus that *kundo* is a noun. This is useful for a learner of a foreign language, who needs to know what part of speech a word is so that she/he can use it correctly in a sentence. But it is not generally useful for a native speaker of the language, who probably already knows how to use the word, or can work out how to use it from looking at its meaning.

Teichelmann and Schürmann also include ethnographic comments, such as the fact that people inherit a tract of land from their fathers. This kind of encyclopaedic information is very useful for learners, whether these are native speakers or foreign language learners. Including the cultural context in which a word is used also often helps to give a better understanding of the meaning of the word.

Kinds of information that are sometimes put into dictionary entries for Aboriginal languages include local or folk classifications for classes of words. Thus, ordinary English speakers classify some plants as grasses, others as trees, shrubs, vegetables, fruit, grains, and so on, while others they find hard to classify (for example, Venus flytraps). Not surprisingly, Aboriginal people have different folk classifications of plants, and these may be included in the dictionary entries for plants (for example, are they seed-bearing? are they edible? what kinds of implements can one make out of them?). Another area that may be included is the mythological significance of something, for instance, if fire is an important dreaming for speakers of a language, they may want this to be included in the dictionary entry for that word.

The heart of a dictionary entry is the explanation it gives of the meaning of a word. The dictionary-maker has to decide how the reader will best grasp the meaning of an unfamiliar word — whether the meaning of the word should be spelled out as a definition, or synonyms should be used, or pictures should be given, or illustrative sentences should be used. It seems that different kinds of words require different types of explanations — it might be more helpful to show a picture of a wombat than to describe it in words, but it would be hard to provide an unambiguous picture of an activity like 'winning'.

Dictionary entries can be ordered in several ways. For languages like English and Aboriginal languages which use the Roman alphabet, a common way is according to the first symbol (letter) representing the first sound of the word, or what we customarily call alphabetical order. Of course, there's no need to arrange the letters in that order. The Russian alphabet, for example, has the letter representing the sound pronounced [v] as the third letter of its alphabet. But English-speaking societies, by and large, have chosen to use the ABCDEF alphabetical ordering, and so have the lexicographers working on Aboriginal languages (with some exceptions, usually relating to sounds written with two letters, such as *ng*).

There are other ways of arranging material. For instance botanists and gardeners have arranged a special way of classifying plants, and in botany books, the plants are often listed in the order of that classification, rather than in alphabetical order.

A thesaurus is a whole dictionary arranged by topics. Two important decisions that have to be taken before making a thesaurus are, first, what will be the topics, and second, what order will the topics be arranged in? For instance, an English thesaurus might have a major topic devoted to architecture, while a thesaurus of Nunggubuyu (a north coast people) might have a major topic on dugong. The order and structuring of topics also reflects the importance of particular concepts in a culture. A society whose main source of meat is dugong, rather than beef, might give a different priority to dugongs and cattle in a thesaurus of its language. Several good thesauri of Aboriginal languages have appeared, including Heath's thesaurus of Nunggubuyu (1982) and Douglas's thesaurus of the Western Desert Language (1977) (the latter contains excellent illustrations).

CONCLUSION

Much work is being done creating dictionaries of Aboriginal languages, and there are some major dictionaries in preparation, including a Warlpiri dictionary and a comparative Arrernte dictionary. The production of dictionaries has been greatly assisted by computerisation. The availability of texts on computer means that concordances (lists of words in a text with references to where they occur) can be created automatically, providing valuable material for compiling dictionary entries. Putting dictionary entries on to a computer simplifies many of the lexicographer's tasks. It is much easier to be consistent in structuring entries and checking cross-references. Furthermore, from one set of entries different dictionaries can be created semi-automatically. These might be alphabetically ordered, ordered by topic, abridged, or, in the case of bilingual dictionaries, reversed. Finally, computerised dictionaries can be useful for creating educational computer games for children, and for providing people using computers for word processing with computer spelling checker programs. On the other end of the continuum, there is growing interest in small vocabularies and picture dictionaries as useful material for Aboriginal Studies courses.

There is a great need to do more basic recording work on the Aboriginal languages which have no dictionaries. While no one ever saved a language just by making a dictionary of it, there is no doubt that, if Aboriginal languages are to achieve their proper place in the education of children, those children and their teachers must have access to good comprehensive dictionaries.

FOR DISCUSSION

1. Consider the validity of comparing the *OED* and Teichelmann and Schürmann's vocabulary, bearing in mind the following points.
a. The *OED* is a monolingual dictionary, while the other is a bilingual dictionary.
b. The people who prepared the *OED* were native speakers of English, whereas the two people who wrote down the vocabulary of the Adelaide language were native speakers of German.
c. In the nineteenth century, when these dictionaries were compiled, English had been a written language for over five centuries, whereas the Adelaide language had not been written down before the European invasion in 1836.
d. It took more than forty-four years to complete and publish the *OED.* By contrast, the two authors of the Adelaide language vocabulary arrived in Adelaide in 1838 to start learning the language, and eighteen months later published their vocabulary.
e. In 1838 there were probably not more than a few hundred speakers of the Adelaide language.

2. In this chapter, partial explanations of words like 'vocabulary', 'glossary' are given together with an explanation of what they meant in the language from which English borrowed the term. The source of a word is called its etymology. Many

dictionaries contain etymologies for words (indeed, etymological dictionaries are devoted to providing etymologies). Why do dictionaries include etymologies? Do they help you understand the meaning of words? Can you know the meaning of a word without knowing its etymology? Look at the list of words below, (taken from a learner's dictionary (Goddard 1987, 62), and provide etymologies for them.

kalatji	glass, mirror
lapatuṟi	toilet
mutuka	car
nipa-nipa	scissors
tjiila	prison, gaol, the lockup
tjapila	shovel
tina	lunch
tiinta	1. tent, canopy on vehicle. 2. piece of canvas, tarpaulin
walypala	white man
waya	1. wire 2. wire handle on billy 3. power cord 4. things made of wire, for example, a cooking-grill

And now some harder ones:

kaliki	canvas
laimi	(noun) plaster
makaṯi	rifle
miita	spouse
tiki	(on) credit
tjaintjimilaṉi	cash a cheque

3. In the nine years between 1838 and 1846 six dictionaries of Aboriginal languages were published. In 1857 Threlkeld wrote to George Grey that he had hoped to publish his updated dictionary by subscription, but Australians showed a lack of interest in science: 'there is but little Encouragement for such things in this Colony'. In 1971 Geoffrey O'Grady (O'Grady 1971) could only think of four dictionaries of Aboriginal languages published in the twentieth century. Think of reasons why people lost interest in publishing dictionaries. Track down O'Grady's article and compare the reasons with his suggestions.

4. You are presented with a dictionary of 'European'. On page one you see the following lists of words:

abercoc	apricot
alamo	poplar tree
aller	to go
antworten	to answer
amba	it's all up!
arktos	bear
alcatraz	pelican

By dint of asking your Catalan, Spanish, French, German, Russian, Greek and Portuguese friends, you find out that these words come from their languages. What uses could you make of such a book?

5. Look at the following entry from the Warlpiri dictionary (provided by Mary Laughren).

JAALJAAL(PA) [Noun or Preverb] (*Yuendumu dialect*)

1. **feeling, hunch, premonition**

   Ngaju karna jaaljaal-jarrimi nyiyakurra. Marda kapulu kurdu ngajunyangu pakarni. *I have a feeling about something. Perhaps they are going to hit my son.* Kari! Nyiyakurra karna jaaljaal-jarrimi miyalu nyampuju? Ngajunyangukurra kajanyanukurra? Jungajuku ngajunyangukurralparna jaaljaal-jarrija manjurruju. Jungajuku wantija miyalu-purdanji. *Oh, why do I have this feeling in my stomach? Is it because of my son? It was because of my son that I had this twitching feeling. He fell down on his stomach.*

   • When used with the Allative case

2. (*Yuendumu and Lajamanu dialects*) **have an urge, desire (to do something), want, feel (like), have a yen for.**

   Jaaljaal-jarrimi, ngulaji yangka kujaka yapa kiyikiyi-jarri manu jalajala-jarrimi nyiyarlanguku majuku marda ngurrjuku marda — ngurrju-maninjaku — yangka nyanungu yangka yapa — wati marda, karnta marda, kurdu marda. Jaaljaal-jarrimi *is when a person feels like or gets the urge to do something, either something bad or something good — to make something — just that person himself — either a man or a woman or a child.* Jaaljaal-jarrimi karna janyungukupurda. *I feel like some tobacco. [Alma Granites Nungarrayi, Y27.9.88]*

   Wara! Janyunguku karna jaaljaal-jarrimi. *Oh I really feel like some tobacco. [Jean Napanangka Brown Y 1988]*

   • When used with the Dative case

Work out the different kinds of information contained in the entry, how they are coded (for example, by typeface), and speculate as to how readers could use this information. [NOTE: 'Allative' is the case of motion towards, expressed by the suffix *-kurra* in the examples. It is roughly equivalent to the English prepositions 'into' and 'onto'. 'Dative' is the case of the recipient, or the thing desired, of the person benefiting from something expressed by the suffixes *-ku* and *-kupurda* in the examples. It is roughly equivalent to the English prepositions 'to' and 'for'].

6. Provide a dictionary entry for the English word 'urge' in 'have an urge to'. Compare your explanation with one given in a large dictionary, such as the *Shorter Oxford English Dictionary* or the *Macquarie Dictionary.*

7. Suppose the sounds of an Aboriginal language are written as follows: *a i u p t ty k m n ng rn ny l rl ly r rr w y* (all the double letters represent a single sound, just as the *sh* sound in 'shop' represents a single sound). How would you order these sounds? Do you foresee any problems with your ordering?

8. Discuss the advantages and disadvantages of organising a word list alphabetically or by topics. You might consider points such as:
- is it a learner's dictionary?
- if it's a learner's dictionary, what's the first language of the learners?
- what uses is the dictionary intended to have? Learning about a particular topic? Searching for synonyms? Checking the spelling of a word? Looking up the meaning of an unfamiliar word?

9. 'A picture is worth a thousand words'. Discuss the truth of this statement with respect to sets of words — for example, compare words for things, such as saucers, bowls and plates, with words for emotions, such as anger, love and hope.

REFERENCES

Austin, P.
1991 'Australian Lexicography'. In F.J. Hausmann, O. Reichmann, H.E. Wiegand (eds), *Encyclopaedia of Lexicography*, Walter de Gruyter, Berlin, 2638–41.

Capell, A.
1971 History of Research in Australian and Tasmanian Languages. In T.A. Sebeok (ed), *Current Trends in Linguistics* 8, Mouton, The Hague, 661–720.

Cooper, H.M.
1952 *Australian Aboriginal Words and Their Meanings*, South Australian Museum, Adelaide.

Curr, E.M.
1886–87 *The Australian Race: Its Origin, Languages, Customs, Place of Landing in Australia, and the Routes by Which It Spread Itself over That Continent*, 4 vols, J. Ferres, Government Printer, Melbourne.

Dixon, R.M.W., W.S. Ramson and M. Thomas
1990 *Australian Aboriginal Words in English: Their Origin and Meaning*, Oxford University Press, Melbourne.

Douglas, W.

1977 *Illustrated Topical Dictionary of the Western Desert Language: Warburton Ranges Dialect, Western Australia*, Australian Institute of Aboriginal Studies, Canberra.

Gaimard

1830–1835 Vocabulaire de la Langue des Habitants de Golfe Saint-Vincent. In *Voyage de Découverte de l'Astrolabe 1826-7-8-9 sous le Commandement de M.J. Dumont d'Urville*, vol 1 Philologie, J. Tastu, Paris, 6–8.

Goddard, C.

1987 *A Basic Pitjantjatjara/Yankunytjatjara to English Dictionary*, Institute for Aboriginal Development, Alice Springs, Northern Territory.

Grey, G.

1845 'On the Languages of Australia', Being an Extract of a Dispatch from Captain G. Grey, Governor of South Australia, to Lord Stanley. Communicated by his Lordship, *Journal of the Royal Geographical Society* 15, 365–367.

Günther, J.

1892 Grammar and Vocabulary of the Aboriginal Dialect Called the Wirradhuri. In J. Fraser (ed), *An Australian Language, as Spoken by the Awabakal* [L. E. Threlkeld], Appendix D, 56–120.

Heath, J.

1982 *Nunggubuyu Dictionary*, Australian Institute of Aboriginal Studies, Canberra.

Kendon, A.

1988 *Sign Languages of Aboriginal Australia: Cultural, Semiotic and Communicative Perspectives*, Cambridge University Press, Cambridge.

Kenyon, J.

1982 *Aboriginal Word Book*, Lothian, Melbourne.

Kilham, C. et al.

1986 *Dictionary and Source Book of the Wik-Mungkan Language*, Summer Institute of Linguistics, Darwin.

Meyer, H.A.E.

1843 *Vocabulary of the Language Spoken by the Aborigines of the Southern and Eastern Portions of the Settled Districts of South Australia*, J. Allen, Adelaide.

Moorhouse, M.

1846 *A Vocabulary and Outline of the Grammatical Structure of the Murray River Language*, A. Murray, Adelaide.

O'Grady, G.N.

1971 Lexicographical Research in Aboriginal Australia. In T.A. Sebeok (ed), *Current Trends in Linguistics* 8, Mouton, The Hague, 779–803.

Praite, R. and J.C. Tolley

1970 *Place Names of South Australia*, Rigby, Adelaide.

Reed, A.H. and A.W.

1965 *Aboriginal Words of Australia*, A.H. and A.W. Reed Pty Ltd, Sydney.

Reuther, J.G.

1981 *The Diari*, microfiche ed. Translated from the German by P.A. Scherer, Tanunda. Australian Institute of Aboriginal Studies, Canberra.

Sandefur, J. and J. Sandefur

1979 *Beginnings of a Ngukurr-Bamyili Creole Dictionary*, Summer Institute of Linguistics, Darwin.

Schürmann, C.W.

1844 *A Vocabulary of the Parnkalla Language*, Adelaide.

Simpson, J.A. and E.S.C. Weiner

1989 *Oxford English Dictionary*, 2nd ed, Oxford University Press/Clarendon Press, Oxford/New York, 20 vols.

Smyth, R.B.

1876 *The Aborigines of Victoria: With Notes Relating to the Habits of the Natives of other Parts of Australia and Tasmania*, 2 vols, John Currey, O'Neil, Melbourne.

Strehlow, C.F.T.

n.d. *Aranda-Loritja–English Dictionary*, Translated from the German by P.A. Scherer. 223-page typescript held at Australian Institute of Aboriginal Studies.

Teichelmann, C.G. and C.W. Schürmann

1840 *Outlines of a Grammar, Vocabulary, and Phraseology, of the Aboriginal Language of South Australia, Spoken by the Natives in and for some Distance around Adelaide*, Published by the authors, at the native location, Adelaide.

Threlkeld, L.E.

1834 *An Australian Grammar, Comprehending the Principles and Natural Rules of the Language, as Spoken by the Aborigines in the Vicinity of Hunter's River, Lake Macquarie, &c. New South Wales*, Stephens and Stokes, Sydney.

Williams, W.

1840-
[1839] A Vocabulary of the Languages of the Aborigines of the Adelaide District, and other Friendly Tribes, of the Province of South Australia,

published privately by A. McDougall, Rundle St, Adelaide, and then republished in *South Australian Colonist*, Adelaide, 297–98.

Wyatt, W.
1879 Vocabulary of the Adelaide and Encounter Bay Tribes, with a Few Words of that of Rapid Bay. In J.D. Woods (ed), *The Native Tribes of South Australia*, (no publisher) Adelaide, 157–82.

Zorc, R.D.
1986 *Yolngu-Matha Dictionary*, School of Australian Linguistics, Darwin Institute of Technology, Batchelor, NT.

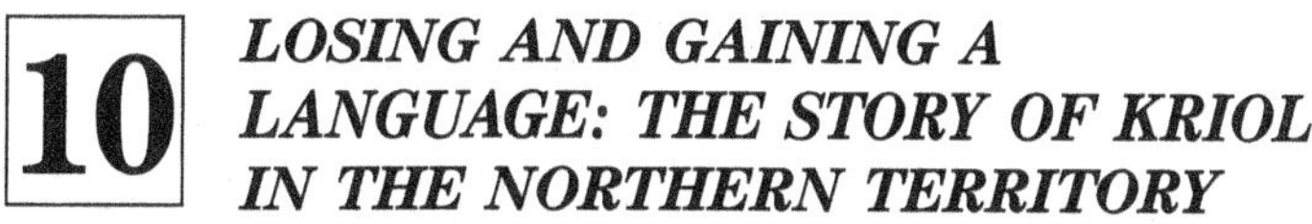

CHAPTER 10

LOSING AND GAINING A LANGUAGE: THE STORY OF KRIOL IN THE NORTHERN TERRITORY

John Harris

PIDGINS: ANSWERS TO A PROBLEM

In the past few hundred years European colonialism has affected many language communities. Disruption of the lives of whole societies has drastically affected normal language transmission from one generation to the next. In extreme cases, indigenous languages have disappeared and new languages arisen. Troy (chapter 3) talks of the origins of a pidgin in early colonial New South Wales. Pidgins have often been viewed with suspicion by those who did not speak them, particularly if they were an elite or politically dominant class while the speakers of the new languages were the colonised, dispossessed or lower classes. Although such prejudice has often been due to elitism or even racism, it has also sometimes been due to ignorance. Many otherwise well-meaning people have simply failed to understand the difference between a restricted pidgin language and a full creole language, nor have they understood why they arise in the first place.

A pidgin is a contact language, used only for limited purposes between groups of people having no common language. Generations of films, novels and comics have produced a derogatory stereotype of pidgins in the minds of many people. This 'me Tarzan, you Jane' kind of language is widely thought to be the result of primitive thought processes, or mental deficiency, or baby talk. This stereotype is wrong. Pidgins are the creation of skilled people faced with a sudden need to communicate with other people who do not speak the same language.

There have been pidgins as long as people from different language communities have been thrust into sudden contact. The period of European colonial expansion, however, brought people into contact much more frequently and much more widely than had happened before.

In the earliest contacts, communication is often restricted to such interactions as trading, where a detailed exchange of ideas is not required. A small vocabulary is sufficient, drawn almost exclusively from the language of the dominant group. The grammar of pidgin is 'simplified' in the sense that it is less complex and less flexible than the structures of any of the languages involved in the contact. It is not, however, merely a jargon: that is, a pidgin has and obeys its own rules.

It is important to realise that simplification of language is not necessarily a backward step. Consider these three sentences: 'I go to Sydney today';

'I went to Sydney yesterday'; 'I will go to Sydney tomorrow'. In an imaginary pidgin, these sentences could become: *I go Sydney today; I go Sydney yesterday; I go Sydney tomorrow.* These sentences are perfectly comprehensible. The meaning is still clear, although there is what some people call a 'loss of grammar'.

A pidgin is nobody's primary language. Both parties privately speak their own full languages. Chinese Pidgin English, for example, which arose in the eighteenth century, was used initially between British traders and Chinese merchants. It was a restricted language, able to cope with simple trade negotiations. Chinese Pidgin English was not the primary language of the Chinese or the British. The Chinese went home and spoke Cantonese while the British went home and spoke English.

Some pidgins remain in use as pidgins for hundreds of years. Others may be only short-lived and then disappear completely. On the other hand, some pidgins expand to fulfil new communicative demands.

CREOLES: RESPONSES TO A NEED

Many pidgins have undergone immense, rapid expansion to become the primary languages of new communities. These new languages are no longer pidgins but are termed 'creoles', a word which originally referred to almost anything which developed in colonial situations. The term is now used by linguists to refer only to new languages which have arisen by the rapid expansion of a pidgin ('creolisation').

Many colonial contexts in which pidgins developed were situations of extreme social disruption in which communities arose consisting of people who did not share a common language. Plantation slavery was a typical context. Slave traders normally supplied slaves from different language backgrounds to prevent them from grouping in large numbers. Their only common language was the plantation pidgin. The slave communities, and particularly their children, had an urgent need to communicate with each other on a wide range of subjects but no language in which to do it. Their response was to create languages of their own, using the local pidgin as the basic raw material, but expanding it to cope with all communicative needs. The resulting languages were creoles.

A creole is a full language, while a pidgin is a restricted special-purpose language. It can be argued that there is no real difference, linguistically, between creoles and other normal languages. The view that a creole is in some way inferior is a delusion, made possible only because, unlike older languages, creoles may still be able to be compared with the languages of which they are believed to be corruptions. Many of the grammatical simplifications for which creole languages are denigrated, such as loss of inflection, are in fact true of modern English when it is compared to its ancestor languages. Changes in English, however, either took a long time or are perceived as having happened long ago, whereas the simplifications of language which occur in pidginisation, and the subsequent preservation of those simplifications in a creole, may all take place within one or two generations.

KRIOL: THE STORY OF A NEW CREOLE

Kriol is a unique Australian creole. Its history well illustrates the relationship between a creole and its pidgin ancestor, and demonstrates that creolisation occurs as a result of rapid social change and the demand for a primary language in a newly emerged community (Harris 1986).

After four unsuccessful attempts by Europeans to invade the Northern Territory between 1824 and 1866, permanent settlement was achieved in Darwin in 1870. Over the next thirty years, there was an influx of English-speaking people. Some came to establish the cattle industry and others came to the gold rushes, where they were outnumbered by the Chinese. There was considerable interaction between Chinese, European and Aboriginal people, particularly in the vicinity of European settlements, such as the emerging townships, the mining camps, and the cattle stations. None of these groups could understand each other's language, so a direct consequence of their need to communicate was the emergence of pidginised forms of English. By the beginning of the twentieth century, these pidgins had converged into one widely understood lingua franca, Northern Territory Pidgin English. At this point, Northern Territory Pidgin English was still a pidgin. It was still a contact language, still used for restricted purposes only, still nobody's primary language; that is, it had not yet creolised. All its speakers spoke other full languages at home.

The first place in the Northern Territory where the pidgin was expanded to become the primary language of a new community was the Roper River Mission (now Ngukurr), where creolisation began to occur shortly after 1908. The invasion of the Roper River region by Europeans had commenced with the construction of the overland telegraph in the early 1870s. Huge cattle drives were then undertaken as the pastoral frontier moved from Queensland into the Northern Territory. Cattle stations were established in the 1870s and 1880s and a small township emerged at Roper Bar, the shallow crossing used by European drovers, miners, settlers, cattle thieves and anyone else who had to cross the Roper River travelling north or south.

These were violent years and a great deal of aggression was directed at Aboriginal people in the region. As one of the early missionaries, R.D. Joynt, wrote in 1918, hundreds had been 'shot down like game'. The massacre of Aboriginal people in a 'war of extermination' was widespread and continuous throughout the whole of the pastoral frontier. Initially, the battle was not entirely one-sided. The Aboriginal people of the Roper River region gained themselves a reputation for fierce and concerted resistance to the European invasion of their lands.

Any hypothetical chance, however, that Aboriginal people may have been able to maintain control over the future of themselves and their society was drastically ended at the turn of the century when a London-based cattle company (The Eastern and African Cold Storage Company) acquired massive tracts of unleased or abandoned land to carve out a pastoral empire from the Roper River north into Arnhem Land. Purchasing all the cattle stations along the western Roper River, they began moving cattle eastward. The company had no intention of allowing Aboriginal resistance to hinder this huge project. Determined to exterminate them, they employed gangs of up to fourteen men to hunt out all inhabitants of the region and shoot them on sight. With the police and other authorities turning a blind eye, the hunting gangs of the cattle company staged an unprecedented, systematic campaign of extermination against the Roper River people. They almost succeeded.

This near annihilation of the Aboriginal people of the region led to the first factor necessary for the genesis of a creole: sudden and drastic social change and the accompanying severe disruption of normal language transmission. The second requirement for the genesis of a creole is a new community. This was made possible by an Anglican mission station.

Challenged by the plight of Aboriginal people, the Anglican Church determined to establish a mission on the Roper River itself. Commenced in 1908, the mission was perceived as a haven of refuge by the scattered people of the region. By 1909 some 200 Aboriginal people gathered there. They were the remnants of the Mara, Wandarang, Alawa, Ngalakan and Ngandi people, together with the easternmost Mangarayi people and the southernmost members of the Rembarrnga and Nunggubuyu. As Barnabas Roberts, an Alawa man who came to the mission as a young boy, once said: 'If the missionaries hadn't come, my tribe would have been all shot down'.

The eight groups spoke separate and distinct languages. As is typical of Aboriginal people, the adults were multilingual. Although they had not lived permanently in such close proximity before, they had met regularly for ceremonial and other purposes. Over the course of a lifetime, these people had always become fluent speakers of each other's languages. The children, however, were not yet multilingual. Approximately seventy children attended school at the mission, each one of them forced into contact with other children whose languages they had not yet had time to learn. They were the new community, they needed a primary language, and they needed it immediately.

Whereas their parents could communicate with other adults by speaking Alawa or Mara or whatever, the children could not. What they had in common was the English pidgin used between Aboriginal and European people, together with the English they were hearing in school. With this limited input, it was this younger generation who, in the course of their lifetime, created the creole, manipulating the linguistic resources available to them to create a language which catered for all their communicative needs. This language is now called Kriol. As one local person, Ralph Dingul, puts it:

> La Ngukurr melabat garrim eitbala langgus. Wen naja traib wandim tok la dis traib, dei tok mijalb garrim Kriol. Jad impotan langgus im Kriol. Olabat gan sabi bla wanim olabat toktok.
>
> (At Ngukurr, we have eight languages. When another tribe wants to talk to this tribe, they talk to each other in Kriol. The important language is Kriol. They all can understand whatever they want to discuss.)

The relationship of the missionaries to the emergence of Kriol is complex. The Aboriginal people accepted the missionaries. They chose the mission site for them and they recognised that the missionaries came as friends, not enemies. They gathered at the mission and there formed the new community for which a new primary language became necessary. Certainly, the mission provided a location for this new community, the location where the demand for a creole would arise; but the mission did not create the creole. The movement of pidgin English towards a creole at other locations — in the Kimberleys, around the cattle stations and at Barunga during World War II, for example — indicates that the process of creolisation would have eventually taken place, provided that Aboriginal people had survived in the region without the mission to protect them. Thus, although the effect of the mission was to expedite the rise of Kriol, it was not the primary cause. Indeed, the truth is that Kriol arose despite the efforts of the missionaries to prevent it.

It is not easy to judge accurately the impact of the missionaries' attitudes to language. Initially, they intended to learn a local language but discovered to their dismay that there were at least eight. They could have chosen one of these — perhaps the language of the actual mission site — but it is still unlikely that this would have prevented the emergence of Kriol.

What the missionaries did was conclude that Standard English was the only choice for the official language of the mission. They therefore tried to discourage what was starting to be called 'Roper Pidgin', and were surprised at their inability to do so. Young people became bilingual, speaking Kriol among themselves and English to the missionaries. Informally, many missionaries also attempted to speak Kriol as a communicative necessity.

The missionaries could not, of course, have known what was happening. Even the scholarly linguistic world did not recognise Kriol until the 1970s. Prior to that, Kriol and its antecedent pidgins were considered 'ridiculous gibberish' (Strehlow 1947, xix), 'broken jargon' (Wurm 1963, 4) and 'lingual bastardisation' (Baker 1966, 316). In this context, the missionaries could not have deduced that a new and viable language was coming into existence. We could hardly expect that the missionaries would have had more linguistic understanding than contemporary linguists. The missionaries discouraged the use of Kriol, banning it in school and especially avoiding it in religious contexts.

Despite the efforts of the missionaries, Kriol was born, and it continued to develop and mature. It is now the language of a new community. For many people it is now both mother tongue and primary language. Kriol is now formally described (Sandefur 1979, 1986) and is beginning to acquire its own distinctive literature.

THE KRIOL BIBLE TRANSLATION

Old prejudices die hard. There are still people today who do not consider Kriol to be a 'proper' language. Furthermore, Kriol-speaking Aboriginal people themselves have held a low view of their language. This is a worldwide phenomenon in creole-speaking communities. Creoles have not normally arisen as the languages of the rich or powerful. Those who speak creoles have endured generations of abuse of themselves and their languages. It is little wonder that they have grown ashamed of their speech.

There is, however, a worldwide trend for creole-speaking people to gain a new sense of self-esteem as they break away from the colonial oppression of the past. The languages which have become their own are invariably part of their emerging identity and gain new respect. In many parts of the world, the new pride that creole-speaking communities have in their languages has been initiated by the translation and publication of something significant and substantial.

This has almost always been the Bible. Whatever one's religious views, the significance of the Bible as a substantial book with powerful symbolic value cannot be denied. Furthermore, the translation of a book with so much deep philosophical and abstract material lays to rest the criticism that creoles are inadequate languages which can only express simple ideas.

The Kriol Bible translation program illustrates this particularly well. Against opposition from some linguists, some missionaries, some educational administrators and even from some older Aboriginal people who believed that Kriol was inferior, a translation program has been in progress since 1973. This Bible translation has played a crucial role in raising the status of Kriol in the eyes of its speakers. When the first small book of selections, *Holi Baibul*, was published in 1985, people at Ngukurr, Barunga, Darwin and in the Kimberleys wore T-shirts depicting the region where Kriol is spoken (*Kriol Kantri*) and a Bible. The slogan read: *Dubala brom God* (Both from God).

Certainly, as is often the case in translation, narrative passages were the easiest to deal with. Yet, even there, the differences between English and Kriol are evident. Here is Luke 2:8, the verse which opens the story of the shepherds visiting the infant Jesus.

English Revised Standard Version:

> And in that region there were shepherds out in the field, keeping watch over their flock by night.

Kriol Holi Baibul:

> *Orait, sambala stakmen deya langa dat Kantri deibin maindimbat ola nenigout langa pedik naitaim.*
>
> 'Alright, some-fellow stockmen there belonging that country they-were minding all-the sheep belonging paddock nighttime'.

Orait replaces 'and' as the normal Kriol commencement of a narrative. The cattle industry, so important in Kriol Kantri, gives *stakmen* (stockmen) as the Kriol word for anyone who minds animals. The first sheep-like animals in the Roper region were goats — hence *nenigout* (nanny goat).

Here are two longer passages containing complex theological ideas from Ephesians 1: 5–10, where St Paul discusses God's plan for humankind.

Revised Standard Version

> He destined us in love to be his sons through Jesus Christ, according to the purpose of his will, to the praise of his glorious grace which he freely bestowed on us in the Beloved. In him we have redemption through his blood, the forgiveness of our trespasses, according to the riches of his grace which he lavished upon us, for he has made known to us in all wisdom and insight the mystery of his will, according to his purpose which he set forth in Christ as a plan for the fullness of time, to unite all things in him, things in heaven and things on earth.

Holi Baibul

> Longtaim God bin jinggabat blanga meigim wi san blanga im, dumaji imbin laigim wi, en bambai after imbin meigim wi im san wen imbin joinimap wi langa Jisas Krais, dumaji imbin gudbinji blanga dum lagijat, en imbin meigim im ron plen. Wal wi garra preisim God en gibit im teingks, dumaji imbin abum detkain filing blanga wi, en imbin shoum wi det filing blanga im wen imbin gibit wi ola enijing friwan thru Jisas det brabliwan san blanga im, dumaji wen Jisas bin weistim im blad, imbin meigim wi fri, en God bin larramgo wi fri brom ol detlot nogudbala ting weya wibin oldei dumbat. Trubala God im brabli kainbala, en brabliwei imbin shoum wi im kainbala. Wal God im brabli sabibala du, en imbin dum wanim imbin wandim, en imbin shoum wi det plen blanga im weya imbin jinggabat blanga dum garram Jisas Krais. Nobodi bin sabi det plen basdam, bat we sabi na. Wi sabi wen im rait taim, God garra joinimap ebrijing weya imbin meigim langa dis wel en langa hebin, en Jisas na garra sidan boswan blanga olabat.

It has been the translators' experience that the task of expressing these concepts in Kriol has made the English more comprehensible to them. Here are a few examples of wording from the above passage:

> (God) destined us...to be his sons
> *Longtaim God bin jinggabat blanga meigim wi san blanga im*
> '(For a) longtime God has thought about making us sons of his'
>
> In him we have redemption through his blood
> *Wen Jisas bin weistim im blad, imbin meigim we fri*
> 'When Jesus shed his blood, he made us free'
>
> He has made known to us...the mystery of his will
> *Imbin shown wi det plen blanga im... Nobodi bin sabi det plan basdam, bat wi sabi na*
> 'He showed us that plan of his... Nobody understood that plan before, but we understand now'.

CONCLUSION

Kriol is now a full language. Over 20,000 people can speak Kriol. For about half of these, Kriol is their mother tongue. Like all languages, Kriol is capable of expressing all that its speakers want to say. Certainly, Kriol speakers on the Bible translation team found themselves saying things that had never been said before in Kriol. But there was nothing, finally, that they could not say.

Living languages do change, and one of the major reasons for change is the need to express new concepts. Kriol has shown itself well able to do that. As time progresses, Kriol speakers will find the need to express and communicate yet newer ideas. That Kriol can do this is proof that it is a full language.

It is possible that some of the changes in Kriol will move it closer to English, because Kriol speakers also speak English as a second or third language. However, the more Kriol comes to symbolise their distinctiveness, the more Kriol speakers will value and preserve it.

FOR DISCUSSION

1. English: If I have no money, I won't come
   Samoan Pidgin English: *No mani, no kam.*

What are the differences between the two sentences? Can one sentence be shown to be inferior to the other? Does one sentence convey more meaning than the other?

2. In a language derived from English the sentence *Me no si man yu tok* means 'I haven't seen the man you are talking about'. Can you tell whether or not the language is a pidgin or a creole? Explain why or why not.

3. Imagine a situation in which an Australian army unit was based in a Berovian-speaking country to oversee a cease-fire. Under what conditions could a pidgin develop there? What language would it be based upon? What could cause this new pidgin to become a creole?

4. In 1582 Richard Mulcaster pleaded for English to be accepted as the language of education and scholarship in England, rather than Latin. English, he said, was: 'our own tung...bearing the ioyfull title of our libertie and fredom, the Latin tung remembering vs of our thraldom and bondage'.

What do you think may have been the objections to English? What was the force of Mulcaster's argument?

REFERENCES

Baker, S.J.

1966 *The Australian Language*, Currawong Publishers, Sydney.

Harris, J.W.

1986 *Northern Territory Pidgins and the Origin of Kriol*, Pacific Linguistics C-89, Canberra.

Joynt, R.D.

1918 *Ten Years among Aborigines*, H. Hearne and Co, Melbourne.

Sandefur, J.R.

1979 *An Australia Kriol in the Northern Territory: A Description of Ngukurr-Bamyili Dialects*, Summer Institute of Linguistics, Darwin.

1986 *Kriol of North Australia: A Language Coming of Age*, Summer Institute of Linguistics, Darwin.

Strehlow, T.G.H.

1947 *Aranda Traditions*, Melbourne University Press, Melbourne.

Wurm, S.A.

1963 *Some Remarks on the Role of Language in the Assimilation of Australian Aborigines*, Pacific Linguistics A-1, Canberra.

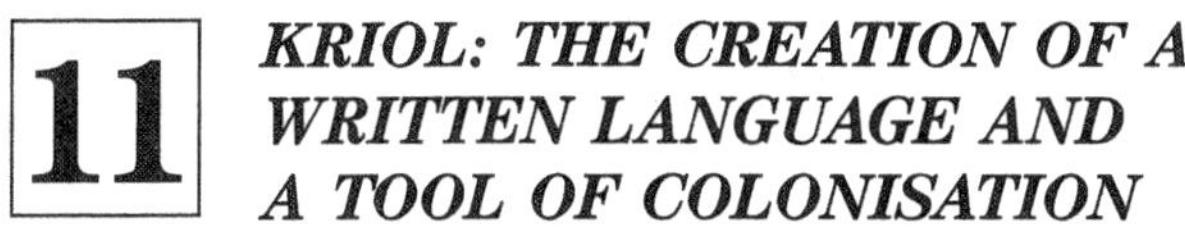

CHAPTER

11 KRIOL: THE CREATION OF A WRITTEN LANGUAGE AND A TOOL OF COLONISATION

Mari Rhydwen

WHAT IS KRIOL?

Kriol is the word 'creole' written in the orthography of the variety of creole spoken in Barunga (formerly Bamyili) and Ngukurr (Roper River). Harris has described the origins of Kriol and the use of the language in Bible translation (chapter 10).

Amongst Aboriginal people in the Northern Territory, the term 'Kriol' is normally used to refer only to the speech of people from Barunga or Ngukurr, although some use the term more widely and in Western Australia one creole is sometimes called 'Fitzroy Valley'. The question that arises is whether there is one language, widely spoken throughout northern Australia, that may be referred to as 'Kriol', or whether there are varieties of creole, of which Kriol is one example. Some linguists argue that there is a single language throughout the area — the name is in fact irrelevant, but call it Kriol. On the other hand, it is well-known that there are language varieties that, although very similar linguistically, are known as different languages for political or other ideological reasons — for example, Serbian and Croatian. In such cases, however, people tend to assert that they are 'really' the same language, thus making a distinction between two kinds of facts, 'scientific facts' and 'social facts'. Because of the dominant scientific paradigm in Western intellectual ideology, facts have status, and real facts have more status than social facts, since it is easier to verify scientific facts. What I call into question is the pre-eminence of scientific arguments in a situation where sociopolitical factors are so evidently significant.

To return to the question of Kriol, many people in the Daly River area do not think that they speak Kriol, even though they acknowledge that they speak a mutually intelligible variety to Barunga Kriol. I could argue for this as a social fact; I could even appeal to a number of 'real' facts to show that there are differences between the two varieties of language. At this point, however, I want to establish that to engage in justifying arguments about the status of Kriol, by drawing on established scientific theory, is to accept a particular view of knowledge and science. To do this, without question, in a cross-cultural situation where the dominant, colonising culture accepts this theory of knowledge, but the colonised group does not, is to be implicated in, at best, colonisation of the mind, at worst, genocide.

There is no simple way through the intellectual labyrinth encountered in the course of doing linguistic work, or indeed any kind of work, in an area so beset by social and political problems far beyond the control of any individual. The reality is that after 200 years of colonisation, no Aboriginal community remains untouched by the influence of that invasion, whether it be in economic, social (including educational) or religious ways. At this stage, the only option which I find appropriate is to approach the question by acknowledging the issues involved — by making explicit the cultural values, pressures and expectations arising from my own cultural environment and by articulating our understanding of other relevant perspectives. I shall be content when a first-language speaker of Kriol/creole revises my arguments.

As mentioned earlier, speakers of creole in northern Australia generally recognise only a few varieties as Kriol. On one level this is insignificant: it does not matter what people call the language they speak and the reality of the language remains unchanged by the terminology used by linguists or others, to describe it. On the other level, it does matter, for the work of linguists is significant in determining educational, and hence social, policy in the Northern Territory.

THE CURRENT USES OF KRIOL LITERACY

In 1972 the government of Australia declared its support for bilingual education programs on the grounds that, in Prime Minister Whitlam's words, 'tribal cultures should be preserved, not crushed' (Dixon 1980, 91). One of the places that a bilingual program was established was Barunga, where the program was in Kriol. Since that time the situation has changed: the Northern Territory government now takes responsibility for education in the area, there have been general shifts in government policy, and there is now a different perspective on bilingual education. There is currently far more emphasis on the efficacy of vernacular literacy in promoting English literacy than on it as a means of ensuring cultural survival. There is, of course, within both Aboriginal and non-Aboriginal intellectual circles, debate about whether vernacular literacy in fact promotes or destroys oral culture; but, aside from that debate, there is also the question of whether vernacular literacy is seen as a tool of assimilation or of liberation.

In a situation where an ancestral language is used in a bilingual program, the justification is that this both aids English literacy acquisition and helps to foster the indigenous language. Many such situations are complicated by the fact that more than one ancestral language is used within the community: the school, by choosing to use one rather than another, alters the status of languages, and by implication, of social groups within the community. Nevertheless, given that the process of schooling cannot but have a homogenising effect, the fact that one or more Aboriginal languages may be used within school programs is at least a concession to the special needs of the community. In many cases the school is viewed as a means of facilitating 'both ways education'. In the words of Bakamana Gayak Yunupingu:

> The school is a place which can do a great deal to help children become successful in language use, but it will work best at this when the community is consulted about how language is to be used. This is because Yolngu draw on the philosophies that will help to sustain sensitive components of Yolngu knowledge through the idea of 'Both Ways' education, to live in, maintain and be proud to live in a Bi-cultural and Bilingual society. (1987, 134)

Whatever the tension between these two ways, there is at least an understanding that cultural maintenance is a significant factor. The situation in Kriol-speaking areas is, however, somewhat different. There is currently, and has only ever been, an official bilingual Kriol program in one school, namely Barunga. At Ngukurr, Kriol is used only orally although there is some informal Kriol literacy. Both these communities comprise groups of speakers of different ancestral languages, many of whom no longer live in their traditional homelands and who live in these communities because of severe social disruption by European settlers. There are substantial differences between the situation of Kriol speakers and that of speakers of other Aboriginal languages. Kriol speakers never identify themselves as Kriol people. They refer to themselves by the name of their ancestral language, even if they do not speak it. Moreover, ancestral languages are often more widely used at places like Barunga than many Europeans realise. People have learned to hide some aspects of their life.

Now, it is apparent that the use of creole as a first language or as a lingua franca, is widespread throughout much of the school-age population in the Northern Territory. The ideology of bilingual education, of biliteracy, is that it allows 'both ways' education, the 'both ways' being Western and Aboriginal. Yet, many children speak a language that gives them access to neither. Children who are creole speakers are, with a few exceptions, treated as though they speak English, albeit 'badly', and there is no provision for them to be taught English as a second language. At the same time, children who speak creole often live in communities where the establishment or continuation of a bilingual program in an ancestral language has been refused on the grounds that the children do not have such a language as their first language. These children not only miss out on adequate access to English, since they are not taught it in ways appropriate to second-language learners, but, in most cases, they miss out on instruction in Aboriginal culture, which is generally assumed to have disappeared.

At Barunga, where there is officially a Kriol bilingual program, this was not the case. It was acknowledged that the children did not arrive at school as English speakers, and ancestral languages were not totally ignored. The inclusion of Kriol, both as a medium and an object of study, gave recognition to the relationship between it and English, while the significance of the ancestral languages, whose names are still used to identify the affiliations of the children within the community, was still acknowledged in the education system. Since the mid 1980s the bilingual program at Barunga has proved vulnerable to changes in school personnel and controversy about the status of Kriol has adversely affected the program there.

KRIOL AT NGUKURR

Ngukurr (previously Roper River) is, like Barunga, a community where it is widely acknowledged that Kriol is spoken. Unlike Barunga, Ngukurr School does not have an official bilingual program, although Kriol is used informally in the school. There appear to be two reasons for this. One is that written Kriol literacy has been used in church-based contexts and the community is generally aware of Kriol and of Kriol literacy. Secondly, almost the entire school staff at Ngukurr is Aboriginal. This is a result of a policy developed by the Department of Education and the community to rectify a situation where there was low school attendance. Hence, most of the teaching staff are themselves Kriol speakers. Although there is little Kriol literacy, Kriol is used extensively orally in the school.

A previous school principal (now dead and therefore, in accordance with local custom, not to be named here) indicated that she wanted a bilingual program but that she wanted the local community to have control over its own literature production and not rely on material produced at Barunga. This issue of local control of literature is central in the debate about literacy in creole-speaking areas. Although it is not a problem for Barunga and Ngukurr speakers to comprehend each others dialects, the differences in pronunciation and a few items of vocabulary are significant markers of identity. The standardising effects of literacy are known, but resisted, much as American spelling and usage may be resisted in Britain and Australia. But, given the importance of maintaining these distinctions, there is no reason why schools in different communities should not be able to produce their own literature, especially since recent developments in computer technology make desktop publishing a real possibility.

CREOLE AT NAUIYU NAMBIYU

At Nauiyu Nambiyu (Daly River) the ancestral languages most widely used are Ngan'gikurunggurr and Ngan'giwumirri, together referred to as Ngan'gityemerri. In addition, older people use a pidgin, known locally as 'Pidgin English', which is mutually intelligible with a creole spoken by younger people and known locally as Ngan'giwatyfala. (*Ngan'gi* is the word for 'language', hence *Ngan'giwatyfala* is 'Europeans' language'.) The crucial distinction between the pidgin and the creole rests on whether it is the first language of the speaker. In the case of all the older speakers whom I recorded, it is an ancestral language that is their first language both in a chronological sense and in the sense that it is the language they use most. They can be heard addressing young people in ancestral languages, even though the young people tend to respond in creole. In the case of people under thirty years of age, creole is the language they use habitually, although they may have some knowledge of their ancestral languages. In addition, they speak some English as well, so that the creole is, for them, not primarily a contact language with English speakers but the language of intra-community communication. For pidgin speakers the pidgin may serve this function but is also the sole means of communication with English speakers.

There is one group who do not fit neatly into either of these categories and this is the group between the ages of about thirty and forty. This was the first generation to attend the Mission School, which was established in the 1950s. This is the generation whose parents were speakers of ancestral languages, and who spoke those languages with their parents as young children, but who lived in dormitories at the school where English was the only language officially spoken. This is the generation who, although they can often speak an ancestral language to some extent, can be heard using creole to each other and to their children. They are presumably the first generation of local creole-speakers.

Kriol speakers and Ngan'giwatyfala speakers generally insist that they do not speak the same language, and it appears to be a matter of significance for both groups to maintain this position. One woman who had family connections with both the Daly River area and with a Kriol-speaking area did speak of creole in the two areas as kinds of Kriol, but she also drew my attention to the differences between the varieties. This was also the case with a Nauiyu Nambiyu woman who was interested in writing creole. It would seem that people who were able to discuss the differences and similarities between Kriol and Ngan'giwatyfala were those who had already acknowledged that Ngan'giwatyfala is widely spoken and has some similarities to Kriol, as opposed to those who were still, in some way, denying its existence. Among the differences were the fact that Daly people say *mifala* and not *mibala* (we); they say *liliwan* for *lilwan* (small); and they say *wulumen* not *olmen* (old man). In addition, when ancestral language words are used in Ngan'giwatyfala, they are different from those used in Kriol-speaking areas. Thus, for people familiar with both varieties, the differences appeared to be either phonological or lexical, with lexical differences mainly restricted to ancestral language words. These are the same kinds of difference that are invoked when one asks about the differences between Barunga and Roper Kriol.

NGAN'GIWATYFALA ORTHOGRAPHY

At this stage it is too early to develop a Ngan'giwatyfala orthography, partly because not enough of the language has been recorded and analysed, but also because of the delicate relationship between members of the community and anyone who wishes to discuss creole. There are, of course, linguistic and pedagogical reasons for aiming at an orthography that corresponds as nearly as possible to the sound system of the language. It is also desirable to use symbols which are available on typewriters and so on, and which are not too different from those used in other languages. But beyond factors such as these, it is important that an orthography is acceptable to those who will use it — the speakers of the languages themselves. This is particularly significant where a language is being written for the first time by those who are not members of the local community. Thus, it is essential that speakers of a language cooperate in the design of an orthography. At Nauiyu Nambiyu there is considerable antagonism towards creole and reluctance to participate in activities that might promote it, such as writing it down. Hence, it is difficult to obtain the kinds of input from the community that would be necessary to create an acceptable orthography.

It is thus important to open up debate about linguistic matters with members of the community, to identify the problems as they appear to an outsider and to offer suggestions about possible courses of action. It cannot be denied that children in the community are speaking creole and that this must have some impact on their progress in the school system in which they are obliged to participate. Not only community members, but those people who are in the community as school teachers, need to be involved in the process of deciding what the implications of creole are for the education of the children.

Furthermore, Ngan'giwatyfala does not exist in isolation. In fact, all over the Northern Territory and Western Australia people speak varieties of creole or non-standard English that are related to each other in some way. It is not only at Nauiyu Nambiyu that children in a community are speaking a creole which is not being acknowledged formally by the school or community and that the children's access to the skills which the community hopes they will gain from a school education is probably being hampered by the fact that they speak a creole.

It is worth noting here that where written Kriol is already in use, it is not necessarily used in all possible situations. At Barunga, Kriol has been used in the bilingual program there for thirteen years, but its use is mainly confined to the school. It is only amongst members of the Christian community that Kriol literacy is used outside the school and only in that context that there is intra-community communication through the medium of Kriol literacy. Within Barunga, English is generally used as the medium for written communication, such as notices in the shop or on the Council notice board. In such a small community there is relatively little need for written communication and no tradition of using it among community members.

So far as communication with the wider community is concerned, English is, and is likely to remain, the medium of communication. The only likely use for written Kriol is for the dissemination of information about government projects and suchlike, but even this seems improbable in view of the increasing use of television and video to perform this kind of function. At Ngukurr, a team of educators from the Northern Territory Power and Water Authority conducted a campaign to teach people about conservation of resources, but they did this through personal contact and videos, not through writing. The widespread ownership of televisions and video equipment, in contrast to the lack of writing materials in Aboriginal communities, suggests that this situation may continue. Indeed, in the wider Australian community it is through the electronic media that information is most rapidly and effectively disseminated to the general public.

Thus it seems reasonable to assume that if written creole is ever used in Nauiyu Nambiyu, its use too may be restricted to educational purposes within the community. In view of this it is worth examining the possibility of devising an orthography specifically for use in that community, or in others that use the same dialect. There are two possibilities, one is using the Ngan'gityemerri orthography, or a modified version of it, the other is to have a completely separate orthography based neither on Ngan'gityemerri nor on Kriol. These two possibilities will be considered in turn.

DESIGNING AN ORTHOGRAPHY

One obvious way to write Ngan'giwatyfala would be to use the local orthography of Ngan'gityemerri. But the sounds of the two languages are in fact rather different. Like most Australian languages, Ngan'gityemerri has no fricative sounds such as [s], [z] and [h]. It is necessary to represent these sounds in Ngan'giwatyfala and a similar need to extend Ngan'gityemerri symbols arises within vowels. Once such additions or changes are made– and reflected in a substantial proportion of the words of the language — it is no longer the case that one is using the local orthography. Any supposed advantage of similarity or compatibility between two spelling systems is undermined.

A second possibility would be to use the Kriol orthography already in use at Barunga and Ngukurr. Some minor modifications would still be needed — for example, the addition of the symbol *f* to cater for Ngan'giwatyfala pronunciations such as *mifala* 'we' rather than Kriol *mibala* — but a strong argument for using the existing Kriol orthography is that it has been developed already and is relatively widely known. It is used not only in scholarly works about Kriol, but there are also many books written in the language for use in schools and a Kriol version of the Bible. If it were used for writing Ngan'giwatyfala and other varieties of creole that have not yet been written, there could ultimately be a very extensive range of communities that would share a writing system. It would be possible to produce written texts that could be used in creole-speaking areas all over the Northern Territory and there would be the potential for the dissemination of written information to large numbers of people.

On the other hand, there are problems that are not so easily overcome as minor modifications to the use of symbols. It is clear that varieties of creole are spoken differently. Moreover, the differences between varieties are important to speakers. Kevin Rodgers, principal of the Ngukurr school and a Kriol speaker, has explained why Ngukurr people do not want Kriol material for their school to be produced at Barunga:

> It is important to write the dialect of Kriol that is spoken in Ngukurr and not that spoken in Barunga, since the sounds and some vocabulary of the Ngukurr dialect is related to the local traditional languages and not to the traditional languages spoken at Barunga. (1988)

Thus, even within the areas where people acknowledge that they all speak Kriol, there are problems about using the written form. Kriol orthography allows dialectal variation to be manifested so that, for example, the word for 'go', can be written *go* or *gu* according to local pronunciation. But this means that written material produced by the speaker of one dialect is regarded as unsuitable teaching material in areas where another dialect is spoken. There is a strong feeling within communities that their identity is reflected in the variety that they use. Thus, there is hostility towards standardising written Kriol, towards creating a written form that is no-one's dialect but that everyone could read. Rodgers writes:

> The Barunga school books were influenced by non-Aboriginal teacher linguists who seem to have developed a 'School Kriol' dialect, which is more than simply the difference between oral and written Kriol modes.

The test of any such orthography will of course be whether it is acceptable to speakers. At present no orthography is acceptable. Moreover, very few people are familiar with the Ngan'gityemerri orthography, making it difficult to consult community members about the extent to which they would like Ngan'giwatyfala orthography to be based upon it. It seems likely that the evolution of an orthography for Ngan'giwatyfala will depend to some extent on whether the community develops a strong interest in writing Ngan'gityemerri. If they do, then using that orthography as a basis for creole orthography may be acceptable. If not, then it might be more appropriate to use the Kriol orthography, if indeed Ngan'giwatyfala is ever written by its speakers. Ngan'giwatyfala speakers may continue to regard the variety as a purely oral mode of communication so that the question of how to write it will remain forever merely a matter of debate among linguists.

THE FUTURE OF CREOLE LITERACY

The issues in creole literacy include both practical linguistic questions relating to the precise form of the orthography and more delicate questions relating to notions of linguistic and cultural identity. The most pressing issue, however, is what linguists and educators should or can do to facilitate language education that is appropriate to the needs of Aboriginal people in communities where creole is spoken. With hindsight, it is easy to identify the mistakes in apparently well-meant efforts. At a local level, consultation and liaison with local Aboriginal people with an interest in education are possible and desirable. More important, in my opinion, is a willingness to share information freely. To empower Aboriginal people in ways that allow them to challenge and debate such issues, they need to have free access to the information with which non-Aboriginal people work. In order to do this they need access to the education system that informs the debate. Yet, when non-Aboriginal people make decisions about language that seem to them necessary to facilitate that access, they may be guilty of cultural imperialism. It is only by making explicit, at every stage, our cultural assumptions; by being prepared to learn about and respect those of others; and, most importantly, by not judging those of others by the criteria intrinsic to our own, that we can hope to maintain the integrity of our culture and that of anyone with whom we are in contact.

A TEXT IN THREE ORTHOGRAPHIES

To illustrate the issues raised in this chapter, the same story is given below in three different orthographies. The story is a spoken narrative, not originally written down. But the three transcriptions of it will show the differences mentioned above. A translation to English is included at the end. (Only the second transcription is punctuated because only it has adopted a punctuation system.)

Ngan'gityemerri orthography

(Names are left in English spelling. Words that break normal rules of Ngan'gityemerri orthography are marked with an asterisk.)

wan satidey* muning mi Kiti en u* nadawan Molly Patricia Mercia Dominica mela bin askim* gida* bla* gu anting langa ada* said* langa wut* dat* pleis* na im kul* Dangerous Gap init Dangerous Gap wel mela bin askim* bla* Patricia asbin* imin drupimuf* mela la rud* en mela bin wuk frum* la dat* kuna* rait* bak la dat* lilwan krik* wen dat wen dey bin syutim wan ulmen gat gan mela bin dringgimbat* wata* de na wel mela bin stat* klaimapbat* untup* la il en ay bin stat* lukranbat* blanga* we dem* pukupany wen dey* bin digimbat mela bin fanydimbat sam* fresywan* uwul* we dey* bin digimbat wel ay bin gu ratybek* la wan kuna* en ay bin fanydim* syugubeg* langa entpit* en imin isiwan bla* tegimat tufala bin afum lilwan eks* en Patricia imin biyany imin sidanabat* la wan lilwan ruk* en im from* samting* imin telim yu luk andanit* en imin luk dat pukupany* wel imin raty* andanit* wel mela kudan tekimetim tyepeka end* Patricia imin telim mi wan pukupany* im iya ay kan tekimbat yu ken alpum mi en imin gifit mi dat ukwaya ay bin tray* tekimbat* nating* wel frum* de mela bin mufimbat wan ruk* wel mi ay bin duwim dat* wek tekimbat* dat* ruk* afta* ay bin pulimat dat* pukupany* bat imin unli* lil bebiwan wel mela bin gudaun* daun* na wel mela ai bin testi* bla* wata* bat nu wata* bin de wal mela bin klaimap* ran* an ran* ai bin get disi mela bin gu en mela bin afum wan dug* im neim* Sopi wel ai bin telim Patricia en Marita bla* gudan lukranabat wata* dey bin fanydim liliwan watahol* bat imin hotwan* dat* wata* ay kudun drinkim* wel mela bin go ratyaran* dat* dug* imin tayid* na frum* klaimapbat* la il imin afta* sidan* la wanim busyisy wal mi ay bin anggri* bla* taka mela bin tekim nu* taka de la dat il ay bin lafta* katimbat* merrepen ay bin itimbat* datan* na ay bin itimbat* itimbat* tu en ay bin megim dem* adamob* katimbat mu*

> tufala bin anggri* frum* de mela bin dringgimbat* wata* imin sey* faif* u* klok* na mela bin wuk bek mela wukbek we Andi bin drupimuf* mela mela luk dat* redwan* ka imin de na weitweitbat* bla* mela en mela bin kambek kemp den

As can be seen almost thirty per cent of words are problematic, and some of those are problematic in several ways. It seems to be clear that the orthography of Ngan'gityemerri is, therefore, unsuitable as a medium for writing Ngan'giwatyfala.

Kriol orthography

(Some minor modifications have been made to usual Kriol.)

> Wan Satidei moning mi Kitty en hu nathawan? Molly, Patricia, Mercia, Dominica mela bin askim githa bla gu anting langa atha said langa, wat that pleis na im kal? (Dangerous Gap intit?) Dangerous Gap. Wel mela bin askim bla Patricia asbin. Imin tekim mela. Imin dropimof mela la rod. En mela bin wok from la thad kona rait bak la thad liliwan krik wen dat wen dei bin shutim wan ulmen deya gat gan. Mela bin dringgimbat wada deya na. Wel mela bin stat klaimapbat ontop la il en ai bin stat lukranabat blanga weya that pokupain wen thei bin digimbat. Mela bin faindimbat sam freshwan owul we thei bin digimbat. Wel ai bin gu raitbek la wan kona en ai bin faindim shugabeg langa entpit en imin isiwan bla tegimaut mela bin abum liliwan eks. En Patricia imin biyain. Imin sidanabat la wan lilwan rok en im from samthing imin telim yu luk andanith en imin luk thad pokupain. Wal imin rait andanith wel mela kudun tekimautim tjepeka. En Patricia imin telim mi 'Wan pokupain im iya ai kaan tekimbat yu kan alpum mi?' En imin gibit mi thad ukwaiya. Ai bin trai teikimaut, nathing. Wel from theya mela bin mubimbat wan rok wel mi ai bin duing that wek tekimatbat that rok afta ai bin pulimat that pokupain bat imin onli lil beibiwan. Wal mela bin gudaun daun na. Wel mela, ai bin testi bla wada. Bat no wada bin deya wal mela bin klaimap ran en ran en ai bin get disi. Mela bin gu en mela bin abum wan dog im neim Sopi. Wel ai bin telim Patricia en Marita bla gudaun lukraunabaut wada. Dei bin faindim lilwan wadahol bat imin hotwan that wada. Ai kudan drinkim. Wal mela bin go raitaran with thad dog imin tayid na bla klaimapbat thad il imin afta sidaun la wanim bushish. Wal mi ai bin anggri bla taka. Mela bin tekim no taka deya la that il. Ai bin lafta kadimbat Merrepen. Ai bin idimbat tharran na. (Idimbat Merrepen?) Mm. (Yu kan idim?) Ai bin idimbat, idimbat tu, en ai bin

mekim that nathamob katimbat mo. Tufala bin anggri tu. From theya mela bin dringgimbat wada. Imin sei faif o klok na mela bin wok bek. Mela wokbek weya Andy imin dropimof mela. Mela luk that redwan ka imin deya na weitweit bla mela. En mela bin kambek kemp den.

Local orthography

wan satidey moning mi Kiti en hu nadawan Molly Patricia Mercia Dominica mela bin askim gida bla gu anting langa ada sayd langa wot dat pleys na im kol Dangerous Gap init Dangerous Gap wel mela bin askim bla Patricia asbin imin drupimuf mela la rod en mela bin wok from la dat kona raty bak la dat lilwan krik wen dat wen dey bin syutim wan ulmen gat gan mela bin dringgimbat wata de na wel mela bin stat klaymapbat ontop la il en ay bin stat lukranbat blanga we dem pukupany wen dey bin digimbat mela bin fanydimbat sam fresywan uwul we dey bin digimbat wel ay bin gu ratybek la wan kona en ay bin fanydim syugubeg langa entpit en imin isiwan bla tegimat tufala bin afum lilwan eks en Patricia imin biyany imin sidanabat la wan lilwan rok en im from samthing imin telim yu luk andanit en imin luk dat pukupany wel imin raty andanit wel mela kudan tekimetim tyepeka end Patricia imin telim mi wan pukupany im iya ay kan tekimbat yu ken alpum mi en imin gifit mi dat ukwaya ay bin tray tekimbat nating wel from de mela bin mufimbat wan rok wel mi ay bin duwim dat wek tekimbat dat rok afta ay bin pulimat dat pukupany bat imin onli lil bebiwan wel mela bin gudaun daun na wel mela ai bin testi bla wata bat no wata bin de wal mela bin klaimap ran en ran ai bin get disi mela bin gu en mela bin afum wan dog im neym Sopi wel ai bin telim Patricia en Marita bla gudan lukranabat wata dey bin fanydim liliwan watahol bat imin hotwan dat wata ay kudun drinkim wel mela bin go ratyaran dat dog imin tayid na from klaimapbat la il imin afta sidan la wanim busyisy wal mi ay bin anggri bla taka mela bin tekim no taka de la dat il ay bin lafta katimbat merrepen ay bin itimbat datan na ay bin itimbat itimbat tu en ay bin megim dem adamob katimbat mo tufala bin anggri from de mela bin dringgimbat wata imin sey faif o klok na mela bin wuk bek mela wukbek we Andi bin dropimof mela mela luk dat redwan ka imin de na weytweytbat bla mela en mela bin kambek kemp den

English translation

One Saturday morning me Kitty and who else, Molly, Patricia, Mercia and Dominica, we all decided amongst ourselves that we would go hunting together over the other side [of the river] at, what's that place called, Dangerous Gap isn't it? Dangerous Gap. Well we asked Patricia's husband to take us and he dropped us off on the road and we walked from the corner all the way back to the little creek where they shot an old man, with a gun. We had a drink of water there then we started climbing to the top of the hill and looking around for where the echidnas had been digging. We found some recent holes where they had been digging. Well I went all the way back to one corner and I found some honey in an antbed and it was easy to get out. Two of them had a little axe and Patricia was further back. She'd been sitting down on a little rock and something told her to look under the rock and she saw an echidna. It was right underneath. Well we couldn't reach it apparently. And Patricia told me, 'There's an echidna here. I can't get it out. Can you help me?' She gave me the hook wire. I tried to take it out but I couldn't. Well after that we were moving the rock, well I was doing the work, moving the rock, and then I pulled out the echidna but it was only a baby. Well we went all the way down then, well we, I, wanted a drink of water and there wasn't any water there. We climbed up again round and round and I got dizzy. We went on and we had a dog with us, called Sopi. Well I told Patricia and Marita to go down and look for water. They found a little waterhole but the water was hot and I couldn't drink it. Well we went all over the place with that dog. It was tired after climbing the hill and it had to rest in the whatchamacallit, the bushes. Well, as for me, I was hungry. We hadn't taken any food there and I had to cut some sand palm nuts. I was eating them, I was eating two of them and I made the others cut more. The other two were hungry too. After that we were drinking water, it was about five o'clock then. We walked back. We walked back to where Andy had dropped us off. We saw that red car. He was waiting for us and we returned to the camp then.

FOR DISCUSSION

1. Consider the ways in which your own spoken dialect and written forms of English reflect your cultural identity. As a group, identify differences or similarities among your dialects and see if you can find correlations with cultural differences or similarities.

2. It has been suggested (Wijk 1977) that the spelling of English should be regularised. An example of the system he proposes is included here:

> It shood be noted, on the wun hand, that certen speech sounds ar reprezented by several fonic units, and, on the uther, that certen fonic units ar uzed to denote more than wun sound. This may seem sumwhot strainge at first.

What is your reaction to his suggestion? Does the fact that Wijk is not a native English speaker affect your feelings about his suggestion?

3. As mentioned in the preceding article, many people, both Aboriginal and non-Aboriginal, consider creole a threat to both access to English and maintenance of indigenous languages. In view of limited funding for language and education programs, discuss your priorities were you to be responsible for language policy in this area.

REFERENCES

Dixon, R.M.W.
1980 *The Languages of Australia*, Cambridge University Press, Cambridge.

Rodgers, K.
1988 Critical Review of Language Survey by John Sandefur, unpublished MS.

Wijk, A.
1977 *Regularized English Regularized Inglish. A Proposal for an Effective Solution of the Reading Problem in the English-Speaking Countries*, Almqvist and Wiksell, Stockholm.

Yunupingu, B.
1986–87 Language-Use in Yirrkala. In *D-BATE: Aboriginal Teachers Write about Their Community Languages*, Deakin University and Batchelor College of Aboriginal Teacher Education, NT.

CHAPTER

12 THE LANGUAGE OF OPPRESSION: THE BOLDEN CASE, VICTORIA 1845

Michael Christie

STICKS AND STONES WILL BREAK MY BONES...

In 1841 in an area we know today as the Western District of Victoria, two Aborigines were killed while crossing the run of the squatter, George Sandford Bolden. The Aborigines were husband and wife. The man was shot at close range, while the woman was horsewhipped so severely that she died from the beating. Their son escaped and reported the incident to the Protector for Aborigines in that district, Charles Sievewright. Sievewright, who doubled as the local justice of peace, took down Bolden's explanation of what had happened and eventually managed to have Bolden stand trial for the killings. The criminal trial briefs are still extant and among them is Bolden's original deposition made in Sievewright's presence.

It is a brief handwritten deposition devoid of detail. In it Bolden stated that, while out mustering with his men, he came upon three Aborigines whom he tried to drive away with stockwhips. The Aboriginal man attempted to pull him from his horse, so he shot him in the stomach. He fired once again as the man took refuge in a waterhole and this second shot was fatal. The woman died from wounds to the head.

Bolden's language is bland and matter-of-fact. It is the language of a man intent on not saying too much, for fear of incriminating himself. The action and movement that must have characterised that brief, tragic encounter are missing. In his deposition Bolden says impassively that 'the second shot was fatal' and that the woman 'died from her wounds'. The young boy who witnessed the killing of his parents and reported it to Sievewright is simply one of 'three Aborigines' (Bolden 1841). The sex and age of the group is not mentioned nor is the fact that they were a family, crossing what was to them traditional tribal land.

There are many ways of describing what happened on that day. A dispassionate coroner, interested only in the events as an explanation of the cause of death, might have described it as follows: 'Two otherwise healthy human beings died, the female because of subdural bleeding caused by heavy blows to the head, the male because of the loss of blood and dysfunction of vital organs caused by gunshot wounds to the body'. As in Bolden's deposition there would be a heavy use of the passive voice.

In my own opening I tried to state the facts of the case as unemotively as possible. The woman was hit with a stockwhip. The correct verb used for this action is 'to horsewhip'. But the phrase stands out simply because the action of whipping a woman to death is horrifying no matter how it is described. Bolden's phrase 'died from head wounds' is as understated as one can get. To the surprised victims the 'incident' of the record book was sudden, unprovoked, cold-blooded murder. To their tribespeople it was an act of war.

How would the boy himself have described this event that so abruptly left him orphaned? His images and the words would certainly be far more graphic than those of Bolden, so anxious to play down what he and other squatters considered a routine 'clearing operation'. At some point, as the family walked across the flats they must have heard, above the sounds of the bush, a sound unlike that of wallabies on the move, a sound that was rhythmic and heavy, and that grew louder as it approached. When Bolden and his men reached the group on their horses, there must have been shouts, running feet, the wheeling of horses, the crack of whips.

The woman did not simply die. She was hit again and again, perhaps with the handle of the whips as well as the leather hide itself. There was blood and horse sweat and cries of pain. There was also a hopeless uneven struggle as the black man tried to protect himself and his family, as he tugged on a whip in the hope of dislodging at least one of his assailants. There was the sound of gunshots, the acrid smell of gunsmoke, a bloody trail to a waterhole, two black bodies in the grass.

The boy was never allowed to give his version of what happened to the court. If he had, we might have some inkling of his terror on that day. Perhaps he hid, listening in horror to the dull thud of the gunshots. Perhaps it was he who first found his mother once the horsemen had ridden away, her head crushed like the heads of the goannas they may have hunted that day. The documents give no hint of the hurt or the despair or the sense of loss of a boy who, in a single afternoon on the river flats, saw both his parents die.

Instead, we have the journalese of a newspaper report, in which we are told that Judge Willis advised the jury to acquit the defendant ('the brother of a near and respected neighbour of mine') because there is 'a clear and distinct right to turn any person off their property, that may come on it for the purpose of aggression or not' (*Port Phillip Gazette* 1841). Bolden escaped without censure and his reputation among white settlers was enhanced among his peers because of 'his firm handling' of the blacks.

The incident was certainly no more horrific than many others that occurred on the Australian frontier. A few years earlier, in June 1838, twenty-eight Aborigines, mainly women and children, had been shot and mutilated and their bodies burned on a run near Myall Creek, in the Liverpool Plains area (*Australian* 1841). In another incident, in February 1842, at Muston's Creek in the Western District, eight whites surrounded a ti-tree clump where two Aboriginal families were sleeping and fired at them indiscriminately. Two men and a woman escaped with gunshot wounds but a child and three women, one of whom was pregnant, were killed. The massacre, according to testimony gathered by Sievewright, was premeditated and carried out to relieve the boredom of a summer evening (*Port Phillip Gazette* 1843).

DESCRIBING VIOLENCE

Until the 1970s such incidents were rarely alluded to in Australian history books and, when they were, they were often glossed over or depicted from the whites' point of view. Our knowledge of the frontier comes mainly from the written record, which is, almost without exception, couched in English. There is some variation in style and perspective among official records and newspapers, which make up the largest proportion of the documents. There is even more diversity in the private letters and journals of individuals. But what is remarkable is the consistency of the language used to describe frontier conflict between whites and blacks. The Aborigines' actions are usually termed 'attacks, incursions, atrocities, outrages, crimes, murders, or depredations', whereas the activities of the squatters and border police are referred to as 'incidents, clearing operations, self defence, punitive expeditions or police actions'. Judge Willis talked about 'turning off' trespassers. Ironically, in the 'flash language' of the convicts, to 'turn off' meant to kill. There are a few diaries (see below) where the authors avoid euphemism and some of the evidence given at contemporary Royal Commissions is often unequivocal and frank regarding the violent treatment of the Aborigines.

Since 1970 revisionist historians have done a great deal to balance our picture of what occurred during the colonisation of Australia. But there is still a need to challenge historical descriptions, to investigate the language used, and to ask who said what, when and why. This is particularly important when the only records remaining are official documents, or when commentary on events is in the form of newspaper reports. For example, in the incidents mentioned above, white men were tried for the deaths of Aborigines but the words of the Aborigines (albeit translated) were never heard, because Aboriginal evidence was inadmissible in court. Although they were theoretically British subjects (because the Crown had claimed Australia and all within it as its own), the Aborigines were excluded as witnesses, because, it was argued, they were heathens and as such could not take the oath by swearing on the Bible.

As a result our knowledge of events is based on descriptions that have been sanitised or wrapped in the cotton wool of euphemism. At the Bolden trial Sievewright put the boy's case to the court: but, according to him, the evidence was ridiculed. He himself, as a public servant, was obliged to concur with Judge Willis's ruling that the blacks had been trespassing because of the legal fiction that Australia had been 'unoccupied and waste' at the time of discovery and, therefore, all land belonged to the Crown by right of discovery. The Crown abrogated the right to dispose of it as it wished, subdividing land into town allotments and leasing land in the interior to the graziers. A ruling, such as that of Judge Willis, set legal precedents for dealing with Aboriginal 'trespassers' and a squatter's lease became, in effect, a licence to kill.

I have focused on the Bolden case because in this incident the squatter himself is brought to trial. In most cases the men involved in frontier atrocities were pastoral workers who were either ex-convicts or ticket-of-leave men. It was important for those who took pride in British culture to see incidents such as Myall Creek (where the ferocity of the killing was hard to deny) as the work of the 'debased and criminal element in society' and unrepresentative of the British type. It is true that shepherds, hutkeepers, bark gatherers, and bullockies, some of whom had themselves been brutalised by the British penal code, were often responsible for offences against the blacks, but they by no means had a monopoly on racial violence.

Bolden was not an ex-convict. Like many squatters he came from a good family and considered himself to be a gentleman. If we can believe the private journals of squatters, written during the frontier period, it would seem that Bolden was not unrepresentative of his class. Henry Meyrick, in describing the activities of his fellow squatters in Gippsland, wrote that Aboriginal 'men, women and children were shot whenever they can be met with' and that although he himself would 'not ride into a camp and fire on them indiscriminately, as is the custom here whenever smoke is seen', he did admit that 'if I caught a black actually killing my sheep I would shoot him with as little remorse as I would a wild dog' (Meyrick 30 April 1846).

Neil Black, another gentleman squatter, deliberately took up a run that had already been 'cleared' of blacks by a former overseer, Frederick Taylor. Black noted in his diary that he had let another do the job because 'I could not stand the thought of murdering them, and to tell the truth I believe it is impossible to take up a new run without doing so, at least the chances are 50 to 1' (Black 1839–41, 43).

What is surprising in Black's diary is his frankness. He refers to the killing of blacks as murder. But it is also important to note that even with Meyrick and Black, language and action are intertwined. Meyrick, in his diary entry, calls the Aborigines 'men, women and children' when they are sitting by their camp fires doing no harm to him, but likens them to wild dogs when they attack his sheep. In the first instance he would never fire on them at random, in the latter he would shoot them remorselessly.

If, as Black claimed, 'two thirds of the squatters does not care a single straw about taking the life of natives', we need to ask what it was that enabled well-educated gentlemen to act in such a manner? Why was it, then, that the second sons of respectable British landholders, who made up a good proportion of the squatters, could kill with such little consideration for the law and such little remorse for the loss of human life? How do we explain their ability to shoot or poison whole groups of Aborigines in their push for new or richer pasture land? And how could they still hold their head high in a society that they claimed represented the acme of civilisation?

The answer is very complicated but part of the explanation is that Aborigines were so often spoken of as less than human that it became possible even for educated people to begin to believe such rhetoric and to treat them as such. The oppression of the Aborigines began with words.

POPULAR THEORISING ABOUT RACE

European philosophers such as Aquinas held that all creatures were arranged in an ascending order from the simplest organism, through primates and humans to spiritual beings. In the seventeenth century philosophers began to apply this concept of 'the Great Chain of Being' to human society. Some concentrated on differences in languages, others on the physical variety among people of different races. Most of them produced schemes for what they called the 'progressive stages of human development'. Had they avoided value judgements, the schemes might have served as a useful categorisation of world economic systems but instead, by ranking those systems in order of excellence and using terms such as 'savagery', these philosophers reinforced the cultural chauvinism of Europeans at the expense of other races, most notably the black races. Their so-called scale of civilisation placed the Europeans first and the blacks last.

As more and more explorers and navigators had contact with the great south land, references to Australian Aborigines increased. Dampier's scathing description of Aborigines began to appear in more intellectual works as evidence of the degrees and differences among human beings. His phrase that the Aborigines '...setting aside the Human Shape...differ little from brutes' is repeated again and again, both in philosophical works and in the books of the early nineteenth century ethnologists (Dampier 1927, 312).

Ethnology, or the study of human groups, blossomed in the early 1800s. One reason was the fierce debate that raged over the rights and wrongs of slavery. The new 'science' of ethnology was employed by both sides in a particularly nasty war of words. The debate did nothing to advance the image of Aboriginal people in the minds of the colonisers, whether they were gentlemen squatters or ex-convicts. Indeed, the slavery debate added a whole new set of racist words and concepts to an already rich literature. In order to justify slavery, proponents drew support from the writings of those philosophers who developed the idea of 'the Great Chain of Being', and argued that slavery benefited the savages because it replaced a life of idleness with a life of sustained work, the basis of progress and civilisation. Others quoted the Bible, saying that the life of a slave under a Christian master was preferable to the life of a 'debased and demoralized savage'. Besides, hadn't Noah cursed the sons of Ham and said that they would serve the sons of Japheth (Genesis 9:18–27)? Conveniently, the black races were held to be descended from Ham and the white races from Japheth. The opponents appealed to Christian charity, claiming that it was precisely because the blacks were inferior that they deserved to be evangelised rather than exploited.

The debate polarised the two main theories of human origin: monogenesis and polygenesis. In simple terms, monogenesists argued that the various races were all descendants of Adam and Eve; but some peoples had degenerated from an original, common excellence. The polygenesists, on the other hand, insisted that such differences could not have emerged in the 6,000 years since creation and that the various races were the result of separate creative acts. The more radical polygenesists claimed that the races not only were created separate and unequal but were in fact distinct species.

One writer who gave support to the polygenesist position was Edward Long. In his popular *History of Jamaica* (1970 [1774]), Long quoted the work of anatomists and biologists to emphasise what he claimed were similarities between blacks and apes. In his opinion, blacks were 'brutish, ignorant, idle, crafty, treacherous, thievish, mistrustful and superstitious' and slavery was a fitting occupation for them. The publication of Charles White's *An Account of the Regular Gradations in Man* (1799) added weight to Long's writing and reinforced the racial prejudices of planters, colonisers and travellers. According to White, Negroes were a distinct species closer to apes than Caucasians. They had 'smaller brains, larger sexual organs, an ape-like odour and an animal-like immunity to pain' (Harris 1968, 89–90). Although most people supported the monegenesist position because it accorded with the Christian version of events, the racial stereotypes put forward by people like Long and White stuck and found their way into the pages of popular magazines and journals.

Unfortunately for the Aborigines, the colonisers who were taking their land seemed to be all too well acquainted with these arguments and assertions. In many cases one hears the exact phrase repeated. On the basis of his brief encounter with the Port Phillip blacks in 1803, Lieutenant Tuckey described them as 'a cruel, crafty, thievish race' without a redeeming feature (1805, 167–85). Barron Field, in his *Geographical Memoirs of New South Wales*, drew on the ethnologist Pritchard's work for his section on the Aborigines, a people he described as the 'lowest among the varieties of human species' (1825, 82). This conclusion crops up again and again in the works of colonial writers.

A good number of these colonial writers had been squatters themselves and many of these books were aimed at the literate landholders and their families. They were also regular subscribers to the *Times* and to periodicals such as *Blackwoods*, the *Quarterly*, and the *Edinburgh Review*, and to their colonial equivalents, the *New South Wales Magazine* and the *Colonial Literary Review*. From such reading they absorbed popularised theories as well as detailed and often derogatory information on the lifestyle and customs of 'savage tribes', including the Australian Aborigines.

JUSTIFYING VIOLENCE

Thus, many of the squatters, even before they arrived in Australia, had internalised a negative way of thinking about Aborigines and acquired a language to express those thoughts. The intellectual argument that the Aborigines more closely resembled 'the ourang outangs than men' made it easier for the squatter to treat the Aborigines as subhuman, to lump them with the dingo and shoot them as a 'rural pest'. In a chilling commentary on Henry Meyrick's words, the Reverend W. Yate told the House of Commons Select Committee on Aborigines in 1838:

> I have heard again and again people say that they (the Aborigines) are nothing better than dogs, and that it was not more harm to shoot them, than it would be to shoot a dog when he barks at you (Yate 1838, 202).

Not all ministers of religion shared Yate's disgust at this. In his book *Kangaroo Land* (1862) the Reverend A. Polehampton insisted that 'the Australian blacks are little less ugly than gorillas, which indeed to my mind they much more nearly resemble than white men or the higher types of blacks' (Polehampton 1862, 154). The Reverend D.M. McKenzie, echoing Charles White, claimed that the Aborigines had a particularly strong and disagreeable odour, 'so strong...that cattle smell it at a distance' (1851, 135).

Squatters like Alexander Majoribanks, who tried their hand at writing, show us just how influenced they were by what they read. Majoribanks quoted and agreed with philosophers who argued that Aborigines not only had thicker skulls but smaller crania than whites. According to another squatter, Hugh Jamieson, who disagreed with the likes of Majoribanks, disdain of the Aborigines was not confined to the colonies. 'The almost universal opinion of the world', he wrote, 'seems to assign the Aboriginal natives of Australia to the very lowest place in the scale of civilisation and of intellect' (Bride 1898, 269).

My contention that words abetted deeds on the frontier is borne out by another colonial writer, Thomas Bartlett. Writing in 1843, a couple of years after the Bolden incident, Bartlett insisted that there was a large group of settlers who did not consider the Aborigines to be fellow creatures at all and used the 'harshest and most severe measures towards them' (Bartlett 1843, 65). Christopher Hodgson agreed, referring to settlers who saw the Aborigines as 'a species of similar acaudata, or tailless monkey', to be hunted down and exterminated (Hodgson 1846, 299). Alexander Majoribanks, quoted above, was one such squatter. 'The Aborigines', he wrote, 'are universally allowed to be the lowest race of savages in the known world and their extirpation would be of great benefit to the whole of the country' (Majoribanks 1847, 82, 249). Such racist language not only paved the way for the oppression of Aborigines but also served as a more acceptable excuse for actions that were motivated by economic greed. As the *Colonist* pointed out in an editorial on 16 January 1839:

> Sordid interest is at the root of all this anti-aborigine feeling. Because the primitive lords of the soil interfere in some of the frontier stations with the easy and lucrative grazing of cattle and sheep, they are felt by the sensitive pockets of the graziers to be a nuisance; and the best plea these 'gentlemen' can set up for their rights to abate the nuisance by the summary process of stabbing, shooting, burning and 'poisoning', is that the offenders are below the level of the white man's species.

The academic theories about racial differences and the intellectuals' disgust at Aboriginal life and culture filtered through to illiterate whites. Most convicts and immigrant labourers also arrived in Australia with a distorted and prejudiced view of the Aborigines. Once in Australia such misconceptions were aggravated by fear, a fear that was often cultivated by jailers and squatters as a means of preventing convicts or workers from escaping. The conclusions of racial theorists were often encapsulated in the form of catchcries, sayings, proverbs and jokes. We have seen how hackneyed phrases such as 'Aborigines are raised but little above brute creation' appear again and again in the literature. Proverbs such as 'never trust a savage' and racist jokes about the smell and sexuality of Aborigines were part of the colonial vernacular.

The language of the rural worker, and the hatred of the Aborigines that it implied, was undoubtedly shaped in part by the literature of the day. But the white workers' interaction with the blacks is at least more easily explained than that of their educated counterparts, who often spoke of the civilising influence of British colonisation.

CONCLUSION

This chapter began with a schoolyard chant 'sticks and stones will break my bones but names will never hurt me'. It is a defiant and somewhat pitiful cry.

The point of this chapter is that names do hurt, that racist language and racist ideas are the precursors of racist action, that it is easier to use sticks and stones, guns and swords, poison or the pox, if you have already named your victims, described them as worthless and subhuman. It is not an original thesis nor a completed one. The squatters who used such general terms of abuse in regard to the Aborigines interacted with them in more ways than those mentioned above. There was an exchange — a two-way process occurring as the frontier moved — that belies some of the language and attitudes outlined above. Words and action went hand in hand on the frontier.

It suited squatters to redefine Aboriginal people when they needed their labour or their sexual favours. But when squatters bought cheap land, Aboriginal land, as they did on the frontier, the exchange between black and white was tragic and one-sided for the Aborigines. It was then that the racist stereotypes were of most use to the land-hungry squatter who might have to kill the original owners in order to take the land. Sticks and stones will break your bones but names will also hurt you.

FOR DISCUSSION

1. List all the words and phrases you can think of that use colour, particularly black and white, for positive or negative purposes. Can you explain or justify these uses?

2. There is a campaign today to eradicate 'sexist' language. Do phrases such as 'blacken one's character', or those you listed above, constitute 'racist' language? Would you advocate eliminating such words or phrases?

3. The comedian Lenny Bruce tried to take the sting out of derogatory terms like 'nigger' and 'wog' by getting those who were insulted to laugh at the labels rather than take offence at them. Do you think this is a solution?

4. Racism has often been bolstered by pseudo-scientific theories. Can you think of any current theories that lend support to racism? Can you discredit them?

REFERENCES

***Australian* [newspaper]**
1841 8 December.

Bartlett, T.
1843 *New Holland*, Smith and Son, London.

Black, N.
1839–41 Diary, typescript copy of original, MS 8996, La Trobe Library, Melbourne.

Bolden, G.S.
1841 Deposition 24 October, Queen v Bolden, Crown Law Office files, Criminal Trial Briefs, series 30, Public Record Office of Victoria.

Bride, T.F.
1898 *Letters from Victorian Pioneers*, Victorian Government Printer, Melbourne.

Byrne, J.C.
1848 *Twelve Years Wandering in the British Colonies from 1835–47*, 2 vols, Bentley, London.

***Colonist* [newspaper]**
1839 16 January.

Dampier, W.A.
1927 *A New Voyage Round the World*, Edited by N.M. Penzer, The Argonaut Press, London.

Field, B. (ed)
1825 *Geographical Memoirs of New South Wales*, Murray, London.

Harris, M.
1968 *The Rise of Anthropological Theory: A History of Theories of Culture*, Routledge and Kegan Paul, London.

Hodgson, C.
1846 *Reminiscences of Australia with Hints on the Squatter's Life*, Wright, London.

Long, E.
1970
[1774] *History of Jamaica*, 3 vols, Cass, London.

Majoribanks, A.
1847 *Travels in New South Wales*, Smith, Elder and Co, London.

McKenzie, D.M.
1851 *Ten Years in Australia*, Orr and Co, London.

Meyrick, H.H.
1840–47 Letters to his family in England, MS 7959, La Trobe Library, Melbourne.

Polehampton, A.
1862 *Kangaroo Land*, Houlston and Wright, London.

Port Phillip Gazette **[newspaper]**
1841 4 December.
1843 2 August.

Tuckey, J.
1805 *An Account of a Voyage to Establish a Colony at Port Philip* [sic], Longman, Hurst, Rees and Orme, London.

White, C.
1799 *An Account of the Regular Gradations in Man*, London.

Yate, W.
1838 Evidence before the House of Commons Select Committee on Aborigines, House of Commons, *British Parliamentary Papers* vol 7.

CHAPTER

13 LANGUAGE AND THE LAW: WHITE AUSTRALIA v NANCY

Diana Eades

INTRODUCTION

Nancy is a twenty-nine-year old Aboriginal woman who lives in a country town in southern Queensland. In May 1990 she was charged with unlawful use of a motor vehicle. She pleaded guilty and was fined $500 and placed on a twelve-month good behaviour bond, but she was innocent. This story is fictional, but it is based on a wide range of real cases studied by the author from the early 1980s.

To understand what happened, we need to know about Nancy, and her family — about their background and way of living, about their values and priorities. We need to know about their experience of being Aborigines in an Australian town, and about the differences between them and the non-Aboriginal people in the town. And, in particular, we need to know about the linguistic and cultural issues faced by Aboriginal people in their dealings with the law.

The next section of this chapter paints a picture of the lives of many Australian Aborigines today, and some of the background which is essential to understanding their dealings with the legal system. The third section, 'Understanding Nancy's Story' provides some of the cultural and linguistic information which is also essential to this understanding. The chapter separates these two sections in order to encourage you to think about cultural and linguistic matters which are relevant to cross-cultural communication in Australia today.

Various parts of the next section are marked by letters (a), (b), and so on; the section following that is divided into numbered subsections, each of which is particularly relevant to one or more of the parts of the second section marked by letters. When you have read the chapter, work out the puzzle of matching the numbered subsections in the third section with the relevant parts of the second section. The chapter was written in such a way that you should be able to match each subsection with one letter — but you will doubtless see additional subsections which are also relevant in some instances.

NANCY'S STORY

Nancy's family had always been proud of being Aboriginal, even in the generations when it was easier (and often safer) for people of mixed Aboriginal descent to hide it. Grannie Lizzie, who died when Nancy was ten years old, often talked of the 'dark ages' when she was growing up. She had been taken from her parents at the age of about seven, and sent to the girls' dormitory at the Cherbourg Aboriginal Reserve (about 200 kilometres northwest of Brisbane). Here she was forbidden to speak her Waka Waka language, and she was only allowed to see her mother and grandmother once a week. At the age of about thirteen years, Lizzie was sent out west as a domestic on a large property. Although she was housed, fed and clothed, she had to work six-and-a-half long days a week, never receiving any payment. After trying to run away several times, Lizzie finally succeeded in getting back to Cherbourg, where she gave birth to her first child, whose father was the aggressive manager she had been determined to escape from.

At the age of twenty Lizzie gained the Reserve Superintendent's permission to marry another Cherbourg resident and move away from the reserve. She eventually had twelve children, the youngest of whom was her seventh daughter Maud. The children received limited schooling, because Aboriginal children were not allowed to attend school if non-Aboriginal parents objected to them being there.

When Maud gave birth to Nancy in 1962, her family was living in humpies on Sandy Creek, about ten kilometres east of the small town of Smithville. It was a happy place with lots of cousins growing up, despite the hard living conditions. There was no electricity, and the only water was what they carted from the creek. Her parents and aunts and uncles worked hard at whatever they could — mainly seasonal fruit and tobacco picking. At times the men worked for the railways, and had to live as far away as north Queensland for months at a time.

The year that Nancy started school was the year that the Australian government, acting on the result of a national referendum, allowed Aboriginal people to register as voters, and to be counted for the first time in the census of the population of Australia.

But school was difficult for Nancy and her relatives in many ways. The white children laughed at them; and, when they learned about 'wild and savage natives', Nancy felt ashamed to be one of the dark people. And it was so hard to keep up with what was going on. The teacher asked so many questions and, when the children didn't answer, she thought they were stupid, or sulky, or both. (a)

There were other problems: Nancy often felt 'shame', and although the teacher seemed annoyed with her, she didn't know what she had done wrong. (b) (c)

And then the teacher was always telling her to speak 'proper English', not that 'bad, slovenly English, with the words left out'. (d)

Besides, it was hard to get to school, walking in about ten kilometres every day. Sometimes it was too hot, sometimes Nancy just felt tired, and other times it was too exciting at home — especially when relations came to stay from

Cherbourg. And then sometimes her relations would take her back to see her people, where she would stay for weeks at a time. (e)

In 1976, Nancy's family moved on to the Aboriginal reserve on the western outskirts of Smithville. They were one of the first families to be allocated a house to rent by the newly formed Aboriginal Housing Cooperative.

When she was sixteen year old Nancy had her first child. During the next three years, while she stayed with her family on the reserve, two more children were born. In 1985 Nancy and her de facto husband Jim moved into town, where they still live today, renting a house through the Aboriginal Housing Co-operative.

Now that they are in town the troubles with the police seem worse than they were on the reserve — maybe it was good to be out of sight, out there past the town dump. In town the police always seem to notice the usual family noise and the fights that happen from time to time, and often someone is arrested.(f)

But Nancy likes being in town: she can walk to the shops, and it is much easier for the children to get to school than it ever was for her. And she wants her children to have a good education.

The hardest part is getting back out to the reserve to see her Mum and Dad, her brothers who still live there, and all her other relatives. If one of the Murries in town is driving out, she can usually get a lift. But often she has to get a taxi. That's all right, unless it's that Harry driving the cab — he just hates blacks.

On Saturday, 5 May, Nancy was very pleased to see her cousin Charlie drive in from Jonesville, some eighty kilometres away. She guessed he'd borrowed a car from up there, and now he was offering to take Nancy and her kids out to see Mum. No good that he was drunk, though — so Nancy drove.

Suddenly the flashing blue light pulled her over, and before she knew it, Nancy was arrested for unlawful use of a motor vehicle.

In the police station, Nancy was scared. She had heard how one of her cousins had been beaten by one of the policemen in Jonesville just last year. She was scared that these two police officers would harass her like that. She was surprised to think that young Charlie would have taken that car, and she wondered whose it was, and where he had found it. She could hardly speak she was so scared. But she hardly had to speak — the policemen seemed to do all the talking. She wished she could read, to see what they were writing down. She told them what happened: she was at home, but she had been out to town earlier in the morning, after the boys left for football, whatever time that was; she came back, Charlie turned up and offered her a lift to the reserve. But there were so many questions that she didn't know what to do. (a)

Nancy was tired, scared and confused. She was worried about young Charlie too – she should help him; after all, his father had helped her so much when she had applied to the Housing Coop for the house. (g)

But then, when the policeman started to raise his voice, Nancy was terrified – it was just like the teachers all those years ago at school. The best thing would be to cooperate, so Nancy quickly said 'yes' to the questions. (h)

The policeman calmed down, soon the questions were over, and he told her to see the Legal Aid man when he came to town the next week.

In the Legal Aid office a few days later, there were more questions. Nancy was confused by the way that the lawyer was asking these questions. Here are some of the problems faced by Nancy in this legal interview.

He asked lots of questions with 'or', like:

> Nancy, were you down at the creek that morning before
> you got a lift with Charlie, or were you at home all morning?

To this Nancy answered 'yes'. (i)

And he wanted prompt answers, so there was no time to think about the answers. (j)

She also felt as if most of the questions about time were too complicated, such as:

> What time did you go to town first?
>
> How soon after that did you return home? (k)

The lawyer seemed kind, and he explained to Nancy that she would have to go to Jonesville for the court case in four weeks' time. Nancy was really scared now. She had been to court before, two years ago, when she was fined $70 for swearing outside the hotel in Smithville late one night. (l)

At least she would be with her cousin Charlie. But the lawyer explained that Charlie would be going on a different day, in two weeks' time, because he was to plead 'guilty'. He had stolen the car, and he had told the police how it happened. He told the lawyer too. The lawyer would ask the magistrate to give him a community service order rather than a gaol sentence. Everyone was very worried about the rising numbers of deaths of Aboriginal people in gaols, particularly young men. It would be better for people like Charlie, who were not dangerous, to pay for their crime and help the community.

The lawyer explained it all to Nancy. If she genuinely had not known that Charlie had stolen the car, then she must plead 'not guilty'. Then she would go to court in four weeks' time, and answer the questions from the police prosecutor, and from her own lawyer.

Nancy's head was spinning. She hated all their questions. Migeloos ask so many questions all the time — it's dangerous to answer them, and it's dangerous not to answer them. Nancy made up her mind.

Two weeks later Nancy was in court. The charge of knowingly driving a stolen motor vehicle was read out to her. She was asked 'How do you plead?'

Her answer was:

'Guilty, eh?'

UNDERSTANDING NANCY'S STORY

(1) Aboriginal English can be regarded as a dialect of English in much the same way as Scottish English and American English. There are different ways of speaking Aboriginal English in different parts of the country, just as there are different ways of speaking American English in different parts of the United States. Think for example of the dialectal differences between American English and Australian English. In Australian English, we say 'She's in hospital', but to American English speakers this sounds a bit weird, and speakers of this dialect say 'She's in the hospital'. Neither dialect is right or wrong, but there are systematic differences between them. This is the same situation with the difference between Standard Australian English and Aboriginal English.

Aboriginal English is also related to traditional Aboriginal languages. For example, in traditional Aboriginal languages (as in many other languages of the world) there is no equivalent of the English verb 'to be'. So the sentence *Geen junggoor* in Waka Waka (Nancy's Grannie Lizzie's language) would translate literally into English as 'Woman sick'. This grammatical structure has remained in many varieties of Aboriginal English and you may hear Aboriginal people say 'woman sick' instead of Standard English 'the woman is sick'.

It is only since the late 1960s that Aboriginal English has been recognised as a distinct dialect of English with its own rules. Most non-Aboriginal Australians still mistakenly think that this dialect of English is 'bad English', or somehow inferior to Standard English, just because it has different rules.

(2) Aboriginal people are often uncomfortable about the way in which non-Aboriginal people ask them questions (see also Yallop's comments on the grammar of questions in chapter 2). This is because there are significant cultural differences between the two groups in the way that information is sought. While the direct question is central to most information seeking in mainstream Australian society, Aboriginal people throughout Australia, whether they speak a traditional language or Aboriginal English, frequently use a range of indirect means of finding

out information. For example, they make a hinting statement and wait for a response:

> I'm wondering about what happened last night. I need to know about why you didn't do your homework.

Or they may volunteer information for confirmation or denial:

> It seems as if everyone went to the creek after school. People might say that no-one likes the Maths teacher. (I think) maybe no-one likes the Maths teacher.

Or they may tell people what they need to find out about, and then wait for a later occasion before receiving an answer.

It is clear that silence — giving people time — is important to all of these Aboriginal ways of finding out information.

Although some questions are used, it is considered rude in Aboriginal cultures to question people about many things, or to put them on the spot. Individual personal privacy is protected by the constraints on direct questions in many situations.

(3) Aboriginal people throughout Australia often answer 'yes' or agree to whatever is being asked by a non-Aboriginal questioner, even if they do not understand the question. This phenomenon, which has been observed for many decades, has recently been labelled 'gratuitous concurrence' (Liberman 1985). Liberman explains this gratuitous concurrence as a way that Aboriginal people have developed to protect themselves in their interactions with non-Aboriginal Australians. It occurs particularly where the questioner, say a teacher or police officer, has authority over the Aboriginal person being questioned.

Thus, a very common strategy for Aborigines being asked a number of questions by non-Aborigines is to agree, regardless of either their understanding of the question or their belief about the truth or falsity of the proposition being questioned. Their apparent agreement often really means something like this: 'I think that if I say "yes" you will see that I am obliging, and socially amenable, and you will think well of me, and things will work out well between us'. This is undoubtedly one of the major problems facing Aboriginal people seeking justice in the legal system.

(4) Questions which ask the respondent to choose one of two alternatives are rarely found in the linguistic structure of traditional Aboriginal languages or in Aboriginal English. So such questions, known as either–or questions, may confuse the Aboriginal person being questioned, who often simply answers: 'yes'.

(5) Silence is an important and positively valued part of many Aboriginal conversations. This is a difficult matter for most non-Aboriginal people to recognise and learn, because in Western societies silence is so often negatively valued in conversations. Between people who are not close friends or family, silence in conversations or interviews is frequently an indication of some kind of communication breakdown. On the contrary, in Aboriginal societies silence usually indicates a participant's desire to think, or simply to enjoy the presence of others in a non-verbal way. Because Aboriginal people are so accustomed to using silence in conversation with other Aboriginal people, many are uncomfortable if they are not given the chance to use silence in their conversations or interviews with non-Aboriginal people.

This difference has serious implications for many interactions in mainstream Australian society where the question–answer method of seeking information is fundamental, such as employment interviews, doctor–patient interviews, school classrooms, and legal interviews, whether in the police station, the lawyer's office or the courtroom. Aboriginal silence in these settings can easily be interpreted as evasion, ignorance, confusion, insolence, or even guilt. In Australian courts of law, silence is not to be taken as admission of guilt, but it would be difficult for police officers, legal professionals or jurors to set aside strong cultural intuitions about the meaning of silence, especially if they were not aware of cultural differences in the use and interpretation of silence.

(6) Another important cultural difference in conversations concerns the use of eye contact. Direct eye contact is frequently avoided in Aboriginal interactions where it is seen as threatening or rude. Conversely, in much non-Aboriginal interaction in Australia, the avoidance of eye contact, especially by someone who has been asked a question, is interpreted as rudeness, evasion or dishonesty. This cultural difference in use and interpretation of eye communication can be very important in the classroom, as well as in police or courtroom interviews.

(7) Speakers of Aboriginal English, like speakers of traditional languages, often reckon time not by the clock or calendar, but in reference to some social or seasonal or climatic event. So, for example, an answer to the question 'When did that happen?', might be 'just before Max turned up', or 'around sunrise'. When asked to give specific clock times, Aboriginal people often find it hard to be accurate and consistent.

(8) Many cultural values and practices which are important in traditional Aboriginal societies are still important in non-traditional Aboriginal societies, such as Nancy's. For example, responsibilities for childrearing are shared among a wide group of relatives, and it is often considered beneficial for a child to move around between various relatives from the extended family.

(9) Another cultural value which is important in non-traditionally oriented Aboriginal societies, as in traditionally oriented societies, is loyalty to kin. Aboriginal people expect each other to be loyal to a wide extended family. In many ways Aboriginal cultural values emphasise the family group rather than the individual, and this is seen in many of the choices and actions of Aboriginal people.

(10) Another cultural practice which can be seen in Aboriginal societies throughout Australia is the preference for outdoor living and the expectation that people will see and hear much of what goes on in Aboriginal family life. Studies of traditionally oriented Aboriginal camps show that physical privacy is a low priority. And in towns and cities today the same is often true. Small houses accommodate large families or many members of an extended family, and by non-Aboriginal standards they are frequently overcrowded. Much day-to-day living takes place in open, outside areas such as the main street of towns, in parks and other public places, or on the verandahs and in the yards of houses. The open way that many members of an Aboriginal family live in towns and suburbs often results in cultural clash with non-Aboriginal neighbours and police officers.

(11) One of the most common offences with which Aboriginal people are charged is that of using obscene language. Aboriginal people are particularly vulnerable to this charge because of their open lifestyle. But the very notion of 'obscene language' involves a significant area of cultural clash between contemporary Aboriginal and mainstream Australian societies. Simply put, what is widely considered to be obscene language in many sectors of mainstream Australian society is much less likely to be offensive in Aboriginal societies. Swearing, like fighting, is considered to be a normal part of Aboriginal social interaction, and in particular a necessary part of settling disputes.

A further difference from most of non-Aboriginal Australia is that there is no gender distinction in this matter. That is, Aboriginal people do not generally consider swearing to be stronger or more offensive if it comes from a woman.

(12) One of the strongest Aboriginal concepts is the feeling of 'shame' which is felt when people are singled out in front of a group, whether it be for praise or for rebuke. This concept of 'shame' has no simple equivalent in non-Aboriginal society, but it is like a mixture of embarrassment and fear.

FOR DISCUSSION

1. Why did Nancy plead guilty to a crime she did not commit?

2. Although this paper has been about speakers of Aboriginal English, many of the cultural and linguistic issues raised here are relevant also to speakers of

traditional Aboriginal languages. What do you think are some of the additional disadvantages faced by speakers of traditional Aboriginal languages in their dealings with the law?

3. Read this summary of the famous 'Ann Arbor case' in the United States.

In America, the dialect of English spoken by Afro-Americans or Blacks, became the subject of a landmark court case in 1979 in Ann Arbor, Michigan. Black parents at an elementrary school in a low-income housing area took the School District Board to court for failing to recognise the language difficulties faced by their children, and to educate them accordingly. The children were all speakers of the Black dialect of English (known as Black English Vernacular, or BEV), which, like Aboriginal English, is a significantly different dialect of English. The children, who were achieving very poorly at school, were classified by the school as learning disabled, or in need of speech therapy. The parents' case depended on whether BEV was sufficiently different from Standard English to constitute a barrier to learning. With the help of linguists, the parents were successful. The judge ordered that the school district must recognise BEV, must develop a program to help teachers to recognise it, and must offer teachers methods of using that knowledge in teaching Black children Standard English.

Now discuss the question:

What are the implications of this American case for educators of Aboriginal English speaking students in Australia?

WIDER BACKGROUND

There has not been room in this chapter to discuss many aspects of Aboriginal English, and of the legal and historical factors involved in Nancy's story, but the following sources will provide more information.

Aboriginal English

Eades, D.

1988 They Don't Speak an Aboriginal Language, or Do They? In I. Keen (ed), *Being Black: Aboriginal Cultures in 'Settled' Australia*, Aboriginal Studies Press, Canberra, 97–115.

1991 Communicative Strategies in Aboriginal English. In S. Romaine (ed), *Language in Australia*, Cambridge University Press, Cambridge, 84–93.

Kaldor, S. and I.G. Malcolm.

1991 Aboriginal English — An Overview. In S. Romaine (ed), *Language in Australia*, Cambridge University Press, Cambridge, 67–83.

Aborigines and the Law

Gale, F., R. Bailey-Harris and J. Wundersitz
1990 *Aboriginal Youth and the Criminal Justice System: The Justice of Injustice?*, Cambridge University Press, Cambridge.

Hanks, P. and B. Keon-Cohen (eds)
1984 *Aborigines and the Law*, George Allen and Unwin, Sydney.

Hazlehurst, K. (ed)
1987 *Ivory Scales: Black Australia and the Law*, NSW University Press, Sydney.

Koch, H.
1991 Language and Communication in Aboriginal Land Claim Hearings. In S. Romaine (ed) *Language in Australia*, Cambridge University Press, Cambridge, 94–103.

Liberman, K.
1985 *Understanding Interaction in Central Australia: An Ethnomethodological Study of Australian Aboriginal People*, Routledge and Kegan Paul, Boston.

Royal Commission into Aboriginal Deaths in Custody (RCIADIC)
1988 *Interim Report*, Australian Government Publishing Service, Canberra.

1991 *Final Report*, Australian Government Publishing Service, Canberra.

A submission by the Queensland Aboriginal Co-ordinating Council to the Royal Commission into Aboriginal Deaths in Custody in August 1990 compared Aboriginal and non-Aboriginal appearances in Queensland Magistrate's Courts. This submission showed that Aborigines are 11 times more likely to be charged with unlawful use of a motor vehicle, 13 times more likely to appear for drunkenness, and 7 times more likely to appear for offensive behaviour (p 52).

History of Aboriginal Reserves in Queensland

FAIRA
1979 Beyond the Act: Queensland Aborigines and Islanders: What Do We Want?

Wearne, H.
1980 *A Clash of Cultures: Queensland Aboriginal Policy (1824–1980)*, Uniting Church, Brisbane.

CHAPTER

14 LANGUAGE AND TERRITORIALITY IN ABORIGINAL AUSTRALIA

Alan Rumsey

INTRODUCTION

Linguists who have studied Australian Aboriginal languages (myself included) often get asked how to translate this or that English expression into 'Aboriginal'. As anyone who has got very far in reading this book will know, there is no such language. Rather, there are, even now, at least 100 quite distinct Aboriginal languages, and 200 years ago there were many more. What relation is there between these language differences and other kinds of Aboriginal social differentiation?

Those who are aware of the diversity of Aboriginal languages generally think of this as a matter of tribal differentiation: each language is (or was) spoken by a distinct tribe. I am going to try to show in this chapter that that is a mistaken view — that language is actually related to the territorial differentiation in a quite different way. My evidence will come from two sources: from recent findings of the Aboriginal Land Commission in the Northern Territory, and from some other recent studies by anthropologists and anthropological linguists. First, I want to review some older ideas about this topic, which were widely held by anthropologists until recently, and probably still are held by most non-Aboriginal Australians.

LANGUAGE AND 'TRIBE'

Onc of the preconceptions most people have about Aborigines (at least those living in central and northern Australia) is that they are 'tribal'. What does that mean? Among other things, it means that they come in 'tribes'. But what is a tribe? Some of the better-known examples of Aboriginal social groupings which are generally referred as to 'tribes' include Pitjantjatjara, Arrernte, Warlpiri, Kamilaroi and Wiradjuri. But what do we mean when we refer to these as 'tribes'? If we look at the ways in which that word has been defined or used in relation to Aborigines, we find that it generally involves one or more of the following characteristics:

1. most or all members of the tribe live, or used to live, in a single, clearly bounded region;

2. they speak a common language or dialect which is unique to them;

3. they tend to marry within the tribe;

4. they share certain customs or cultural traits which are unique to their tribe.

Where do we get all these ideas about the nature of tribes? One thing to notice right away about them is that they are also characteristics which we attribute to the kind of social grouping which non-tribal peoples are thought to have instead of tribes, namely the nation-state. Indeed, what are now called Aboriginal 'tribes' in Australia were also commonly referred to in the nineteenth century as 'nations'. Even as recently as 1976, an eminent linguist claimed of northeast Queensland that 'the only major difference' between 'the (so-called) "tribes"...and what are called nations in Europe and other parts of the world...was in terms of population size' (Dixon 1976, 219–20).

But the idea of the nation-state is a very recent and historically specific one. Despite the fact that they are now everywhere, very few nation-states existed 200 years ago, and 400 hundred years ago they were unheard of. Since Australian Aboriginal cultures developed largely independently of outside influences for at least 40,000 years, we should be very cautious about assuming that a kind of institution developed here which just happens to include a good many of the characteristics of the nation-state. This is not to say that it could not have happened but, rather, that any such claim must be examined carefully. We cannot assume that any particular attribute will necessarily be found in combination with any other: so, each of the presumed ones must be considered separately in light of the available evidence. I will now do this for each of the four characteristics listed above, in reverse order.

The third and fourth characteristics may be quickly disposed of, as even those few scholars who have included them in their definition of tribe, have generally seen them as tendencies only. The rates of in-marriage ('endogamy') vary greatly from one 'tribe' to another, and are often lower than they are in a given area among 'countrymen' from more than one 'tribe'. And there may be important cultural differences within named 'tribes'. Circumcision, for instance, was practised by the southern Jawoyn people (east of Katherine, Northern Territory) in common with neighbouring 'tribes' to the east, south and west, but not by the northern Jawoyn. Thus, traits (3) and (4) cannot be taken as necessary attributes of the 'tribe'.

In the end, those who have seriously tried to define the 'tribe' have generally fallen back on only the first two traits mentioned above: common links to a definite territory and common language. See, for example Howitt (1904, 41), Spencer (1921, lxiii), and Woodward (1974, 142) to be discussed below.

But this apparently simple definition has proven difficult to apply, for several reasons. First, regarding territoriality, the correlation between 'tribal' affiliation and residence is only a very loose one. This is true even in outback regions such as the Northern Territory. A very thorough statistical study which was based on data gathered there in the 1950s (Milliken 1976) showed that most

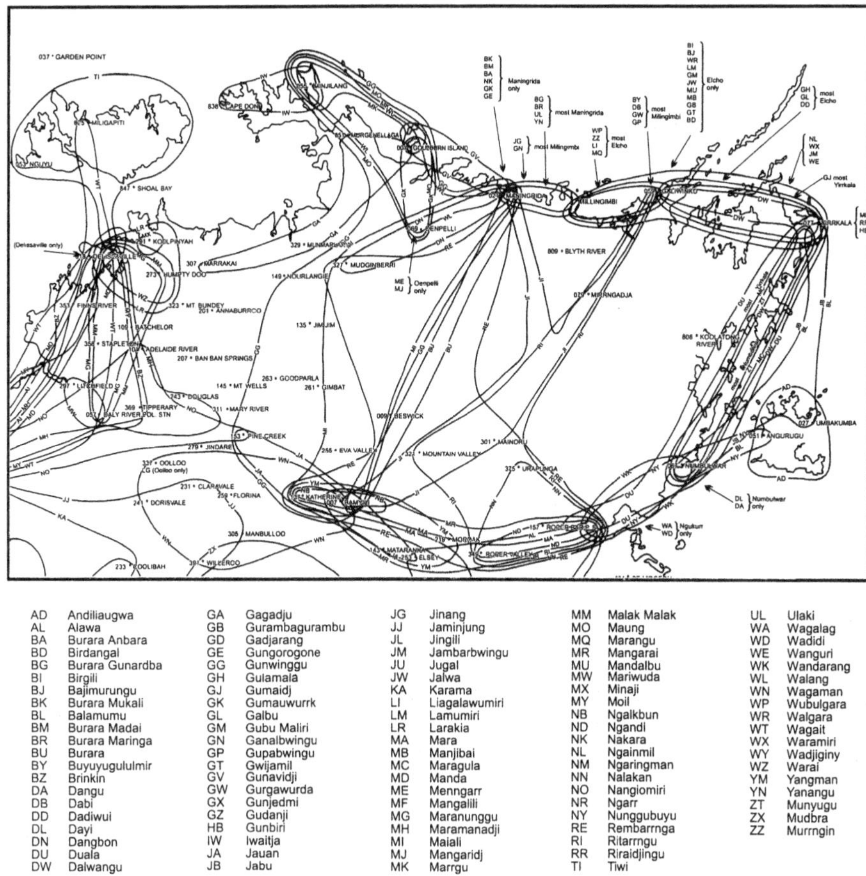

Map 8: Aboriginal group distribution according to residential patterns (from Milliken 1976, inside back cover)

members of most tribes did indeed live within a single identifiable region of the Territory, but that none of these regions was clearly bounded off from the others. Rather, there was an enormous amount of overlap among them, such that the membership of every 'tribe' was residentially dispersed among that of many others. The degree of dispersal has no doubt increased since European colonisation and the wholesale movement of Aboriginal people onto large government settlements and into towns. But it would be a mistake to read backwards from this to a situation in which we assume that tribes were sharply bounded residential groups. For, as far as we can tell from the available details of life history and genealogy going back to the pre-European past, a significant portion of Aboriginal marriages have always been between people of different 'tribes', especially in areas where differences at the level of 'tribe' are of greatest political importance. In such cases, one of the marriage partners usually ends up spending most of his/her time in the 'tribe' territory of the other, and the children may end up living in either, or yet another. Moreover, the life histories of many men show a high degree of residential mobility, within and beyond their 'tribal' territories' (see Myers 1986, 77–102; Warner 1964, 467–90 for examples from the Western Desert and northeast Arnhem Land).

This is not to say that there is no connection at all between tribal identity and territoriality. On the contrary, despite all the complications regarding residence, it is clear from what Aboriginal people say all around Australia that they think of the land as divided up into more-or-less clearly bounded regions, each associated with a label such as Warlpiri, Wiradjuri, and so forth. In this respect, there is a striking contrast between the residential map resulting from Milliken's study, cited above, which is full of crossing lines and multiple overlaps, and that of Tindale (1974), which shows the whole of Australia neatly divided into a jigsaw puzzle of named tribal territories (see Maps 8 and 9). While the precise location of some of the boundaries drawn by Tindale has been disputed, no one has seriously challenged the idea that each 'tribal' name is associated in principle with a more-or-less clearly bounded region. Confusion arises only when we try to think of the tribal name as referring, in the first instance, to a group of people, and then to delimit its territory according to where those people live. Rather, it refers, in the first instance, to a piece of land.

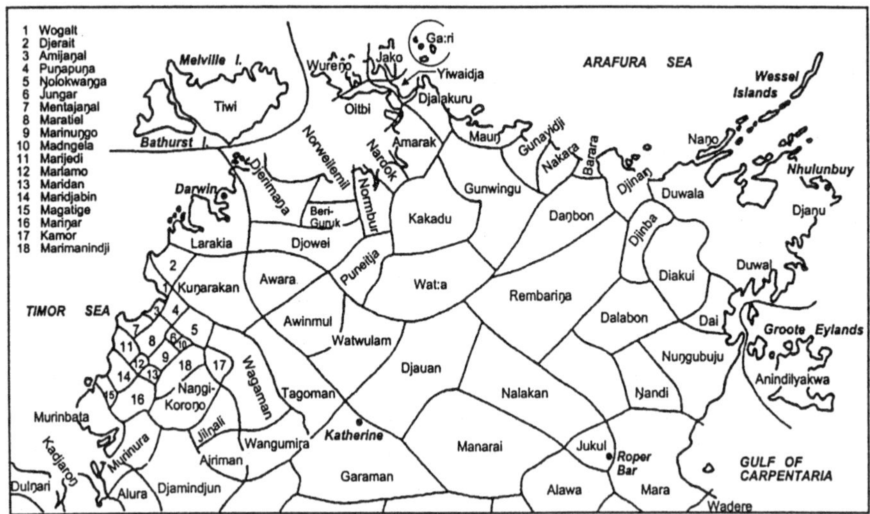

Map 9: An example of Aboriginal group distribution according to Tindale (after Tindale 1974).

Almost every such label (Warlpiri, Wiradjuri, et cetera) also refers to a language. Why should this be so? Presumably because there is some kind of link between language and territory. Most people who have offered definitions of 'tribe' in Australia have assumed that that link is established by the fact that there is a distinct group of people, the tribe, who both occupy (and/or 'own') the territory and speak the language. Hence, the second of the two basic definitional features of the tribe: that its members are distinguished from others by speaking a common language.

But this assumption has now proven untenable. For, as more and more studies are made of Australian Aboriginal languages and their patterns of use, it becomes ever more obvious that almost no one speaks only one of them. As one linguist has put it: Australian Aborigines are 'the leading contenders for being the most multilingual people in the world' (Laycock 1979, 82). To this day, in mainland areas where Aboriginal languages are spoken, almost every fluent speaker is fluent in at least two of them, and it is not uncommon for one person to speak four or five, even in areas where the languages differ greatly in grammar and vocabulary. Nor does speakership cluster in such a way that, for example, languages A and B are spoken by all and only the members of some particular 'tribe' (Sutton 1978). Unlike in most parts of the world, language boundaries in Aboriginal Australia are not significant communicative boundaries, because people tend to be able to speak the languages of neighbouring regions as well as their own.

Here we are faced with an apparent paradox: the names for Aboriginal languages seem to identify them clearly with tribal territories, but it is not possible to delimit any clear-cut, non-overlapping groups of people on the basis of the languages they speak. To show how this paradox can be resolved, I turn now to some developments that have taken place during the course of recent land claim hearings in the Northern Territory.

THE ABORIGINAL LAND COMMISSION

During the past twenty years, especially in the Northern Territory, traditional Aboriginal forms of land tenure have been the subject of more intensive expert investigation than ever before. Much of this work has been done in connection with the passage and implementation of the *Aboriginal Land Rights (Northern Territory) Act 1976*, which for the first time gave some groups of Aboriginal Australians secure legal title to some or all of their traditional territories. This was done in two different ways. First, areas of the Northern Territory that had already been set aside as Aboriginal reserves (Arnhem Land, for example) were immediately converted to Aboriginal Land. Second, certain other kinds of land, chiefly vacant crown land, could become the subject of Aboriginal land claims, to be presented before a kind of royal commission — the Aboriginal Land Commission — which was specifically created to hear such claims and, after deliberating upon them, to make recommendations to the federal Minister for Aboriginal Affairs.

These land claim hearings have proven far more arduous and protracted than anyone had expected. Masses of data have had to be gathered for them concerning Aboriginal people's relation to land, and thousands of hours of oral evidence from Aboriginal and other expert witnesses have been heard by the commission, resulting in hundreds of volumes of transcript. By contrast, among anthropologists specialising in Australian Aboriginal cultures, traditional land tenure had not been one of the major topics of investigation before the 1960s, and little had been published on it in comparison with topics such as kinship and ritual.

Under those circumstances, the work of the Aboriginal Land Commission was bound to produce some surprises, and it did. Most of them are beyond the scope of this chapter, which is specifically concerned with the role of language in relation to land and people. But in that regard, there is much to learn from the way Aboriginal people have chosen to present their claims.

The 1973–74 Royal Commission on whose inquiry the Land Rights Act was based — the Woodward Commission — clearly did not expect 'tribes' or 'language groups' to put themselves forward as claimants for land. Their finding was that the kind of Aboriginal groups that customarily held land were a kind of subdivision of the language group rather than the whole language group. In some areas the land-owning groups were thought to be 'dialect groups'. More commonly, they were what it called 'clans'. As for the more inclusive groups, which it called 'language groups' or 'tribes', the commission, adopting the minimal definition I have discussed above, saw each of them as having 'a common language, a commonly used name for that language and thus for the people speaking it, and an identifiable tract of country where those people live or used to live' (Woodward 1974, 142). Tribes were in this view dismissed as of little or no relevance for land tenure. In the words of the report: 'In no sense can the tribe be regarded as the basis of Australian social organization' (142). In all these respects, the Woodward Commission Report carries over a very influential view of Australian land tenure propounded by the first Australian Professor of Anthropology, A.R. Radcliffe-Brown (1930–31), who saw the 'clan' or 'horde' as having exclusive proprietary rights in land.

The Land Rights Act itself would seem to have incorporated the Woodward Commission's views when it defined 'traditional Aboriginal owner' in such a way as to require Aborigines claiming land to show (among other things) that they comprise a 'local descent group'. For language groups, if their membership is distinguished solely by their speaking a common language, cannot be 'descent groups', whereas clans clearly are. Where clans exist — in northeast Arnhem Land, for example — everyone belongs to one of them, namely that of his or her father (in other words, they are what anthropologists call 'patrilineal' clans). That is why such groups have always been readily accepted, in terms of the Act's definition of 'traditional Aboriginal owner', as descent groups. And since each such clan is also associated with a particular set of sites or an 'estate', they are 'local' descent groups.

In the first nine land claims heard by the Aboriginal Land Commissioner (during 1977–80) the claimants presented their case for traditional ownership in groupings which were readily recognisable as patrilineal clans of the orthodox Radcliffe-Brownian sort. There was extensive testimony and deliberation concerning issues such as: Is this particular claimant group a clan? Does this particular clan qualify as traditional owner for this particular bit of claimable land? Can people with links to the clan other than through their father (for example, through their mother or grandmother) be included among the traditional owners of its estate? But there was no serious challenge to the assumption that the estates in question were clan estates, to which the points of possible linkage were provided by a core of kinsmen related through the male line, even if links to that 'core' might sometimes be through women.

The first real challenges to this assumption came in the early 1980s, when the commissioner first began hearing claims over land within the area of earliest and greatest impact from colonisation in the Northern Territory: the western half of the Top End. At the Finniss River hearing in 1980, the claimants presented themselves in groupings which, in terms of the Woodward Report, were not 'clans' but 'tribes': Maranunggu, Kungarakany and Warai (Aboriginal Land Commissioner 1981). On the evidence presented at the hearing, it is not clear that anything like the clan ever existed in this area. Certainly by 1980, there was no clear evidence for even a vestigial system of patrilineal clans or discrete clan estates. The claimants related themselves to land at the level of what they themselves called 'tribes', each of which was in principle associated with a well-bounded region, a language, and a name for that language.

In the following year a similar grouping, called the Malak-Malak/Madngele, presented themselves as claimants in the Daly River region, about 100 kilometres south of the Finniss River claim area. This claim differed from the Finniss River one in that, here, there was also at least a vestigial system of clan-like groupings, each of which was associated with certain sites within the larger

Malak-Malak/Madngele region. Some of these groups had no surviving members. Sites or estates formerly associated with those extinct groups were said to have been 'taken over' by the Malak-Malak/Madngele group as a whole (Sutton and Palmer 1981; Aboriginal Land Commissioner 1982).

Further up the Daly River system, a claim was heard in 1983–84 over crown lands in the vicinity of Katherine, where a tradition also survives (among older people at least) of clan-like groupings, albeit with less clear-cut territorial associations than among the Malak-Malak/Madngele. The whole area under claim was said in Aboriginal testimony to have belonged to the Jawoyn people (Aboriginal Land Commissioner 1988) — a grouping which, again, would have been considered by Radcliffe-Brown to be a 'tribe', of which the various 'clans' were component parts.

In each of these three claims, as in some subsequent ones, the 'tribal' groupings not only chose to present themselves as such but were in the end accepted by the Aboriginal Land Commissioner as traditional owners of at least some of the land in question (Aboriginal Land Commissioner 1981, 1982, 1988). Indeed, in the Katherine claim (and perhaps in the Malak-Malak one, though the judge's report is ambiguous on the matter) they were acknowledged in preference to the clan-like units even for areas where the latter were clearly of some relevance as local descent groups. This is in spite of the Woodward Commission's conclusion of a few years before that 'the language group was never a social or political unit, and so never a land-holding group' (Woodward 1974, 145).

What are we to make of the apparent disparity between those earlier conclusions and the outcome of the land claim process in the Northern Territory? Part of the answer is that language groups have probably become more important as clans have become less viable as a result of European invasion and settlement. Consider, for example, the history of the Alligator Rivers region, just to the west of Arnhem Land. It has been estimated that, as a direct result of colonisation which began there in the 1880s, the Aboriginal population within the next two generations was reduced to about 5 per cent of what it had been (Keen 1980). As a result, many clans died out altogether, and whole language groups were reduced to about the same size as some single clans had been before.

A hundred miles to the south, in and east of Katherine, a similar, if somewhat less drastic decline was being experienced by the Jawoyn people, to whom I have referred above in my review of land claim proceedings. By 1940, only a small fraction of the Jawoyn population were living on or near country associated with their particular clan, and by 1980 it was impossible to find out, for most of the clans, where that country had been. But there was a very clear understanding where Jawoyn country was, and most Jawoyn people were still living on it (as indeed they still are, along with many other non-Jawoyn Aboriginal people). Most of the younger people had no clear idea what clan they belonged to, but their identity as Jawoyn was known by all, and of very great importance to them.

But what exactly is the basis of that identity? In our review of the notion of 'tribe' above, we were left with only two features — common territory and common language — and it seemed impossible to relate even those two to each other, since almost no one speaks only one Aboriginal language.

Here is where the evidence from land claim hearings has proven very enlightening. For, in land claims where language groups have been recognised by the Aboriginal Land Commissioner, the ability to speak the language in question has proven to be neither a necessary nor a sufficient condition for inclusion within the group. If it had been a necessary condition, many of the younger claimants — including almost all of them in the Finniss River hearing — would have to have been excluded, as their main linguistic competence is in various forms of English. Conversely, if it had been a sufficient condition, some people would have been included among the claimants — in the Katherine claim and probably elsewhere as well — who had had little or no association with the area in question, and who were not identified with it by themselves or anyone else. More generally, although many Aboriginal people in this area speak three or four Aboriginal languages, no one is equally identified with that many language names or 'identifiable tracts of country': not everyone who speaks Jawoyn, even fluently, feels entitled to say 'I am Jawoyn' or 'Jawoyn is my language' (Merlan and Rumsey 1982). The relevant relationship to language is not one of speakership, but one which is better glossed as language ownership (as in Sutton 1978; Sutton and Palmer 1981).

LAND, LANGUAGE AND PEOPLE

In order to see how that relationship is constructed in Aboriginal terms, let us reconsider the interrelationships among the three terms I mentioned above: land, language, people. I said that Westerners tend to assume that any link between territory and language will be established by the fact that there is a distinct group of people, the tribe, who both occupy (and/or 'own') the territory and speak the language. But in the land claim process, the links between language and land which have proven most relevant have not been of the kind which are mediated by links between language and people (as in Western ideologies of 'tribe' and nation) but, rather, are direct links between particular languages and particular tracts of country. Thus, it is not the case that, for example, Jawoyn country is called that because it is or was occupied by people who speak the Jawoyn language. Rather, it is called Jawoyn country because it is the region in which that language was directly installed or 'planted' in the landscape by Nabilil 'Crocodile', a Dreamtime creator figure who moved up the Katherine River, establishing sites and leaving names for them in the Jawoyn language (Merlan and Rumsey 1982). In this formulation, language and country are directly linked, and the mediated link is between language and people: Jawoyn people are Jawoyn not because they speak Jawoyn, but because they are linked to places to which the Jawoyn language is also linked.

What is the basis of that linkage? In all the land claims hearings where this matter has been taken up, it turns out to be a matter of what anthropologists call filiation — links through one or both parents. Thus, for example, when helping the Jawoyn claimants to prepare their case, the assisting anthropologists, Francesca Merlan and I, compiled a list of all living persons — approximately 400 of them — who were identified by Aboriginal people in the area as Jawoyn. We recorded the family trees of all these people, including, among other information, the clan and language group membership of their parents, and what languages they could speak. The latter did not correlate closely with language group membership. But parentage did. In every single case, it turned out that one or both of the Jawoyn claimant's parents were also identified as Jawoyn. (In a very few cases these were what we would call 'adoptive' parents instead of 'biological' ones, but in all such cases, they were the ones who had actually reared the person.) From this and from claimants' explanations about why they were considered Jawoyn, we concluded that filiation provided the basis for language group membership, and that ability to speak the language did not.

This conclusion was well-supported in the claimants' evidence at the land claim hearing. When witness after witness was asked why he, she, or somebody else was considered to be Jawoyn (or of some other language group), the answer was never 'Because I speak Jawoyn', but almost always 'Because my father was' or 'Because my mother was'.

Thus, contrary to Justice Woodward's conclusions concerning 'language groups', it became possible to regard them as local descent groups. They were 'descent groups' in that their membership was determined not, as he had supposed, by speaking a common language, but by filiation from a member of the group. And they were local in that each is clearly identified with a particular region, with which the language is also identified.

It is in the latter respect — in the postulation of direct links between land and language — that Jawoyn and European world views are most different. But it is clear that the Jawoyn are not unusual in this respect among Aboriginal groups. The more one comes to understand the principle involved, the more evident

Plate 5: Claimant Peter Jatbula gives evidence in Jawoyn (Gimbat area) land claim hearing, October 1992 (photograph by Alan Rumsey).

it becomes just how widespread is its application. Let us consider some other examples, from anthropological sources rather than from Aboriginal Land Claim hearings.

OTHER EXAMPLES OF THE LINK BETWEEN LANGUAGE AND LAND

Southwest of Jawoyn country, in the Roper River region, the Mangarrayi people tell a story of the Dreamtime, in which the landscape in the eastern part of their territory was created by two Olive Pythons. As the story was told to Francesca Merlan, the Pythons speak in the Mangarrayi language, until they get to a place called Jambarlin. The place must be steep, for they climb slowly. When they get there, they start speaking a different language, Alawa. As the narrator tells the story, she herself switches from Mangarrayi to Alawa, and quotes them in that language as saying 'Let's you and I go quickly'. The narrator comments on the switch of language and says that now, from that point on [to the east] 'people always talk Alawa' (Merlan 1981, 144).

A thousand kilometres to the west, in the Kimberley district of Western Australia, the Ngarinyin people have told me of how their language originated at a place called Gulemen, 'Beverly Springs', where it was first spoken in the Dreamtime by Possum. From there he carried it all over present-day Ngarinyin country, and that is why the language is there today.

Far to the east, at Doomadgee in northwestern Queensland, the territories of the Ganggalida, Garawa, and Waanyi people are:

> where particular languages are said to 'belong', implying that they fit there appropriately with other features of the landscape. When in that area using bush resources, and certainly when formally dealing with many totemic and other extra-human features of the landscape, it is appropriate to speak the language which belongs there. Other Aboriginal languages would not be effective in ritual matters; indeed use of another language may well bring forth hostility from totemic forces.
>
> The concept of language as a fundamental characteristic of landscape is also evident from mythic accounts where travelling totemic figures change their language on reaching the boundary of a linguistic territory – as, for example, in the story of a snake who switches from Jingalu to Waanyi at the present border between the two. (Trigger 1987, 217–19).

In central Australia, T.G.H. Strehlow, who grew up among Arrernte (Aranda) people at Hermannsburg Mission, was told of how a Dreamtime horde of native cats:

> after travelling from Port Augusta in South Australia through the territory of the Jankuntjatjara and Matuntara, entered the Aranda area at Ilbirla —a series of springs... As soon as they crossed the Palmer River their ears were deafened by the chirping of crickets in the river grass; ...in their confusion, they began to speak in a mixture of Aranda and 'Loritja' [Luritja, Western Desert Language] after speaking only 'Loritja' during their previous travels over many hundreds of miles of Western Desert Country.
>
> From this point on they...began to address each other by [class-] names. And after they had gone on, night overspread the land behind their sterns, while they went forward in broad daylight.
>
> And they laid down [as a barrier] that great expanse of sandhills,...those sandhills covered with stands of desert oaks. (Strehlow 1965, 133)

The 'class names' to which Strehlow refers are part of a system which divides the whole of society into four or eight 'skins', and specifies who may or may not marry each other. (This system is similar to that described earlier by Bavin for Warlpiri in chapter 6.) Strehlow reports that the Luritja narrator of this myth concluded by saying that the native cats:

> through raising a sandhill barrier between the Aranda and themselves...and through causing night to fall on the people living south of this border, had authorized [them]...to marry indiscriminately...prohibitions on marriage operated only for the Aranda. (Strehlow 1965, 134)

Strehlow's conclusion from this is that, in the Aboriginal view, these systems of marriage classes:

> were *based on the land itself* [emphasis in the original]: for it was the same wandering horde of ancestral beings which had validated the 'classless' kin-grouping system of the Western Desert groups south of the sandhill barrier...and which had instituted the rule that all groups living north of this barrier had to address one other by [class-] names. (Strehlow 1965, 134)

This conclusion was very sound as far as it went, and at the time it represented a real advance over most Europeans' understanding of the Aboriginal world view, in its emphasis on meaningful features of the landscape as the basis of the world order. But in light of what we have learned since Strehlow's time about the links between Aboriginal languages and land, it seems likely that, in the Western Desert view which is represented in this myth, it is not only the distinctive Arrernte (Aranda) marriage system that is 'based on the land itself', but also their language. Indeed, this myth seems to show this at an even greater level of specificity than the myths from other areas I referred to above.

To this day, Western Arrernte country is linguistically 'mixed' between the two languages referred to in the myth: all Western Arrernte speakers also understand the nearby Luritja dialects, and those whose clan countries are near the Palmer River speak Luritja as well, and often mix in Luritja words when speaking Arrernte (Diane Austin-Broos, personal communication). The myth would seem to be establishing a connection between this linguistic mix and the landscape. As in the other myths, the travelling Dreamtime hero who creates the landscape switches language at a certain point, and by doing so creates a socially significant boundary (which in this case he also marks by laying down a series of sandhills). But rather than switching from one language to another, he switches from one language to a mixture of two — the same mixture which is still characteristic of that area.

Moreover, the myth at least indirectly (through a chain of cause and effect) relates specific features of the landscape at Ilbirla to its 'mixed' linguistic identity. Arrernte country, which begins there, is much more well-watered than the neighbouring Western Desert ('Luritja') area, and its spring-fed rivers grow the grass that feeds the crickets whose deafening chirps produced the confusion which caused the native cats to produce a mixed language.

I have dwelt at some length on this central Australian myth partly because it provides a particularly clear example of the direct link between land and language in Aboriginal Australia, and of how different it is from the Western notion of a 'national language'. In the latter, the nation is thought of as, first of all, a group of people with a common history, common language, and common territory with which the language is thereby associated. The association between territory and language is a contingent one, subject to change as one people conquers or assimilates another.

By contrast, in the Aboriginal myths which associate language and land, no account at all is taken of people, or peoples. Languages, or even mixtures of them, are directly placed in the landscape by the founding acts of Dreamtime heroes. From that point on, the relation between language and territory is a necessary rather than a contingent one. People too, or their immortal souls, are similarly grounded in the landscape, in the form of spirit children (or 'conception spirits') associated with specific sites, and via links through their parents to more extensive regions. But the languages were already placed in those regions before any people came on the scene. The links between peoples and languages are secondary links, established through the grounding of both in the landscape.

ACKNOWLEDGEMENTS AND CONCLUSION

I wish to thank Diane Austin-Broos and Harold Koch for their advice on aspects of this chapter; Wilma Merlan and Francesca Merlan for their comments on a draft of it; and Francesca Merlan for the benefit of our many conversations about land, language and social identity, and for bringing to my attention the passage from Strehlow cited here. Portions of this chapter have previously appeared in *Anthropological Forum* 6 (1), and we thank its editors for permission to reprint them here. Thanks also to the many Aboriginal people in Katherine and the Kimberleys who have discussed these matters with me. I am particularly indebted to David Mowaljarlai, who in 1976 concisely summed up the point of this chapter by explaining to me that 'everything goes back to the land'.

FOR DISCUSSION

This chapter is about the way Aborigines formulate the relationships among land, language and people.

1. To what other aspects of Aboriginal social life might that kind of formulation be related?

2. Why do you think there are so many different Aboriginal languages?

3. If the idea of the nation-state has led to false assumptions about Aboriginal social life, what other common Western preconceptions do you think might have to be overcome in order to understand it better? Do you think it is ever possible to start trying to understand another culture without any preconceived ideas? If so, how? If not, is the task a hopeless one? Why or why not?

REFERENCES

Aboriginal Land Commissioner

1981 *Finniss River Land Claim*, Australian Government Publishing Service, Canberra.

1982 *Daly River (Malak Malak) Land Claim*, Australian Government Publishing Service, Canberra.

1988 *Jawoyn (Katherine Area) Land Claim* Australian Government Publishing Service, Canberra.

Dixon, R.M.W.

1976 Tribes, Languages and other Boundaries in Northeast Queensland. In N. Peterson (ed), *Tribes and Boundaries in Australia*, Australian Institute of Aboriginal Studies, Canberra, 207–38.

Howitt, A.W.

1904 *The Native Tribes of Southeast Australia*, Macmillan, London.

Keen, I.

1980 *Alligator Rivers Stage II Land Claim*, Northern Land Council, Darwin.

Laycock, D.

1979 Linguistic Boundaries and Unsolved Problems in Papua New Guinea. In S. Wurm (ed), *New Guinea and Neighbouring Areas: A Sociolinguistic Laboratory*, Mouton, The Hague.

Merlan, F.

1981 Land, Language and Social Identity in Aboriginal Australia, *Mankind* 13, 133–48.

Merlan, F. and A. Rumsey

1982 *The Jawoyn (Katherine Area) Land Claim*, Northern Land Council, Darwin.

Milliken, E.P.

1976 Aboriginal Language Distribution in the Northern Territory. In N. Peterson (ed), *Tribes and Boundaries in Australia*, Australian Institute of Aboriginal Studies, Canberra, 239–42.

Myers, F.

1986 *Pintubi Country, Pintubi Self*, Smithsonian Institution Press, Washington, and Australian Institute of Aboriginal Studies, Canberra.

Radcliffe-Brown, A.

1930–31 *The Social Organization of Australian Tribes*, Oceania Monographs, Sydney.

Spencer, B.

1921 Presidential Address. In Report of the Fifteenth Meeting of the Australian Association for the Advancement of Science.

Strehlow, T.G.H.

1965 Culture, Social Structure and Environment in Aboriginal Central Australia. In R.M. and C.H. Berndt (eds), *Aboriginal Man in Australia* Angus and Robertson, Sydney.

Sutton, P.

1978 Wik: Aboriginal Society, Territory and Language at Cape Keerweer, Cape York Peninsula, Australia, PhD thesis, University of Queensland.

Sutton, P. and A. Palmer

1981 *Daly River (Malak Malak) Land Claim*, Northern Land Council, Darwin.

Tindale, N.

1974 *Aboriginal Tribes of Australia*, University of California Press, Los Angeles.

Trigger, D.

1987 Languages, Linguistic Groups and Status Relations at Doomadgee, an Aboriginal Settlement in North-West Queensland, Australia, *Oceania* 57, 217–38.

Warner, W. L.

1964 *A Black Civilization*, Harper and Row, New York.

Woodward, J.

1974 *Aboriginal Land Rights Commission Second Report*, Australian Government Publishing Service, Canberra.

CHAPTER 15 NEW USES FOR OLD LANGUAGES

Paul Black

INTRODUCTION

The Australian television series *Unknown Australia* recently spoke of the Northern Territory as being 'where an ancient people cling to a way of life 40,000 years old.' For some reason many Australians like to think of Aboriginal people in just this way, even though most are now wearing Western clothes, living in Western-style houses, and participating to a great extent in a Western-style economy. It would be just as fair to characterise non-Aboriginal Australians as 'clinging' to ways of life one or two thousand years old, at least, because many of their social, political, and religious practices go back that far — and we seldom know for sure which Aboriginal practices go back much further than this.

As the Aboriginal writer Colin Johnson (1985, 21) put it, the notion of:

> a stone-age culture (static and unchanging) is a myth created by those who should have known better and still put forth by those who should know better. All societies and cultures change and adapt, and this is fact not theory.

As Aboriginal lifestyles change, Aboriginal languages must change with them or they will increasingly be put aside in favour of a language that *can* cope with the new circumstances.

This may seem to make language and culture maintenance a paradox: what can it mean to 'maintain' something that must either change or go out of use? We'll return to this question at the end of this chapter, after considering in more detail what it means for Aboriginal languages to adapt to new uses.

THE NEW USES AND THEIR EFFECTS

Many Aboriginal languages have already died out, of course, but those still spoken in dozens of communities across northern and central Australia are being used for a variety of new purposes. The language situation at Kintore, in the Northern Territory, seems typical. As described by Amery (1986, 15–18), the local Pintupi/Luritja language is used not only in connection with more traditional activities, such as hunting, ceremonies, and everyday camp life, but also in the local clinic, school, church and store, for council meetings, card playing, and discussing Aboriginal art business, and even for long-distance communication over two-way radio. In such locations as Alice Springs Aboriginal languages have also been used in broadcast radio for over a decade and are being used in videos and for occasional television broadcasts.

Such new uses can actually affect the language itself. Most obviously they often require new vocabulary. They can also involve new discourse patterns and may require the relatively new medium of writing, and this can have less obvious effects on the structure of the language.

Let's consider some examples. Clinics in many communities now depend heavily on Aboriginal health workers, who generally interact with patients in the local language. Amery (1986, 23–24) notes that this not only involves much new vocabulary relating to diseases and treatments but also that it can lead to less traditional patterns of interaction as the health workers adopt Western practices in asking more direct questions in taking a medical history.

Local government meetings often deal with Western institutions and resource management, and they may thus bring new topics and vocabulary to the community. The pattern of discourse may also be somewhat different. As a specific example, a few years ago there was a day-long meeting in Galiwin'ku (on Elcho Island) about whether tourism should be introduced to the island. The meeting was held in a public area outdoors, with the audience strung out in quite a wide circle. Speakers took turns coming to a microphone in the centre of the circle and stating their case for or against tourism. There was little or no interaction with the audience, which did not, for example, ask questions. The meeting was not run in a Western style, but there clearly were some less traditional elements, such as the use of the microphone. And at the end, a few people circulated around the audience to record people's vote on whether or not they wanted the proposed tourist facilities — surely not a traditional practice.

Church services in Aboriginal communities are often partly in English and partly in the local language. When I attended a Catholic mass on Bathurst Island, for example, much of the liturgy was in English, but the sermon was delivered in the local Tiwi language. (The speaker referred to written notes, whether in English or Tiwi.) The hymns were also in Tiwi, and to aid the memory an overhead projector was used to project the written lyrics against a wall in a front corner of the church. The hymns, some scripture and other church literature are also available in book form. Prayers are sometimes also said in Tiwi. In Wadeye (formerly Port Keats) people use the local Murrinh-Patha language for prayer both at mass — where *Yile dingarrayepup kathu* is the local equivalent of 'Lord hear our prayer' — and more privately (Brother Vince Roche, personal communication). The literature and the oral sermons, hymns and prayers represent new genres of language use, although some of them (such as sermons) may well be similar to more traditional genres. They also involve many new concepts as well as expressions that become endowed with special meaning, such as Koko-Bera *ngerr wethárr*, the 'good news' of the gospel.

Broadcasting is quite different from other language use in Aboriginal settings in that the broadcaster cannot see the listeners, or generally even be sure who is listening. It is thus very different from talking to a group of friends or relatives. Since the broadcaster can't be sure how much the audience already knows, and since they can't ask for clarification, the language needs to be relatively decontextualised, that is, self-contained. Broadcasting can also cover a wide variety of topics, whether relatively traditional or modern, and the latter may involve the use of new vocabulary. Because it can reach so many people, broadcasting can actually play a crucial role in promoting new vocabulary and language standards in general; see Poulson, Ross, Shopen, and Toyne (1986). Broadcasting can also make use of writing, such as for notes on news or announcements.

In school programs the role of Aboriginal languages can vary from being the object of study for a hour or two per week to being one of the main media of instruction, normally along with English, in what is a bilingual program. We'll

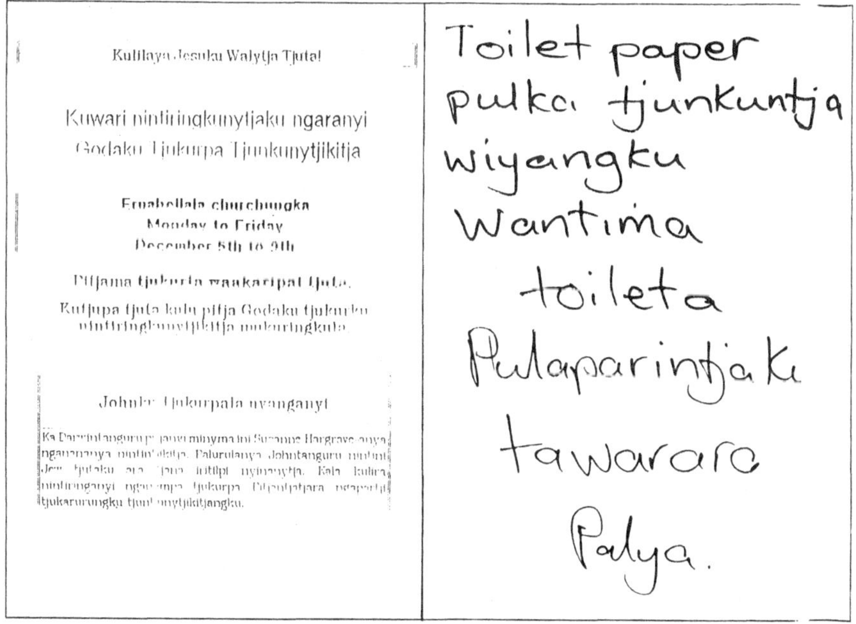

Plate 6: Examples of notices, Ernabella, 1988. Left is an announcement of coming Bible Translation Workshop, and right is a notice from the clinic telling people not to use too much paper lest the toilet block up (reproduced from *Australian Aboriginal Studies* 1990/number 2).

consider bilingual programs at some length because of their impact on the children and hence the transmission of culture, and also because some readers may wonder if their benefits justify their cost.

THE CASE OF BILINGUAL EDUCATION

Some thirty bilingual programs have been operating in recent years in Aboriginal communities in northern and central Australia. The following list is based on Bubb (1990) for Northern Territory communities and on Black (1983) and M. Gale (1990) for programs in other locations (and see Map 10).

Language	*Locations (and year started)*
Arrernte (Aranda)	Yipirinya School in Alice Springs (1983), Ltyentye Purte (Santa Teresa, NT) (1989)
Burarra	Maningrida, NT (1986)
Dhuwaya and others	Yirrkala, NT (1974)
Djambarrpuyngu	Galiwin'ku, NT (1974)
Gupapuyngu	Milingimbi, NT (1973)
Kukatja	Balgo Hills, WA (about 1987)
Luritja	Haasts Bluff (1974), M'Bunghara (1981), Papunya (1984), Watiyawanu, NT (1981)
Manyjiljarra	Strelley, WA
Maung	Warruwi, NT (1973)
Murrinh-Patha	Wadeye, NT (1976)
Ndjébbana	Maningrida, NT (1981)
Ngaanyatjarra	Warburton, WA (mid-1970s only)
Nyangumarta	Strelley, WA
Pintupi/Luritja	Walungurru, NT (1983)
Pitjantjatjara	Ernabella and other S.A. communities (since the 1960s), Areyonga (1973) and Docker River, NT (1979), Yipirinya School in Alice Springs (1983)
Thayorre	Edward River, Qld (discontinued)
Tiwi	Nguiu, NT (1974)
Walmajarri	Noonkanbah, WA (briefly after 1980)
Warlpiri	Lajamanu (1982), Nyirrpi (1986), Willowra (1977), Yuendumu, NT (1974)
Wik-Mungkan	Aurukun, Qld (suspended)

Nowadays bilingual education is often thought to be important for local language maintenance, but most of the programs were in fact started in order to improve the general education of the children. In most programs children begin schooling in their own language but over the next few years are taught increasingly in English, which typically comes to be used more than the local language by grade

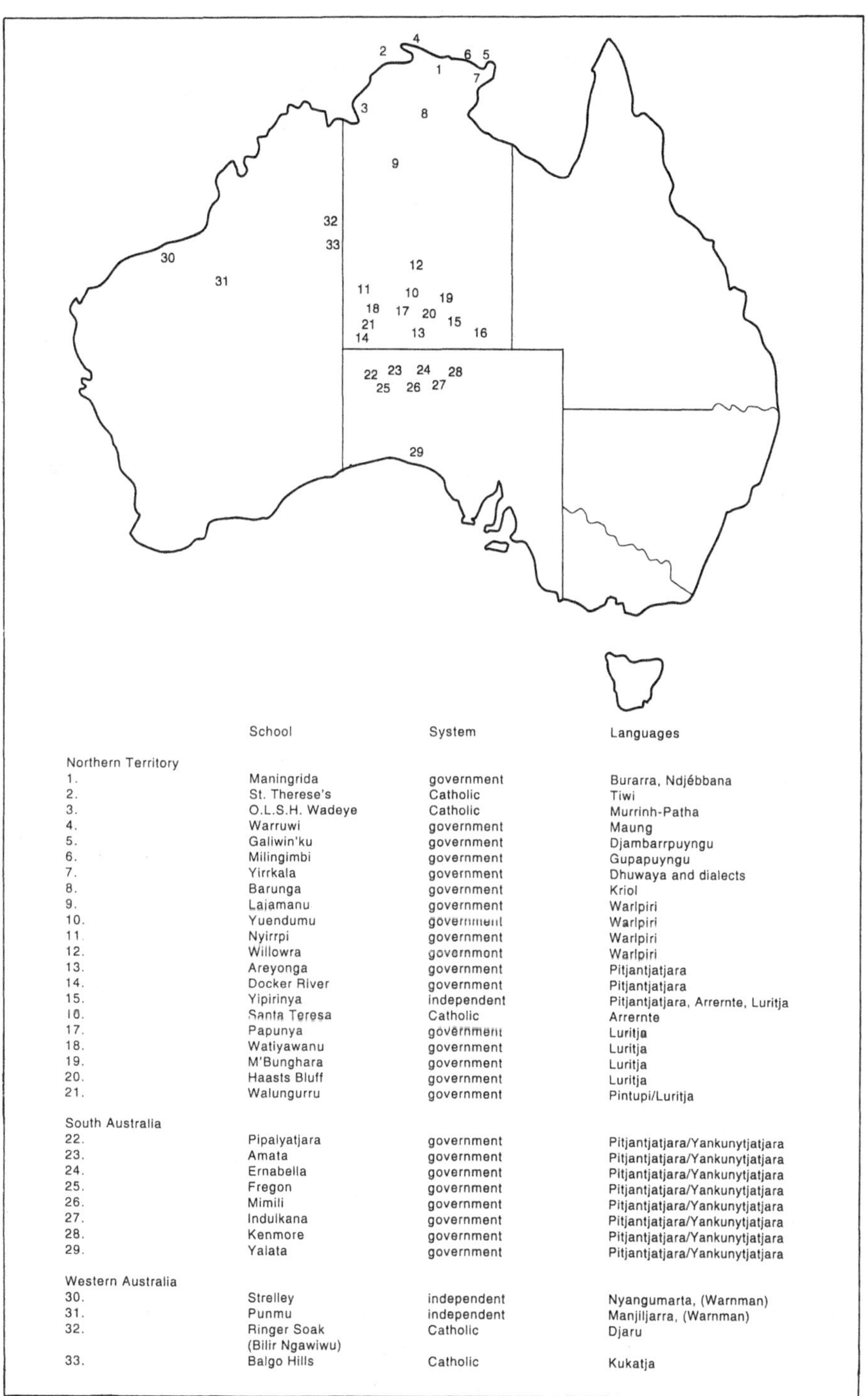

	School	System	Languages
Northern Territory			
1.	Maningrida	government	Burarra, Ndjébbana
2.	St. Therese's	Catholic	Tiwi
3.	O.L.S.H. Wadeye	Catholic	Murrinh-Patha
4.	Warruwi	government	Maung
5.	Galiwin'ku	government	Djambarrpuyngu
6.	Milingimbi	government	Gupapuyngu
7.	Yirrkala	government	Dhuwaya and dialects
8.	Barunga	government	Kriol
9.	Lajamanu	government	Warlpiri
10.	Yuendumu	government	Warlpiri
11.	Nyirrpi	government	Warlpiri
12.	Willowra	government	Warlpiri
13.	Areyonga	government	Pitjantjatjara
14.	Docker River	government	Pitjantjatjara
15.	Yipirinya	independent	Pitjantjatjara, Arrernte, Luritja
16.	Santa Teresa	Catholic	Arrernte
17.	Papunya	government	Luritja
18.	Watiyawanu	government	Luritja
19.	M'Bunghara	government	Luritja
20.	Haasts Bluff	government	Luritja
21.	Walungurru	government	Pintupi/Luritja
South Australia			
22.	Pipalyatjara	government	Pitjantjatjara/Yankunytjatjara
23.	Amata	government	Pitjantjatjara/Yankunytjatjara
24.	Ernabella	government	Pitjantjatjara/Yankunytjatjara
25.	Fregon	government	Pitjantjatjara/Yankunytjatjara
26.	Mimili	government	Pitjantjatjara/Yankunytjatjara
27.	Indulkana	government	Pitjantjatjara/Yankunytjatjara
28.	Kenmore	government	Pitjantjatjara/Yankunytjatjara
29.	Yalata	government	Pitjantjatjara/Yankunytjatjara
Western Australia			
30.	Strelley	independent	Nyangumarta, (Warnman)
31.	Punmu	independent	Manjiljarra, (Warnman)
32.	Ringer Soak (Bilir Ngawiwu)	Catholic	Djaru
33.	Balgo Hills	Catholic	Kukatja

Map 10: Location of bilingual educations schools (after Schmidt 1990).

four. After less than a decade of operation, some such programs were indeed found to be more successful, in general academic terms, than the English-only programs that they replaced (Gale, McClay, Christie and Harris, 1981; Murtagh, 1980).

The reasons for the effectiveness of bilingual education are not hard to imagine. Most obviously, it's much easier for children to learn in a language they understand than in one that they don't (see also Macnamara 1967). They can begin developing important academic skills, such as reading and writing, even before they are ready to learn much through the medium of spoken English. Many of the fundamentals they learn transfer readily to their later studies in English. In the area of literacy, for example, these fundamentals include such basics as the fact that books, unlike people, always 'tell the same story,' and that we read from left to right and from top to bottom. They also include most of the letters and punctuation required for English.

A well-designed and properly staffed bilingual program can also make the students considerably more comfortable and confident about attending school (see also Cummins 1986). Even the fact that the local language is being used in written form can be a source of pride, allowing people to say, 'Now we are the same as white people — we can write our own language too' (Leeding, 1984, 11). On the other hand, to be confined to interaction in an alien language can be stifling:

> the missionaries didn't realise that when they stopped us speaking Yolngu [that is, Aboriginal] language in the school, they were stopping our way of thinking. How could we use our Yolngu thinking if school was run by Balanda [that is, Europeans] with Balanda language? (Yunupingu 1989, 1).

As this passage suggests, the benefits of effective bilingual education come not just from the use of the local language in school but also from who is there to use it. Such programs tend to depend on employing local people in professional capacities, at least as teaching assistants and literacy workers, but increasingly also as teachers and principals. This helps make both the children and the local community feel that the school is something of their own, rather than an alien and perhaps colonial institution. As Wunungmurra (1989, 13) says,

> Yolngu [that is, Aboriginal people] must own the school program. Without this we will feel crushed and lose our self respect and self identity — we will be living on other people's programs like it was in the past, in the mission days.

Bilingual programs involve uses of Aboriginal language that differ considerably from traditional uses. The subject matter taught in the language often requires the development of new vocabulary. This includes some words required largely for academic purposes alone, such as ones relating to written language (for example, 'letter', 'sentence', 'full stop') and mathematical concepts and processes (for example, 'minus', 'fraction', 'set'). Furthermore, the teacher–pupil relationship can involve quite different patterns of oral language use than is otherwise normal in the community, and the development of a written version of the language tends to be especially important. Let's consider the discourse patterning and writing at more length before examining ways in which new vocabulary can arise.

DISCOURSE PATTERNING

Western-style schooling provides an especially fertile environment for speakers of Aboriginal languages to interact quite differently in their languages than they have in the past. Even in Western society the patterns of verbal interaction in schools tend to be rather different from those in non-school situations. Since teachers are expected to be in control of their classes, students are generally not allowed to talk whenever they wish, and in many circumstances they are expected to direct their talk only to the teacher, rather than to other students. Often the teacher-directed talk also falls into a 'question-answer-evaluation' pattern of exchange that is unusual outside of schools. Consider this example:

Teacher: What's the capital of South Australia? Ken?
Student: Adelaide.
Teacher: Right!

Outside of classrooms (or quiz programs) we don't normally ask such 'display' questions — that is, ones for which we already know the answer. To the extent that Aboriginal teachers follow such Western practices in their own teaching they may be deviating even more severely from the normal patterns of exchange in their languages, where even an attempt to gain answers that one does not already know may involve less direct questioning than we might use in English. See also Eades's comments on questioning in chapter 13 of this book, and also Harris (1990, 38–39).

Some other new patterns (or genres) of oral language were mentioned earlier, including hymns and prayers in church and the way Aboriginal health workers are coming to take medical histories. Some of these may be similar to more traditional genres, of course. For example, sermons and radio broadcasts are new to Aboriginal languages, but there were traditional situations in which people similarly spoke in a kind of 'broadcast' mode, rather than to particular individuals. Among the Koko-Bera (of western Cape York Peninsula) for example, such a broadcast mode was used as certain preparations were carried out following a person's death. One elder would have the responsibility of speaking out, to nobody in particular, on the relevant obligations and taboos, such as how people should not visit the part of the country owned by the deceased. This was called *path-kun wičhirrm* — essentially 'carrying the country of the deceased' and translated into the local English as 'preaching'.

The new uses of Aboriginal language may lead not only to new patterns of exchange but also to changes in the way in which respect and avoidance are signalled in language. People normally adjust their speech to suit the relationship between them and the other participants; in English this is what makes the difference between such pairs of sentences as 'Shut up!' and 'Could you please be quiet?'. Relative age is often an important factor in this, and in English such factors as social position and occupation can also be important: we tend to speak in a different way to our doctor than to a taxi driver, for example. In Aboriginal cultures, on the other hand, how people speak to each other, and indeed whether they can speak to each other at all, has usually depended heavily on how they are related or classified as kin; see Alpher's discussion in chapter 7.

Consider what this means in relation to schooling. In a Western-style school an Aboriginal teacher may have to accept responsibilities over a class that are not in accord with expectations based on kinship. Aboriginal teachers undoubtedly find ways of coping with the situation, and it may also be that children of primary school age are not really expected to have mastered the appropriate ways to talk to and behave towards various kin. In any case, however, the school environment certainly provides more support for learning Western-style role relationships — for example, teacher–student — than it does for mastering the kinship obligations.

It's thus not surprising that children do not seem to be mastering the appropriate behaviour towards kin in some communities. In both Kowanyama (on Cape York Peninsula) and Nguiu (on Bathurst Island), for example, I have heard certain children described as exceptional precisely because of how conscientious they were about following the more traditional rules of behaviour. In addition, it seems typical for special 'respect' forms of Aboriginal languages to go out of use much more quickly than the language as a whole. Undoubtedly such changes are promoted by a variety of changes in lifestyle and not solely by schooling.

THE IMPACT OF WRITING

One of the most striking new uses for Aboriginal and Islander languages is their use in written form. As mentioned elsewhere in this book, some languages began to be written quite early in colonial times (as for example in the dictionary of the Adelaide language described by Simpson in chapter 9). But for many Aboriginal languages, a written form has come only since the late 1960s or early 1970s.

Much Aboriginal language writing has been for the purposes of early primary education in bilingual programs. This includes the preparation of primers, story books and other classroom material, as well as the writing of the children themselves. As noted earlier, this first language literacy has important academic and motivational benefits regardless of whether literacy in the language has any real functions outside the school. In some communities, nonetheless, Aboriginal language literacy is gradually coming to be used for a variety of purposes, ranging from occasional public notices to scripture and hymn books in church and sometimes even well-read newsletters in the community at large (see Rhydwen's comments in chapter 11, and also Goddard 1990).

The introduction of literacy to a previously non-literate culture can have tremendous consequences. Writing is more than just a representation of spoken language: it is a tool for doing new things, such as communicating over distance or time and keeping records for posterity or simply to jog one's own memory. Nowadays such electronic devices as the telephone, radio, and tape recorder let us do many of the same things with spoken language, and yet all larger societies around the world still rely heavily on writing. It is a powerful medium, and it is thus accorded a special status in many societies. Western societies value written contracts over oral promises, for example, and the idea that the written word is safer or stronger than the spoken is a compelling one.

One may thus wonder about the effects of literacy on Aboriginal cultures, and whether it can cause changes in lifestyle or ways of thinking that people might someday regret. Two things make this somewhat an ideal question, however. Firstly, whether or not Aboriginal people become literate in their own languages, Australian schooling aims to ensure their literacy in English, and it seems clear that the effects of this literacy will not somehow be confined to some 'English' corner of the brain. Secondly, literacy is only one of a number of factors, including schooling and urbanisation, that are known to affect thought patterns; see the excellent study by Scribner and Cole (1981) for evidence on these matters.

It has sometimes been suggested that a reliance on literacy may inhibit oral storytelling and thus interfere with the oral transmission of traditional stories. One may well be left with this impression by seeing young Aboriginal adults who have been schooled in the written language seek out written versions of traditional stories because they have not learned to tell the story properly themselves. But it is clear that oral traditions are also being lost in communities that have never had the benefit of literacy in their own languages or in some cases even in English, as I found during research on Kurtjar and Koko-Bera languages and traditions in southwestern Cape York Peninsula. It is not literacy that is killing off oral traditions.

Since written and spoken language serve different functions, they often come to be noticeably different in structure and vocabulary, and written language also tends to be somewhat more conservative than speech. One might imagine that the conservatism would require many decades to develop, but in fact it has already begun to appear in written languages that are less than twenty years old. On Bathurst Island, for example, the school uses a much more conservative form of the local Tiwi language than the children actually speak (Black 1990b, 82). Similarly, younger Yolngu Matha speakers in Yirrkala are certainly writing a more conservative form of the language than the so-called 'Baby Gumatj' (or Dhuwaya) many of them actually speak (see Amery forthcoming). Cataldi (1990, 84) has noted how a similar conservatism in written Warlpiri in Lajamanu can be seen as a positive factor in support of language maintenance.

Plate 7: Desmond Taylor recording and transcribing Warnman stories with his father Waka Taylor at the Pilbara Aboriginal Language Centre in 1989 (photograph by Nicholas Thieberger).

SOURCES FOR NEW VOCABULARY

As we noted earlier, using Aboriginal languages in new ways often requires new vocabulary: words for products and prices in the local shop, for medicines and treatments in the clinic, for the processes and subject matter of education in the school, and so on. English is similarly gaining new words and expressions all the time. When Europeans first came to live in Australia, for example, they borrowed such words as *billabong* and *boomerang*, and coined such others as *paperbark* and *platypus*, in order to talk about their new situation and experiences. In the same way the Aboriginal people borrowed or coined words for things that were old in Western culture but new to theirs, such as types of food, drink and clothing. Since that time both English and Aboriginal languages have also gained new words for a variety of innovations that we take for granted today, such as the aeroplane, electricity, motor vehicle, radio, refrigerator, telephone and television. People sometimes take such things to represent change in Aboriginal traditions without noting that they represent change in Western traditions as well.

New vocabulary can be produced from the resources of the language itself or it can be borrowed from other languages. The simplest version of the former is to 'extend' the meaning of an existing word to cover a new concept, just as the meaning of English 'bonnet' was extended to refer to the engine cover of a car. A well-known Aboriginal example is the use of the word for 'ghost' or 'spirit' (for example, *kardiya* in west central Northern Territory, *mánpich* in Koko-Bera) to refer also to white people. Other examples include the extension of Kurtjar *mook* 'bone' to mean 'wheel', of Yolngu Matha *mäkirri* or *buthuru* 'ears' to refer to the dots above the Yolngu Matha letter *ä* (which represents long *aa*), and of Tiwi *yinjanga* 'name' to also mean 'number'.

New vocabulary can also be created as a combination of old elements. One possibility is to extend an old word to cover a new meaning, as described above, but also to qualify the word by another whenever necessary to distinguish the new meaning from the old. Thus, the Kurtjar originally referred to horses as *ruaak* 'dog(s)' or more distinctively as *ruaak ngkuaath* 'big dog(s)', and to sugar as *loongkird* 'sand' or more precisely as *maay loongkird* 'sand food'. Another possibility is to make a compound expression in which both (or all) elements must always occur. Thus, the Warumungu of central Australia came to refer to the rabbit as *kuwarta junmarn* 'long ears' (Simpson 1985, 16). It's also possible to derive new vocabulary by adding affixes to familiar words, as in Warumungu *jina-kari* (foot-belong) for 'shoe', *warli-kari* (thigh-belong) for 'trousers', and *kunapa-jangu* (dog-having) for 'Greyhound bus' (Simpson 1985, 15).

Aboriginal languages have also drawn on English (or in some cases an English-based pidgin or creole) for much new vocabulary: for example,

Pitjantjatjara *rayipula* 'rifle', *mutuka* 'motor car', *turawutja* 'trousers', *tjaata* 'shirt', and *pulangkita* 'blanket' (Amery 1986, 19). As these examples show, the words are often pronounced in a way which conforms to the normal sound pattern of the language but which is rather different from the original English pronunciation.

English is not the only source of borrowing. Languages generally tend to borrow occasional words from their neighbours, and in Australia these have sometimes been words for newly introduced concepts. For example, Warumungu *murrkkarti* 'hat' seems to have originally come from the Kaurna language, far to the south (Simpson 1985, 19). The languages along the coast of Arnhem Land have also borrowed words from the Macassan language of Indonesia in the past few hundred years: for example, Yolngu Matha *jorra*' 'paper', and *rrupiya* 'money'.

Speakers of some languages are anxious to keep their languages as free of foreign influences as possible. Thus, the Germans went through a period of casting out words derived from Latin or Greek, such as *hydrogen*, and replacing them by Germanic compounds, in this case *wasserstoff* (that is, 'water-stuff'). The French have also legislated against the use of foreign vocabulary. Some Torres Strait Islanders I have worked with have also been concerned about keeping their languages as pure as possible by building new vocabulary out of traditional elements. At the same time speakers of languages as diverse as English, Albanian, Filipino and Japanese have happily borrowed some fifty per cent or more of their vocabularies from various other languages — notably French, Latin, and Greek in the case of English. The fact that such a 'mongrel' language as English grew from the speech of a sometime colonised island to a language of international importance demonstrates that borrowing itself is not a threat to the existence of a language. Language 'purity' is largely a matter of personal, or societal, preference.

THE PARADOX OF LANGUAGE AND CULTURE MAINTENANCE

Nowadays many people are concerned with maintaining Aboriginal cultures and languages; see for example Devlin (1990), Schmidt (1990) and McConvell (1991). However, this can't mean 'freezing' the culture or language at some point in time, whether at the time of first European contact or at the present. As a culture or language stops keeping up with the changes in daily life it becomes increasingly less useful and less likely to survive. To 'maintain' a culture or language it seems that you often have to let it change or even help it change. As Poulson, Ross, Shopen and Toyne (1986, 7) note, 'A major aspect of cultural maintenance is the adaptation of language to talking about new things'.

If cultures and languages must change, however, what does it mean to 'maintain' them? As Harris (1990, 39–44) points out, Aboriginal culture will change, but it need not lose its distinctiveness. Perhaps one can identify a variety of characteristics that are currently distinctive of Aboriginal culture, as Harris (1990, 21–39) does. But which characteristics are important to maintain is a matter for Aboriginal people to work out among themselves. To a great extent, cultural demise is simply cultural change that is unwanted by the people involved, perhaps often because it is forced upon them from outside (see Black 1990b).

Aboriginal people certainly seem happy to absorb many Western ideas into their cultures, as long as they do it on their own terms. With respect to education Wäli Wunungmurra (1989, 12–13) pointed out that Aboriginal and Western knowledge

> will only come together if there is respect for our knowledge and where Aboriginal people are taking the initiative, where we shape and develop the educational programs and then implement them. In other words Yolngu [that is, Aboriginal people] must own the school program.

However Aboriginal people decide to maintain their cultures, their languages will have to remain in step if they hope to maintain them too. For promoting language maintenance, Fishman (1987, 14–15) stresses the importance of making sure that it is used in all primary aspects of daily life, such as the home, the school and the workplace, and to whatever extent possible even to promote its use in the 'secondary institutions of intergenerational mother tongue continuity'; see also Black (1990a). As McConvell (1984, 51–52) puts it, the language should

> grow in the hands of Aboriginal people themselves, to challenge the domination of English not in everything, but in the situations [in which] the people themselves feel capable of putting up the alternative.

FOR DISCUSSION

1. The chapter focuses on Aboriginal languages, but many other languages also develop new uses with the passing of time. How many new uses of English can you think of that have developed within the last century or two? As starters you might consider where these bits of English are from: (a) Roger, over and out; (b) Number please; (c) And now a word from our sponsor. As these examples may suggest, you can also consider to what extent the new uses have given rise to distinctive patterns of speech.

2. One reason given for having bilingual education is that people learn better in their first language. Even so, many children throughout the world have had to get their schooling through a second language. Sometimes they seem to do this quite successfully, one known case being children of English-speaking background studying through French in Quebec. Can you see reasons why the status of the language of instruction — as a 'mainstream' or minority language in the community — might tend to affect students' success in studying through the medium of that language?

3. The chapter says that writing is 'more' than just a representation of spoken language, but this should not be to suggest that spoken language is any less important than writing. List as many things as you can that are (a) best done through speech, and (b) best done through writing. For example, to which list would you add (1) communicating in the dark, and (2) stating a complicated mathematical formula? Think about the properties of speech and writing that cause you to add each item to one list or the other.

4. With regard to the relation between literacy and thought patterns, some scholars have claimed that that there are actually deep psychological differences between literate and non-literate people, although Scribner and Cole (1981, 251–525) found no evidence that this was so. What sorts of evidence might one hope to find to confirm or reject such a possibility?

5. The chapter claims that borrowing should not be considered a threat to languages. Some scholars would disagree, and they might point out that the situation of Aboriginal languages is far different from such international languages as English. What arguments can you find for and against such a view?

REFERENCES

Amery, R.

1986 Languages in Contact: The Case of Kintore and Papunya (with Particular Reference to the Health Domain), *Language in Aboriginal Australia* 1, 13–38.

forthcoming An Australian Koine: Dhuwaya, a Variety of Yolngu Matha Spoken at Yirrkala in North East Arnhem Land. In *International Journal of the Sociology of Language.*

Black, P.

1983 *Aboriginal Languages of the Northern Territory*, School of Australian Linguistics, Darwin Community College, Batchelor, NT.

1990a Rethinking Domain Theory, Part I: How Should It Be Applied?, *Ngoonjook* 3, 22–32.

1990b Some Competing Goals in Aboriginal Language Planning. In R.B. Baldauf (Jr) and A. Luke (eds), *Language Planning and Education in Australasia and the South Pacific*, Multilingual Matters, Clevedon, 80–88.

Bubb, P.

1990 Information on Bilingual Programs and Personnel, *NT Bilingual Newsletter* 90-1, 6–9.

Cataldi, L.

1990 Language Maintenance and Bilingual Education at Lajamanu School. In C. Walton and W. Eggington (eds), *Language: Maintenance, Power and Education in Australian Aboriginal Contexts*, NTU Press, Darwin, 83–87.

Cummins, J.

1986 Empowering Minority Students: A Framework for Intervention, *Harvard Educational Review* 56, 18–37.

Devlin, B.

1990 Some Issues Related to Vernacular Language Maintenance: A Northern Territory View. In C. Walton and W. Eggington (eds), *Language: Maintenance, Power and Education in Australian Aboriginal Contexts*, NTU Press, Darwin, 53–74.

Fishman, J.A.

1987 Language Spread and Language Policy for Endangered Languages. In P.H. Lowenberg (ed.), *Language Spread and Language Policy: Issues, Implications and Case Studies*, Georgetown University Press, Washington, 1–15.

Gale, K., D. McClay, M. Christie and S. Harris

1981 Academic Achievement in the Milingimbi Bilingual Education Program, *TESOL Quarterly* 15, 297–314.

Gale, M.

1990 A Review of Bilingual Education in Aboriginal Australia.In *Australian Review of Applied Linguistics* 13(1), 40–80.

Goddard, C.

1990 Emergent Genres of Reportage and Advocacy in the Pitjantjatjara Print Media, *Australian Aboriginal Studies* 1990(2), 227–47.

Harris, S.
1990 *Two-Way Aboriginal Schooling: Western Education and the Survival of a Small Culture*, Aboriginal Studies Press, Canberra.

Haviland, J.B.
1979 How to Talk to Your Brother-in-law in Guugu Yimidhirr. In T. Shopen (ed), *Languages and Their Speakers*, Winthrop, Cambridge, MA, 160–239.

Johnson, C. [Mudrooroo Narogin]
1985 White Forms, Aboriginal Content. In J. Davis and B. Hodge (eds), *Aboriginal Writing Today*, Australian Institute of Aboriginal Studies, Canberra, 21–30.

Leeding, V.
1984 Loanwords: Ours or Theirs? In G.R. McKay and B.A. Sommer (eds), *Further Applications of Linguistics to Australian Aboriginal Contexts*, Applied Linguistics Association of Australia, Parkville, Vic, 7–16.

Macnamara, J.
1967 The Effects of Instruction in a Weaker Language, *Journal of Social Issues*, 23(2), 121–35.

McConvell, P.
1984 Domains and Domination, *NT Bilingual Education Newsletter* 1–2, 48–52.

1991 Understanding Language Shift: A Step towards Language Maintenance. In S. Romaine (ed), *Language in Australia*, Cambridge University Press, Cambridge, 143–55.

Murtagh, E.J.
1980 Creole and English Used as Languages of Instruction with Aboriginal Australians [microfilm], PhD thesis, Stanford University, University Microfilms, Ann Arbor MI.

Poulson, C.J., T.N. Ross, T. Shopen and P. Toyne
1986 Warlpiri Language and Culture: Adaptation to Contemporary Needs, *Language in Aboriginal Australia* 1, 7–12.

Schmidt, A.
1990 *The Loss of Australia's Aboriginal Language Heritage*, Aboriginal Studies Press, Canberra.

Scribner, S. and M. Cole
1981 *The Psychology of Literacy*, Harvard University Press, Cambridge, MA.

Simpson, J.
1985 How Warumungu People Express New Concepts, *Language in Central Australia* 4, 12–25.

Wunungmurra, W.
1989 'Dhawurrpunaramirri': Finding the Common Ground for a New Aboriginal Curriculum, *Ngoonjook* 2, 12–16.

Yunupingu, M.
1989 Language and Power: The Yolngu Rise to Power at Yirrkala School, *Ngoonjook* 2, 1–6.

NOTE

I am grateful to Br Vince Roche for information on prayer in Aboriginal languages and to Rob Amery, Mary-Anne Gale, Stephen Harris, Patrick McConvell, my wife Tina, and my daughter Barbara for taking the trouble to read and comment on this chapter.

CONTRIBUTORS

BARRY ALPHER has recently been an editor for Mouton de Gruyter publishers in Berlin. He has taught linguistics and anthropology for varying periods at Arizona State University, the School of Australian Linguistics in Darwin, Sydney University, the State University of New York at Albany, and Cornell University; has acted as Head of the School of Australian Linguistics; has done applied linguistics in the employ of the Coalition of Indian Controlled School Boards in Denver; has worked with Puerto Rican migrant labourers at the Labor Education Center, Rutgers University, New Jersey; and acted as consultant in Aboriginal land claim work in Central Australia. He has compiled one of the most comprehensive dictionaries of an Australian language: *Yir-Yoront Lexicon: Sketch and Dictionary of an Australian Language* (Mouton de Gruyter, Berlin 1991).

EDITH BAVIN is a Senior Lecturer in Linguistics at La Trobe University. She received her PhD in linguistics from the State University of New York at Buffalo in 1980. Since moving to Australia in 1981, her primary research has been in cross-linguistic aspects of first language acquisition, in particular the acquisition of Warlpiri. Edith is currently doing cross-linguistic research with children from a number of linguistic backgrounds, as well as writing a book on first language acquisition from a cross-linguistic perspective. Other research interests include the West Nilotic languages, and also language change.

PAUL BLACK is a Senior Lecturer in Applied Linguistics in the Education Faculty of Northern Territory University. An American by birth, he came to Australia in 1974 after receiving a Yale doctorate involving linguistic research in Ethiopia. Before assuming his current position in 1990 he worked as a research fellow and later a linguistic archivist for the Australian Institute of Aboriginal and Torres Strait Islander Studies (AIATSIS) in Canberra, and then spent eight years working with Aboriginal literacy workers, interpreters and teachers at the former School of Australian Linguistics (in Batchelor, Northern Territory). From 1991 to early 1993 he was a visiting lecturer in English at Waseda University in Tokyo.

MICHAEL CHRISTIE is a Senior Lecturer in Adult Education at the Northern Territory University. He has a mixed academic background. He majored in English and History but concentrated for his doctoral degree on race relations between Aborigines and colonists in early Victoria. Since then he has worked as an English language teacher (while travelling), as a freelance writer, a potter and a university lecturer. During 1991 he was a guest lecturer in the English Department at Stockholm University.

TERRY CROWLEY gained his PhD at the Australian National University, and now lectures in linguistics at the University of Waikato in New Zealand, and before this he taught at the University of the South Pacific and the University of Papua New Guinea. His current research interests cover Pacific pidgins and creoles, concentrating on Melanesian Pidgin, as well as Oceanic languages. He has also published on the Aboriginal languages of northern New South Wales, as well as Cape York Peninsula in northern Queensland.

DIANA EADES has been working with speakers of Aboriginal English since 1973, mainly in Queensland and New South Wales. She is particularly interested in how Aboriginal culture is continued in the way that Aboriginal people use English. In recent years she has applied her research to a number of areas of cross-cultural communication, particularly in education and the law. Currently she lectures in linguistics at the University of New England, Armidale.

JOHN HARRIS spent many years teaching in Aboriginal communities in the Northern Territory. His doctoral studies dealt with the origin of Kriol. He is now Warden of New College at the University of New South Wales. He is the author of *One Blood, 200 Years of Aboriginal Encounter with Christianity: A Story of Hope* (Albatross, Sydney, 1990) the award-winning history of Aborigines and the Christian Church.

MARI RHYDWEN is completing her PhD thesis on Kriol literacy at Sydney University. In 1992 she completed a report on the extent of the use of Kriol in the Northern Territory and its implications for access to English literacy. She has worked for several years on Kriol and Aboriginal English in the Northern Territory.

ALAN RUMSEY is a senior lecturer in anthropology at the University of Sydney. He is interested in the relationship between language and other aspects of social life, and has been studying Aboriginal languages of the Kimberley region of Western Australia since 1975.

MARGARET SHARPE lectures in sociolinguistics in the Department of Aboriginal and Multicultural Studies, University of New England. She has spent her academic life studying the Alawa and Bundjalung languages of the Northern Territory, northern New South Wales and southern Queensland; Kriol in the Northern Territory; and Aboriginal English in Queensland, Alice Springs and northern New South Wales. Since 1979 she has published three monographs and numerous articles and chapters on these languages, and a children's novel based on her research in these areas.

JANE SIMPSON is presently teaching at the University of Sydney and is working on dictionaries of Kaurna and Warumungu. She has participated in the Warlpiri Dictionary Project and in establishing an archive of machine-readable dictionaries at the Australian Institute of Aboriginal and Torres Strait Islander Studies. She is the author of *Warlpiri Morpho-Syntax: A Lexicalist Approach* (Kluwer 1991).

JAKY TROY has concentrated her research in the area of language contact in Australia since 1788. In 1985 she completed a BA (Hons) at the University of Sydney in linguistic anthropology. Her thesis focused on early language contact in New South Wales, and was later published in a revised form as: *Australian Aboriginal Contact with the English Language in New South Wales: 1788 to 1845* (Pacific Linguistics, B–103. Canberra 1990). She is currently completing a PhD in the Research School of Pacific Studies at the Australian National University.

MICHAEL WALSH teaches linguistics and Aboriginal studies at the University of Sydney. He has carried out fieldwork on Aboriginal languages along the west coast of the Northern Territory since 1972. He has also provided anthropological documentation for a long-running land claim near Darwin.

COLIN YALLOP teaches English and linguistics at Macquarie University in Sydney. He has done linguistic field work in Central Australia and is the author of *Australian Aboriginal Languages* (André Deutsch, 1982).

www.ingramcontent.com/pod-product-compliance
Lightning Source LLC
LaVergne TN
LVHW081259100826
845148LV00005B/915

9780855752415